THE KEY

STUDENT STUDY GUIDE

Science 10

THE KEY student study guide is designed to help students achieve success in school. The content in each study guide is 100% curriculum aligned and serves as an excellent source of material for review and practice. To create this book, teachers, curriculum specialists, and assessment experts have worked closely to develop the instructional pieces that explain each of the key concepts for the course. The practice questions and sample tests have detailed solutions that show problem-solving methods, highlight concepts that are likely to be tested, and point out potential sources of errors. ***THE KEY*** is a complete guide to be used by students throughout the school year for reviewing and understanding course content, and to prepare for assessments.

Rao, Gautam, 1961 –
THE KEY –Science 10
Alberta

1. Science – Juvenile Literature. I. Title

Published by
Castle Rock Research Corp.
2340 Manulife Place
10180 – 101 Street
Edmonton, AB T5J 3S4

14 15 16 FP 13 12 11

Publisher
Gautam Rao

Contributors
Richard Clayton
Rick Bookham
Sandy Grewal

Reviewers
Robert Cadonic
Margaret Pitts

CASTLE ROCK
RESEARCH CORP

Dedicated to the memory of Dr. V. S. Rao

THE KEY—Science 10

THE KEY consists of the following sections:

KEY Tips for Being Successful at School gives examples of study and review strategies. It includes information about learning styles, study schedules, and note taking for test preparation.

Class Focus includes a unit on each area of the curriculum. Units are divided into sections, each focusing on one of the specific expectations, or main ideas, that students must learn about in that unit. Examples, definitions, and visuals help to explain each main idea. Practice questions on the main ideas are also included. At the end of each unit is a test on the important ideas covered. The practice questions and unit tests help students identify areas they know and those they need to study more. They can also be used as preparation for tests and quizzes. Most questions are of average difficulty, though some are easy and some are hard—the harder questions are called *Challenger Questions*. Each unit is prefaced by a ***Table of Correlations***, which correlates questions in the unit to the specific curriculum expectations. Answers and solutions are found at the end of each unit.

KEY Strategies for Success on Tests helps students get ready for tests. It shows students different types of questions they might see, word clues to look for when reading them, and hints for answering them.

Practice Tests includes one to three tests based on the entire course. They are very similar to the format and level of difficulty that students may encounter on final tests. In some regions, these tests may be reprinted versions of official tests, or reflect the same difficulty levels and formats as official versions. This gives students the chance to practice using real-world examples. Answers and complete solutions are provided at the end of the section.

For the complete curriculum document visit http://education.alberta.ca/teachers/program/science/programs.aspx

THE KEY *Study Guides* are available for many courses. Check www.castlerockresearch.com for a complete listing of books available for your area.

For information about any of our resources or services, please call Castle Rock Research at 780.448.9619 or visit our website at http://www.castlerockresearch.com.

At Castle Rock Research, we strive to produce an error-free resource. If you should find an error, please contact us so that future editions can be corrected.

TABLE OF CONTENTS

KEY Tips for Being Successful at School

KEY TIPS FOR BEING SUCCESSFUL AT SCHOOL

KEY FACTORS CONTRIBUTING TO SCHOOL SUCCESS

In addition to learning the content of your courses, there are some other things that you can do to help you do your best at school. Some of these strategies are listed below.

- **Keep a positive attitude:** Always reflect on what you can already do and what you already know.
- **Be prepared to learn**: Have ready the necessary pencils, pens, notebooks, and other required materials for participating in class.
- **Complete all of your assignments:** Do your best to finish all of your assignments. Even if you know the material well, practice will reinforce your knowledge. If an assignment or question is difficult for you, work through it as far as you can so that your teacher can see exactly where you are having difficulty.
- **Set small goals for yourself when you are learning new material:** For example, when learning the parts of speech, do not try to learn everything in one night. Work on only one part or section each study session. When you have memorized one particular part of speech and understand it, then move on to another one, continue this process until you have memorized and learned all the parts of speech.
- **Review your classroom work regularly at home:** Review to be sure that you understand the material that you learned in class.
- **Ask your teacher for help**: Your teacher will help you if you do not understand something or if you are having a difficult time completing your assignments.
- **Get plenty of rest and exercise:** Concentrating in class is hard work. It is important to be well-rested and have time to relax and socialize with your friends. This helps you to keep your positive attitude about your school work.
- **Eat healthy meals:** A balanced diet keeps you healthy and gives you the energy that you need for studying at school and at home.

How To Find Your Learning Style

Every student learns differently. The manner in which you learn best is called your learning style. By knowing your learning style, you can increase your success at school. Most students use a combination of learning styles. Do you know what type of learner you are? Read the following descriptions. Which of these common learning styles do you use most often?

- **Linguistic Learner**: You may learn best by saying, hearing, and seeing words. You are probably really good at memorizing things such as dates, places, names, and facts. You may need **to write and then say out loud** the steps in a process, a formula, or the actions that lead up to a significant event.

- **Spatial Learner**: You may learn best by looking at and working with pictures. You are probably really good at puzzles, imagining things, and reading maps and charts. You may need to use strategies like **mind mapping and webbing** to organize your information and study notes.

- **Kinaesthetic Learner**: You may learn best by touching, moving, and figuring things out using manipulative. You are probably really good at physical activities and learning through movement. You may need to **draw your finger over a diagram** to remember it, **"tap out" the steps** needed to solve a problem, or **"feel" yourself writing or typing** a formula.

Scheduling Study Time

You should review your class notes regularly to ensure that you have a clear understanding of all the new material you learned. Reviewing your lessons on a regular basis helps you to learn and remember ideas and concepts. It also reduces the quantity of material that you need to study prior to a test. Establishing a study schedule will help you to make the best use of your time.

Regardless of the type of study schedule you use, you may want to consider the following suggestions to maximize your study time and effort:

- Organize your work so that you begin with the most challenging material first.
- Divide the subject's content into small, manageable chunks.
- Alternate regularly between your different subjects and types of study activities in order to maintain your interest and motivation.
- Make a daily list with headings like "Must Do," "Should Do," and "Could Do."
- Begin each study session by quickly reviewing what you studied the day before.
- Maintain your usual routine of eating, sleeping, and exercising to help you concentrate better for extended periods of time.

CREATING STUDY NOTES

MIND-MAPPING OR WEBBING

Use the key words, ideas, or concepts from your reading or class notes to create a *mind map* or *web* (a diagram or visual representation of the given information). A mind map or web is sometimes referred to as a knowledge map.

- Write the key word, concept, theory, or formula in the centre of your page.
- Write down related facts, ideas, events, and information and then link them to the central concept with lines.
- Use coloured markers, underlining, or other symbols to emphasize things such as relationships, time lines, and important information.
- The following examples of a Frayer Model illustrate how this technique can be used to study scientific vocabulary.

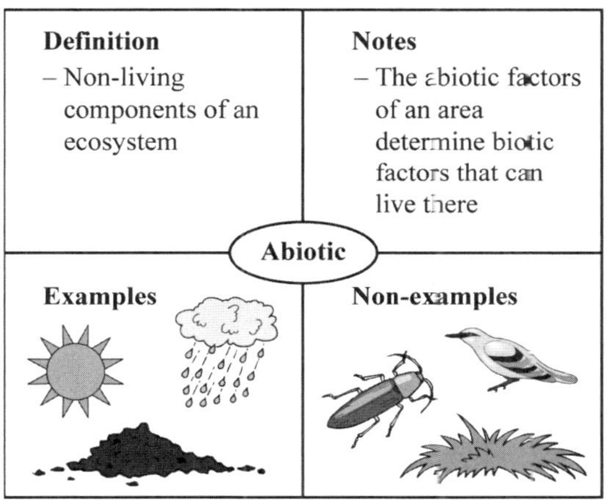

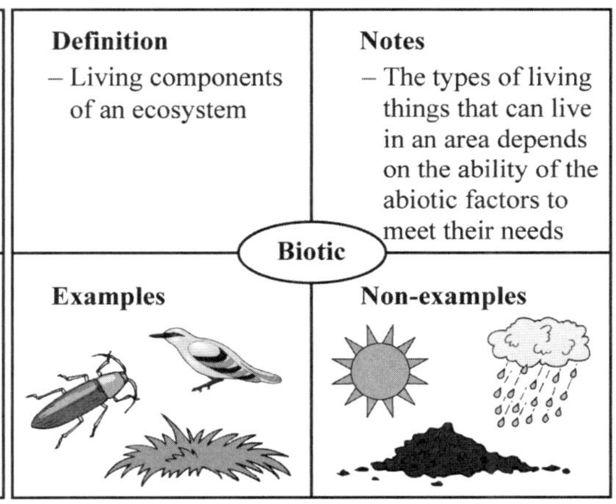

INDEX CARDS

To use index cards while studying, follow these steps:

- Write a key word or question on one side of an index card.
- On the reverse side, write the definition of the word, answer to the question, or any other important information that you want to remember.

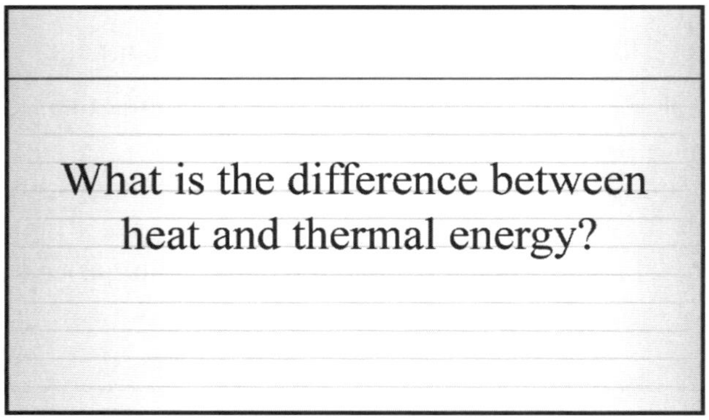

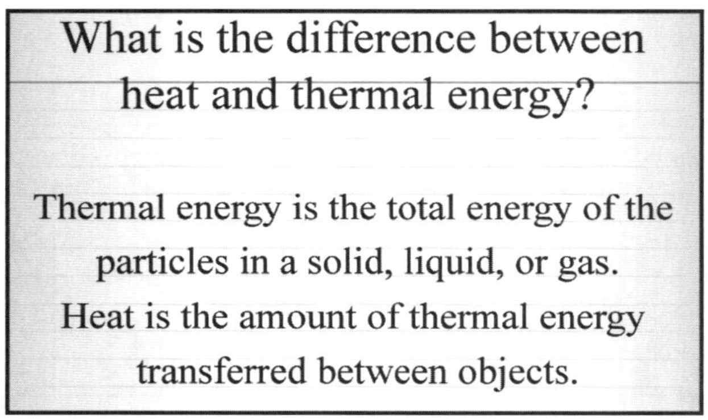

SYMBOLS AND STICKY NOTES—IDENTIFYING IMPORTANT INFORMATION

Use symbols to mark your class notes. For example, an exclamation mark (!) might be used to point out something that must be learned well because it is a very important idea. A question mark (?) may highlight something that you are not certain about, and a diamond (◊) or asterisk (*) could highlight interesting information that you want to remember.

- Use sticky notes when you are not allowed to put marks in books.
- Use sticky notes to mark a page in a book that contains an important diagram, formula, explanation, etc.
- Use sticky notes to mark important facts in research books.

MEMORIZATION TECHNIQUES

- **Association** relates new learning to something you already know. For example, to remember the spelling difference between *dessert* and *desert*, recall that the word *sand* has only one *s*. So, because there is sand in a desert, the word *desert* only has on *s*.
- **Mnemonic** devices are sentences that you create to remember a list or group of items. For example, the first letter of each word in the phrase "**E**very **G**ood **B**oy **D**eserves **F**udge" helps you to remember the names of the lines on the treble clef staff (E, G, B, D, and F) in music.
- **Acronyms** are words that are formed from the first letters or parts of the words in a group. For example, **RADAR** is actually an acronym for **Ra**dio **D**etecting **A**nd **R**anging, and **MASH** is an acronym for **M**obile **A**rmy **S**urgical **H**ospital. **HOMES** helps you to remember the names of the five Great Lakes (**H**uron, **O**ntario, **M**ichigan, **E**rie, and **S**uperior).
- **Visualizing** requires you to use your mind's eye to "see" a chart, list, map, diagram, or sentence as it is in your textbook or notes, on the chalk board or computer screen, or in a display.
- **Initialisms** are abbreviations that are formed from the first letters or parts of the words in a group. Unlike acronyms, initialisms cannot be pronounced as a word themselves. For example, **BEDMAS** is an initialism for the order of operations in math (**B**rackets, **E**xponents, **D**ivide, **M**ultiply, **A**dd, **S**ubtract).

KEY STRATEGIES FOR REVIEWING

Reviewing textbook material, class notes, and handouts should be an ongoing activity. Spending time reviewing becomes more critical when you are preparing for tests. You may find some of the following review strategies useful when studying during your scheduled study time.

- Before reading a selection, preview it by noting the headings, charts, graphs, and chapter questions.
- Before reviewing a unit, note the headings, charts, graphs and chapter questions.
- Highlight key concepts, vocabulary, definitions and formulas.
- Skim the paragraph and note the key words, phrases, and information.
- Carefully read over each step in a procedure.
- Draw a picture or diagram to help make the concept clearer.

KEY STRATEGIES FOR SUCCESS: A CHECKLIST

Review, review, review: review is a huge part of doing well at school and preparing for tests. Here is a checklist for you to keep track of how many suggested strategies for success you are using. Read each question and then put a check mark (✓) in the correct column. Look at the questions where you have checked the "No" column. Think about how you might try using some of these strategies to help you do your best at school.

***KEY* Strategies for Success**	**Yes**	**No**
Do you attend school regularly?	✓	
Do you know your personal learning style—how you learn best?	✓	
Do you spend 15 to 30 minutes a day reviewing your notes?	✓	
Do you study in a quiet place at home?		✓
Do you clearly mark the most important ideas in your study notes?	✓	
Do you use sticky notes to mark texts and research books?	✓	
Do you practise answering multiple-choice and written-response questions?	✓	
Do you ask your teacher for help when you need it?		
Are you maintaining a healthy diet and sleep routine?		
Are you participating in regular physical activity?		

Energy and Matter in Chemical Change

ENERGY AND MATTER IN CHEMICAL CHANGE

Table of Correlations				
Specific Expectation	**Practice Questions**	**Unit Test Questions**	**Practice Test 1**	**Practice Test 2**
By the end of this course, students will:				
A1 Describe the basic particles that make up the underlying structure of matter, and investigate related technologies.				
A1.2 outline the role of evidence in the development of the atomic model consisting of protons and neutrons (nucleons) and electrons; i.e., Dalton, Thomson, Rutherford, Bohr	1, 2, 13, 14, 15, 16, 17	1, 2, 3, 4, 19	NR1, 4	NR1, 2, 4, 5
A2 Explain, using the periodic table, how elements combine to form compounds, and follow IUPAC guidelines for naming ionic compounds and simple molecular compounds.				
A2.1 illustrate an awareness of WHMIS guidelines, and demonstrate safe practices in the handling, storage, and disposal of chemicals in the laboratory and at home	WR2c	5		1
A2.2 explain the importance of and need for the IUPAC system of naming compounds, in terms of the work that scientists do and the need to communicate clearly and precisely	18, 20		13	8
A2.3 explain, using the periodic table, how and why elements combine to form compounds in specific ratios	7, 8, 9, 10, 11, 12,		1, 2, 3, 5	3
A2.4 predict formulas and write names for ionic and molecular compounds and common acids, using a periodic table, a table of ions, and IUPAC rules	NR1, NR2, 19, 21	6, 9	11, 13	7
A2.5 classify ionic and molecular compounds, and acids and bases, on the basis of their properties; i.e., conductivity, pH, solubility, state	WR2a, WR2b	7, 8, 10, 11, 12, 13	7, 10	6, 10, 13, 14
A2.6 predict whether an ionic compound is relatively soluble in water, using a solubility chart	33		9	
A2.7 relate the molecular structure of simple substances to their properties	3, 4, 5		10	

A3 Identify and classify chemical changes, and write word equations and balanced chemical equations for significant chemical reactions, as applications of Lavoisier's law of conservation of mass.				
A3.1 provide examples of household, commercial, and industrial processes that use chemical reactions to produce useful substances and energy	30			
A3.2 identify chemical reactions that are significant in societies	27		WR3	
A3.3 describe the evidence for chemical changes; i.e., energy change, formation of a gas or precipitate, colour or odour change, change in temperature	6, 31	14, WR1b	9	
A3.4 differentiate between endothermic and exothermic chemical reactions	26, 29			11
A3.5 classify and identify categories of chemical reactions; i.e., formation (synthesis), decomposition, hydrocarbon combustion, single replacement, double replacement	NR3, 27		12	12
A3.6 translate word equations to balanced chemical equations and vice versa for chemical reactions that occur in living and non-living systems	22, 23, 24, 32	WR1a, 20	NR2, NR3, 6, 13	NR2, 9
A3.7 predict the products of formation (synthesis) and decomposition, single and double replacement, and hydrocarbon combustion chemical reactions, when given the reactants	25		8	
A3.8 define the mole as the amount of an element containing 6.02×10^{23} atoms (Avogadro's number), and apply the concept to calculate quantities of substances made of other chemical species	NR4, 28	15, 16, 17, 18, WR1d, e, f, g		
A3.9 interpret balanced chemical equations in terms of moles of chemical species, and relate the mole concept to the law of conservation of mass	WR1	WR1c		

ENERGY AND MATTER IN CHEMICAL CHANGE

A2.3 explain, using the periodic table, how and why elements combine to form compounds in specific ratios

The Periodic Table of Elements

The periodic table of elements organizes elements according to their physical and chemical properties. The elements of the periodic table are listed in order according to atomic number—the number of protons in the nucleus. Each horizontal row of the periodic table is called a **period**. Each vertical column of the periodic table is a **group**, or **family**.

All members of a chemical family have similar chemical properties. That is, they react with the same elements in a similar way. For example, all members of Group 2 can combine ionically with two atoms of members of Group 17 ($BeCl_2$, $MgCl_2$, $CaCl_2$, $SrCl_2$, and so on). Members of Group 18 are gases that, under normal circumstances, never react to form compounds.

Periodic Table of Elements

1	H 2.20																	He
2	Li 0.98	Be 1.57											B 2.04	C 2.55	N 3.04	O 3.44	F 3.98	Ne
3	Na 0.93	Mg 1.31											Al 1.61	Si 1.90	P 2.19	S 2.58	Cl 3.16	Ar
4	K 0.82	Ca 1.00	Sc 1.36	Ti 1.54	V 1.63	Cr 1.66	Mn 1.55	Fe 1.83	Co 1.88	Ni 1.91	Cu 1.90	Zn 1.65	Ga 1.81	Ge 2.01	As 2.18	Se 2.55	Br 2.96	Kr 3.00
5	Rb 0.82	Sr 0.95	Y 1.22	Zr 1.33	Nb 1.6	Mo 2.16	Tc	Ru 2.2	Rh 2.28	Pd 2.20	Ag 1.93	Cd 1.69	In 1.78	Sn 1.96	Sb 2.05	Te 2.1	I 2.66	Xe 2.67
6	Cs 0.79	Ba 0.89		Hf 1.3	Ta 1.5	W 2.36	Re 1.9	Os 2.2	Ir 2.20	Pt 2.28	An 2.54	Hg 2.00	Tl 1.62	Pb 2.33	Bi 2.02	Po 2.0	At 2.2	Rn
7	Fr 0.7	Ra 0.9		Rf	Db	Sg	Bh	Hs	Mt	Ds	Rg	Uub	Uut	Uuq	Uup	Uuh	Uus	Uuo

La 1.1	Ce 1.12	Pr 1.13	Nd 1.14	Pm 1.13	Sm 1.17	Eu 1.2	Gd 1.2	Tb 1.1	Dy 1.22	Ho 1.23	Er 1.24	Tm 1.25	Yb 1.1	Lu 1.27
Ac 1.1	Th 1.3	Pa 1.5	U 1.38	Np 1.36	Pu 1.28	Am 1.13	Cm 1.28	Bk 1.3	Cf 1.3	Es 1.3	Fm 1.3	Md 1.3	No 1.3	Lr

* A larger version of the periodic table of the elements with group numbers can be found in the Appendix.

Ions are atoms that have gained or lost electrons. When that happens, they become negatively or positively charged. Nitrogen contains five valence electrons. It needs three more to become stable, and when it gains three electrons it becomes N^{3-}, a nitride ion. Sodium must get rid of one electron to become stable. It becomes Na^{+}, a sodium ion. Positively charged metal ions retain the same name, but negatively charged non-metal ions change their endings to -ide. Argon contains a full valence of electrons, so it does not become an ion. Ion models are shown in the given chart.

		Nitride Ion	Chloride Ion	Oxide Ion	Sodium Ion	Calcium Ion
Symbol		N^{3-}	Cl^{-}	O^{2-}	Na^{+}	Ca^{2+}
Electrons	Level 3		8			8
	Level 2	8	8	8	8	8
	Level 1	2	2	2	2	2
Protons		7	17	8	11	20
Neutrons		7	18	8	12	20
Electrons gained/lost		Gained 3	Gained 1	Gained 2	Lost 1	Lost 2

Note: The outermost energy level is full in each case.

Groups 1 and 2 and the non-metal elements of the periodic table are called **the representative elements,** or the **main-group elements,** and are quite predictable in nature. Group 1 elements always donate one electron. Group 2 elements donate two electrons. Group 17 elements accept one electron, and Group 16 elements accept two electrons. The metals of Groups 3 through 12 are not as easily predictable. They are called the **transition elements**. They may form ions with more than one possible charge. The periodic table indicates the most common ion charge for the transition metals, along with other possible ion charges. This information is given on the right side of the box of each transition metal.

Practice Questions: 7, 8, 9, 10, 11, 12

A1.2 outline the role of evidence in the development of the atomic model consisting of protons and neutrons (nucleons) and electrons; i.e., Dalton, Thomson, Rutherford, Bohr

Structure of Matter

In the early nineteenth century, John Dalton hypothesized that atoms were tiny indivisible particles that all substances were composed of and that different kinds of atoms reacted to form compounds.

Around the turn of the twentieth century, J. J. Thomson described atoms as being like raisin buns—the raisins being the negatively charged electrons stuck on a positively charged sphere. A few years later, Ernest Rutherford proposed that atoms were composed of a central nucleus containing most of the mass and the protons, with tiny negatively charged electrons spinning rapidly around the nucleus. In 1913, Niels Bohr put forth the idea that electrons travel in circular orbits around the nucleus. They would only do so at distinct energy levels, each with its own maximum number of electrons. If an electron got a boost of energy, it could move to a higher energy level farther from the nucleus.

Scientists now assume that atoms are composed of **protons, electrons,** and **neutrons** with the properties shown in the given chart.

Particle	Symbol	Charge	Mass (Atomic Mass Units)
Proton	p	+1	1
Electron	e	–1	$\frac{1}{1\ 823}$
Neutron	n	0	1

Practice Questions: 1, 2, 13, 14, 15, 16, 17

A2.2 explain the importance of and need for the IUPAC system of naming compounds, in terms of the work that scientists do and the need to communicate clearly and precisely

A2.4 predict formulas and write names for ionic and molecular compounds and common acids, using a periodic table, a table of ions, and IUPAC rules

A2.5 classify ionic and molecular compounds, and acids and bases, on the basis of their properties; i.e., conductivity, pH, solubility, state

A2.6 predict whether an ionic compound is relatively soluble in water, using a solubility chart

A2.7 relate the molecular structure of simple substances to their properties

Compounds

Chemicals, many of which are potentially hazardous, are shipped all around the world for use in research, industry, and medicine. It is important to have a clear, concise, and standard way of identifying them. The International Union of Pure and Applied Chemistry (IUPAC) is responsible for the standardized names for chemical compounds. People around the globe now use the same names for compounds with the same chemical formulas, improving communication and reducing confusion.

Ionic Compounds

Generally, when a metal reacts with a non-metal, the metal donates one or more negatively charged electrons to the non-metal. After the atoms donate or gain electrons, they become ions. This gives the metal a positive (+) charge and the non-metal a negative (–) charge. The metal and non-metal ions then come together because opposite charges attract. This is called an **ionic bond**, and compounds formed in this way are called **ionic compounds.** Ionic compounds are always solids at room temperature and normal pressure, and when they form solutions, they conduct electricity.

The IUPAC rules state that for the names of ionic compounds, the metal is named first, followed by the non-metal. For most compounds, the non-metal's name is changed to end in -ide. Some examples of ionic compounds are shown in this table.

IUPAC Name	Formula	How the Compound Formed
Sodium chloride	$NaCl_{(s)}$	One sodium atom donated one electron; one chlorine atom gained one electron.
Sodium oxide	$Na_2O_{(s)}$	The two sodium atoms each donated one electron; one oxygen atom gained two electrons.
Calcium fluoride	$CaF_{2(s)}$	One calcium atom donated two electrons; two fluorine atoms each gained one electron.

Transition metals appear in the periodic table from Group 3 over to the non-metals. Most transition metals can have more than one possible charge. When writing the names of ionic compounds that contain transition metals, it is necessary to use **Stock's system**—roman numerals to indicate the charge of the ion. Examples are copper(I) or copper(II), iron(III) or iron(II). The next table shows some compounds containing transition metals.

Name	Formula
Copper(I) chloride	$CuCl_{(s)}$
Copper(II) chloride	$CuCl_{2(s)}$
Iron(II) oxide	$FeO_{(s)}$
Iron(III) oxide	$Fe_2O_{3(s)}$

Polyatomic ions are ions that contain two or more elements (see the Appendix for a list of some polyatomic ions). Polyatomic ions cannot be split up, and you must enclose the ion in parentheses before adding any subscripts. Two examples are shown below.

sodium + hydroxide = $NaOH$
calcium + hydroxide = $Ca(OH)_2$

Molecular Compounds

Ionic compounds are created by atoms losing or gaining electrons. Molecular compounds are created by sharing electrons in **covalent bonds**. As a result, molecular compounds have physical properties that are different from those of ionic compounds.

Molecular compounds share some common physical properties. They do not conduct electricity when in solution with water, and they have relatively low melting and boiling points. They generally have stronger bonding forces than ionic compounds, and they can be solids, liquids, or gases at room temperature.

The following is a list of some common molecular compounds:

- Water (H_2O)
- Glucose ($C_6H_{12}O_6$)
- Carbon dioxide (CO_2)
- Hydrogen peroxide (H_2O_2)
- Sucrose, or table sugar ($C_{12}H_{22}O_{11}$)

All the elements that make up molecular compounds are classified as non-metals.

These diagrams show the bonds formed in the diatomic molecule oxygen (O_2) and in water (H_2O).

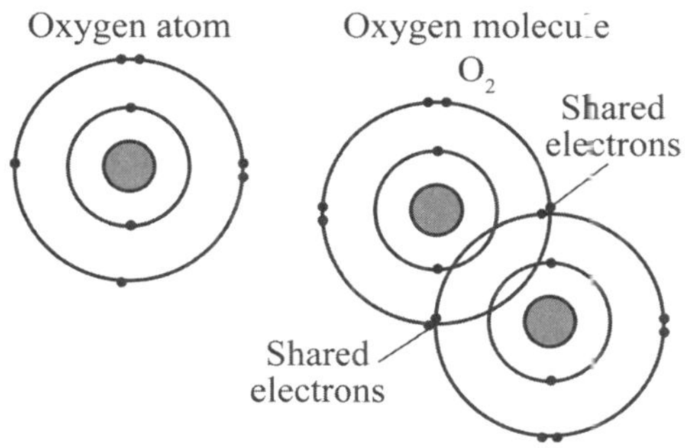

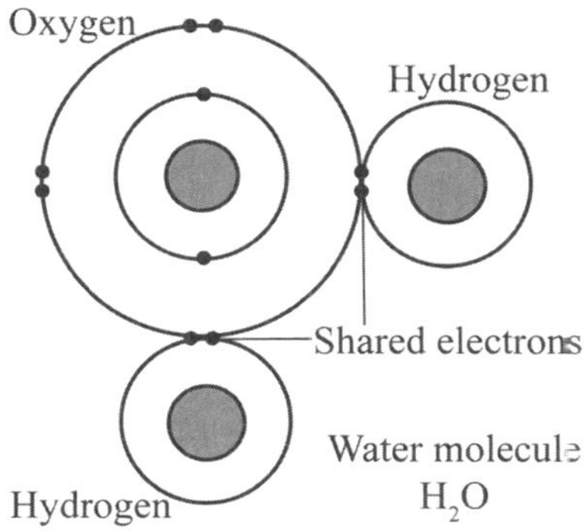

Naming and Writing Molecular Compounds

A prefix naming system is used to name molecular compounds composed of two different non-metallic elements.

Prefix	Number
Mono-	1
Di-	2
Tri-	3
Tetra-	4
Penta-	5
Hexa-	6
Hepta-	7
Octa-	8
Nona-	9
Deca-	10

The first word in the name is a prefix plus the complete element name (omit mono- on the first word).

The second word is a prefix, plus the stem of the element name, plus the ending -ide. Two examples are shown below.

P_2O_5—diphosphorous pentoxide
CO_2—carbon dioxide

Example

Which of the following compounds is **not** named correctly?

PCl_5—monophosphorous pentachloride
N_2O_4—dinitrogen tetroxide
SF_6—sulfur hexafloride
IF_7—iodine heptafloride

Solution

Monophosphorous pentachloride is an incorrect name for PCl_5. The prefix mono- is never used on the first name in a compound. The correct name is phosphorous pentachloride. The other compounds are named correctly.

Properties of Water

Water Polarity and Hydrogen Bonds

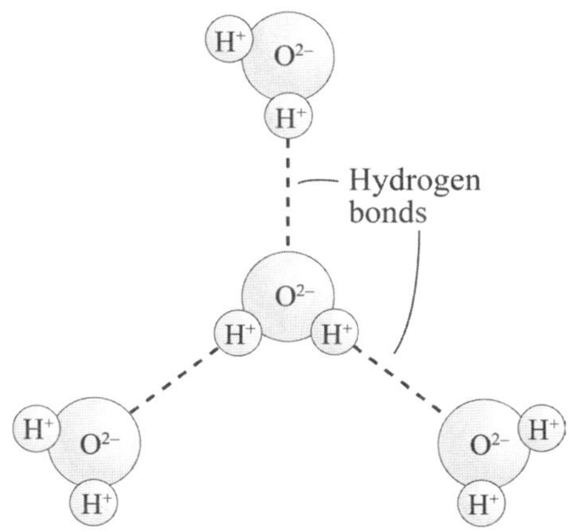

Water is essential for life as we know it to exist. Most organisms are between 70 and 99% water. Water's importance can be seen in its properties. These properties are related to water's molecular structure and the hydrogen bonds that attract one water molecule to another. The hydrogen bonds are the result of a slightly positive charge on the hydrogen atoms and a slightly negative charge on oxygen atoms. Water is referred to as a polar molecule because it has a positive pole and a negative pole. As a result, water molecules hang on to one another. Some of the important properties of water are as follows:

Cohesion—This is the force of attraction between molecules. A raindrop is round because of the cohesion of the water molecules pulling one another together.

Adhesion—This is the force of attraction between water and molecules of a different type. Adhesion causes water to creep up the edge of a drinking glass.

Surface tension—This is a result of cohesion. Since water molecules hang on to one another forming a cohesive film on its surface, water can support a small mass on its surface without breaking. That is how small insects can stand on the surface without falling through.

High melting and boiling point—Most small molecules, such as oxygen and carbon dioxide, are gases at a temperature at which water is still a solid. Because the hydrogen bonds hold water molecules together, it takes a lot of heat energy to make water molecules move fast enough to change from a solid to a liquid or from a liquid to a gas.

Density—When liquid water changes to solid water (ice), the molecules form themselves into an arrangement called a crystal. To do this, the molecules have to move themselves apart a little. As a result, ice is less dense than liquid water. Water is most dense at 4°C. Most matter is most dense as a solid. If ice were denser than liquid water, the ice that forms on a lake would sink. As a result, it would be impossible for fish and other water animals to survive in a lake over winter.

pH OF A SUBSTANCE

The measure of a substance's **pH** indicates whether a substance is acidic, basic, or neutral. A pH of 7 is neutral, less than 7 is acidic, and more than 7 is basic. Physical properties of **acids** are that they dissolve in water, conduct electricity, turn blue litmus paper red, and taste sour. Physical properties of **bases** are that they dissolve in water, conduct electricity, turn red litmus paper blue, taste bitter, and feel slippery. Some common acids and bases are shown here.

Acids

Name	Formula
Hydrochloric acid	$HCl_{(aq)}$
Sulfuric acid	$H_2SO_{4(aq)}$
Carbonic acid	$H_2CO_{3(aq)}$
Nitric acid	$HNO_{3(aq)}$
Ethanoic acid (acetic acid)	$CH_3COOH_{(aq)}$

Bases

Name	Formula
Sodium hydroxide	$NaOH_{(aq)}$
Potassium hydroxide	$KOH_{(aq)}$
Calcium hydroxide	$Ca(OH)_{2(aq)}$

The (aq) indicates that a substance is dissolved in water. In water, acids release hydrogen ions, H^+, and bases release hydroxide ions, OH^-. When an acid is mixed with a base, the H+ combines with the OH^- to produce H_2O in a process called neutralization. The negative ion associated with the acid and the positive ion associated with the base, Cl^- and Na^+ for example, make a salt.

SOLUBILITY

A typical set of chemical reference tables will include a solubility chart. This chart indicates whether an ionic compound has high solubility or low solubility in water. When a substance is dissolved in water, it is described as **aqueous**.

Example

A sodium chloride solution is mixed with a lead nitrate solution. A solubility chart shows that both $Pb(NO_3)_2$ and NaCl are soluble.

$$Pb(NO_3)_2 \rightarrow Pb^{2+}_{(aq)} + 2NO^{-}_{3(aq)}$$
$$NaCl \rightarrow Na^{+}_{(aq)} + Cl^{-}_{(aq)}$$

The solubility chart shows that lead chloride is not soluble. Therefore, when the solutions are mixed, $PbCl_2$ forms a solid precipitate.

$$Pb(NO_3)_{2(aq)} + 2NaCl_{(aq)} \rightarrow 2NaNO_{3(aq)} + PbCl_{2(s)}$$

Practice Questions: 3, 4, 5, NR1, 18, 19, 20, 21, NR2, 33, WR2a, WR2b

A3.1 *provide examples of household, commercial, and industrial processes that use chemical reactions to produce useful substances and energy*

A3.2 *identify chemical reactions that are significant in societies*

A3.3 *describe the evidence for chemical changes; i.e., energy change, formation of a gas or precipitate, colour or odour change, change in temperature*

REACTIONS AND CHANGE

A **chemical change** results when a chemical reaction occurs and a new chemical substance is created. Evidence that a chemical change has occurred may be the release of energy (heat), the formation of a gas or precipitate, a colour change, or an odour change.

Chemical reactions can be used to produce useful chemical products. In agriculture, ammonia is a vital component in fertilizers. The production of ammonia involves the following chemical reaction:

$$N_{2(g)} + 3H_{2(g)} \rightarrow 2NH_{3(g)}$$

In human health, an antacid is used to neutralize excess stomach acid, HCl. Sodium bicarbonate is a common antacid that reacts with stomach acid in the following way:

$$NaHCO_{3(aq)} + HCl_{(aq)} \rightarrow NaCl_{(aq)} + H_2O_{(l)} + CO_{2(g)}$$

A3.8 *define the mole as the amount of an element containing 6.02×10^{23} atoms (Avogadro's number), and apply the concept to calculate quantities of substances made of other chemical species*

Practice Questions: 6, 30, 31

THE MOLE

A chemical reaction always involves a very large number of atoms or molecules. It would be possible to identify the exact number of atoms or compounds involved in a chemical reaction, but it would be very inconvenient because the numbers would be so large. It is a lot easier to speak of the number of moles of reactants and moles of products. A **mole** is a convenient number of particles. The mole was described by Amedeo Avogadro as the number of atoms in 12 g of carbon-12. That number happens to be 6.02×10^{23} and is now referred to as Avogadro's number.

Practice Questions: NR4, 28

A3.4 differentiate between endothermic and exothermic chemical reactions

Endothermic and Exothermic Reactions

Endothermic changes involve the absorption of heat (energy) into the new substance. Photosynthesis is an endothermic reaction, since light energy is taken in. **Exothermic** reactions involve the release of heat (energy). The burning of gasoline, for example, is an exothermic reaction. All combustion reactions are exothermic.

Practice Questions: 26, 29

A3.5 classify and identify categories of chemical reactions; i.e., formation (synthesis), decomposition, hydrocarbon combustion, single replacement, double replacement

A3.6 translate word equations to balanced chemical equations and vice versa for chemical reactions that occur in living and non-living systems

A3.7 predict the products of formation (synthesis) and decomposition, single and double replacement, and hydrocarbon combustion chemical reactions, when given the reactants

A3.9 interpret balanced chemical equations in terms of moles of chemical species, and relate the mole concept to the law of conservation of mass

Categories of Chemical Reactions

Chemical reactions can be classified into a number of different groups, including formation, decomposition, single replacement, double replacement, and combustion.

Formation—In formation reactions, the two reactants are elements that combine to form a product that is a compound; i.e., $A + B \rightarrow AB$.

Example

Word equation: Two moles of sodium plus one mole of chlorine gas react to form two moles of sodium chloride.

Balanced chemical equation:
$2Na_{(s)} + Cl_{2(g)} \rightarrow 2NaCl_{(s)}$

Example

Word equation: Four moles of solid iron plus three moles of oxygen gas react to form two moles of solid iron(III) oxide (rust).

Balanced chemical equation:
$4Fe_{(s)} + 3O_{2(g)} \rightarrow 2Fe_2O_{3(s)}$

Decomposition—In decomposition reactions, a reactant that is a compound is broken down into products that are simpler compounds or elements; i.e., $AB \rightarrow A + B$.

Example

Word equation: Two moles of solid calcium oxide react to form two moles of solid calcium and one mole of oxygen gas.

Balanced chemical equation:
$2CaO_{(s)} \rightarrow 2Ca_{(s)} + O_{2(g)}$

Example

Word equation: Two moles of solid aluminum oxide react to form four moles of solid aluminum plus three moles of oxygen gas.

Balanced chemical equation:
$2Al_2O_{3(s)} \rightarrow 4Al_{(s)} + 3O_{2(g)}$

Single replacement—In single replacement reactions, the reactants are an element and a compound, as are the products; i.e., $AB + C \rightarrow A + BC$.

Example

Word equation: One mole of solid copper plus two moles of aqueous silver nitrate react to form one mole of aqueous copper(II) nitrate plus two moles of solid silver.

Balanced chemical equation:

$$Cu_{(s)} + 2AgNO_{3(aq)} \rightarrow Cu(NO_3)_{2(aq)} + 2Ag_{(s)}$$

Example

Word equation: One mole of chlorine gas plus two moles of aqueous sodium bromide react to produce two moles of aqueous sodium chloride plus one mole of liquid bromine.

Balanced chemical equation:

$$Cl_{2(g)} + 2NaBr_{(aq)} \rightarrow 2NaCl_{(aq)} + Br_{2(l)}$$

Double replacement—In double replacement reactions, the reactants and the products are both compounds. The metal from one reactant combines with the non-metal from the other reactant. There will always be a metal with a non-metal. A double replacement reaction can be shown as $AB + CD \rightarrow AD + CB$.

Example

Word equation: One mole of aqueous lead(II) nitrate plus two moles of aqueous potassium iodide react to produce one mole of solid lead(II) iodide plus two moles of aqueous potassium nitrate.

Balanced chemical reaction:

$$Pb(NO_3)_{2(aq)} + 2KI_{(aq)} \rightarrow PbI_{2(s)} + 2KNO_{3(aq)}$$

Example

Word equation: One mole of aqueous hydrochloric acid plus one mole of sodium hydroxide react to produce aqueous sodium chloride plus one mole of liquid water.

Balanced chemical equation:

$$HCl_{(aq)} + NaOH_{(aq)} \rightarrow NaCl_{(aq)} + HOH_{(l)}$$

Combustion—In combustion reactions, a fuel combines with oxygen to form products that are oxides. They are all exothermic.

Example

Word equation: One mole of methane gas plus two moles of oxygen gas react to form two moles of water vapour plus two moles of carbon dioxide gas.

Balanced chemical equation:

$$CH_{4(g)} + 2O_{2(g)} \rightarrow 2H_2O_{(g)} + CO_{2(g)}$$

Example

Word equation: Four moles of solid aluminum react with three moles of oxygen gas to produce two moles of solid aluminum oxide.

Balanced chemical equation:

$$4Al_{(s)} + 3O_{2(g)} \rightarrow 2Al_2O_{3(s)}$$

Practice Questions: 22, 23, 24, NR3, 25, 27, 32, WR1

2.1 *illustrate an awareness of WHMIS guidelines, and demonstrate safe practices in the handling, storage, and disposal of chemicals in the laboratory and at home*

Safety Guidelines and Practices

WHMIS stands for Workplace Hazardous Materials Information System. WHMIS symbols are used to identify and classify hazardous materials. As well, every chemical used in laboratories, including school labs, is supplied with a Material Safety Data Sheet (MSDS). An MSDS provides specific information about each chemical, including how to dispose of it in a safe and environmentally responsible manner. These guidelines are used not only by chemists but by those in a number of fields, including chemical engineering, transportation, plumbing, and biomedical research.

WHMIS Symbols

	Class A: Compressed gas
	Class B: Flammable and combustible material
	Class C: Oxidizing material
	Class D: Division 1: Poisonous and infectious material—immediate and serious toxic effects
	Class D: Division 2: Poisonous and infectious material—other toxic effects
	Class D: Poisonous and infectious material—biohazardous infectious material
	Class E: Corrosive material
	Class F: Dangerously reactive material

Practice Question: WR2c

PRACTICE QUESTIONS—ENERGY AND MATTER IN CHEMICAL CHANGE

1. What subatomic particle has a +1 charge and is found in the nucleus?
   A. Proton
   B. Photon
   C. Neutron
   D. Electron

2. The nucleus of an atom can be defined as the central dense region that
   A. makes up most of the mass of the atom
   B. takes up most of the volume of the atom
   C. makes up about half the mass of the atom
   D. takes up about half the volume of the atom

Use the following information to answer the next question.

In 1993, a 14-year-old girl in British Columbia fell through the ice of a fast-moving river and became trapped underneath. The current carried her 1.7 km downstream under the ice before she found open water. Amazingly, she was able to breathe under the ice by floating on her back and keeping her nose and mouth in a thin layer of air that had formed between the ice and water.

3. Ice floats on top of water because ice is
   A. less dense than water
   B. slightly more dense than water
   C. composed of different atoms than water
   D. positively charged, whereas water is negatively charged

Use the following information to answer the next question.

The water strider is an insect that can walk on the surface of ponds. It has long legs that spread out to distribute the insect's weight over a relatively large area. The surface tension of water allows the strider to move across the water without sinking.

4. The property of water that creates this surface tension is its
   A. high specific heat capacity
   B. high boiling point
   C. hydrogen bonds
   D. low density

5. Which of the following diagrams represents the polar nature of water?

   A.

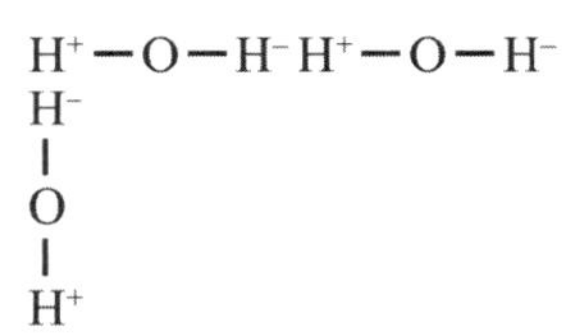

   B.

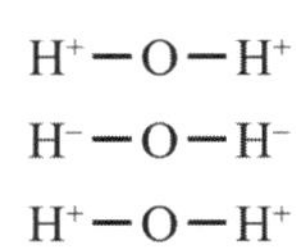

   C.

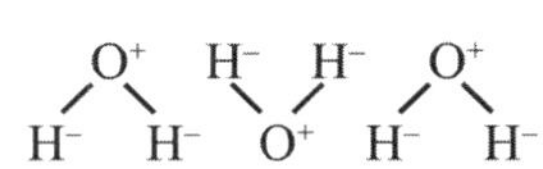

   D.

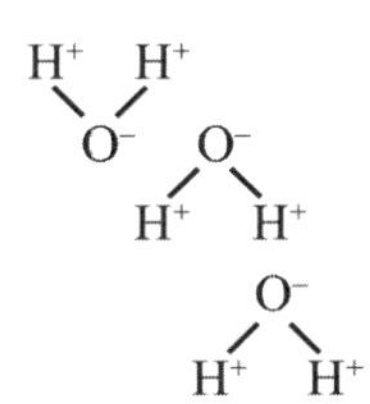

6. Which of the following events is an example of a chemical change?
   A. A Popsicle melting
   B. A metal bar rusting
   C. Pulling copper into a thin wire
   D. Heating iodine to produce violet fumes

Use a periodic table to answer the next two questions.

7 If lithium (Li) reacts moderately with water and sodium (Na) reacts vigorously with water, which of the following metals would be expected to react **most vigorously** with water?
   A. Fe
   B. Al
   C. Be
   D. Cs

Use the following information to answer the next question.

> In 1962, Canadian chemist Neil Bartlett synthesized a compound that most chemists thought could never be synthesized, because it contained an element that was thought to be non-reactive. Bartlett's synthesis showed that although this element had very low reactivity, it could be reactive under the right circumstances.

8. Which of the following compounds did Bartlett **most likely** synthesize?
   A. $KPtF_6$
   B. $SePtF_6$
   C. $XePtF_6$
   D. $RhPtF_6$

Use the following information to answer the next question.

> Red blood cells contain hemoglobin proteins. Each hemoglobin protein is tightly bound to an iron(II) ion. The iron(II) ion binds oxygen molecules, allowing blood to transport oxygen to various parts of the body.

9. Iron(II) and iron(III) ions are represented respectively as
   A. Fe^{2+} and Fe^{3+}
   B. Fe^{2+} and Fe^{3-}
   C. Fe^{2-} and Fe^{3+}
   D. Fe^{2-} and Fe^{3-}

Use a periodic table to answer the next three questions.

10. The element that makes up the major portion of air that humans breathe is located in Group
   A. 14
   B. 15
   C. 16
   D. 17

11. Elements that form ions that have a charge of –1 are from Group
   A. 1
   B. 2
   C. 17
   D. 18

12. The substance that forms a colourless, odourless, and extremely flammable gas and is also believed to make up about 75% of the atoms in the universe has an atomic number of
   A. 1
   B. 2
   C. 6
   D. 8

Use the following information to answer the next question.

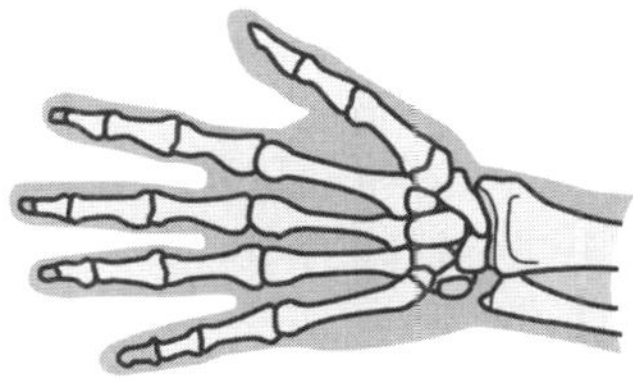

Using a cathode-ray tube, Wilhelm Roentgen accelerated electrons emitted from a hot tungsten surface onto a screen. When Roentgen placed his hand behind the screen, he saw an image of his hand bones on the wall. Roentgen named the unknown radiation, which had illuminated his hand, X-rays.

13. After electrons were emitted from the tungsten surface, the tungsten

A. remained neutral

B. became positively charged

C. became negatively charged

D. alternated between a positive charge and a negative charge

Use the following information to answer the next question.

Carbon-14, unlike carbon-12, is a radioactive isotope of carbon. All organic matter contains a certain amount of carbon-14. After an organism dies, the carbon-14 within it begins to decay at a constant rate. Earth scientists at the University of Alberta use carbon dating to estimate the age of organic material from the last glacial era. Such information enables them to predict the location of natural resources and minerals.

14. One difference between carbon-14 and carbon-12 is that carbon-14 has

A. more protons than carbon-12

B. more neutrons than carbon-12

C. a lower ionic charge than carbon-12

D. a higher ionic charge than carbon-12

15. Which of the following statements regarding the masses of atomic structures is **true**?

A. Protons and electrons have greater masses than neutrons.

B. Electrons and neutrons have greater masses than protons.

C. Neutrons and protons have greater masses than electrons.

D. Protons, neutrons, and electrons have approximately the same mass.

Use the following information to answer the next question.

Some of the strongest known acids are formed by dissolving hydrogen halides in water. A hydrogen halide is formed when an atom from one of the Group 17 elements (the halogens) forms a compound with hydrogen. Four examples of hydrogen halides are shown here.

1. Hydrogen chloride (HCl)
2. Hydrogen fluoride (HF)
3. Hydrogen bromide (HBr)
4. Hydrogen iodide (HI)

Numerical Response

1. Listed in order of increasing molecular mass, these four hydrogen halides are _____, _____, _____, and _____.

16. With respect to their location in an atom, electrons are **best** described as

A. orbiting the atom

B. being contained within the nucleus

C. being evenly distributed throughout the nucleus

D. occupying a large space surrounding the nucleus

17. A potassium atom has 19 protons and 19 electrons. From the lowest energy level to the highest, the electrons in a potassium atom are arranged in the order

A. 1, 2, 8, and 8

B. 1, 8, 2, and 8

C. 2, 8, 8, and 1

D. 8, 8, 2, and 1

18. When a potassium atom forms an ion, its name and symbol respectively are

A. potasside and K^+

B. potasside and K^-

C. potassium ion and K^+

D. potassium ion and K^-

19. Which of the following ionic formulas represents the reaction of potassium with another element?

A. K_2S

B. KN_3

C. KCl_2

D. K_3Al

20. The formulas for iron(II) oxide and iron(III) oxide respectively are

A. FeO and Fe_2O_3

B. Fe_2O and Fe_3O_2

C. FeO_2 and Fe_2O_4

D. Fe_2O_2 and Fe_2O_3

Use the following information to answer the next question.

Automobile exhaust is a major contributor to air pollution in many industrialized cities. New automobile technology is helping to cut down on the pollutants within automobile emissions. For example, new automobiles are designed to cut down on CO emissions. When the engines of these cars are idling, they produce emissions that contain a maximum of 0.1% CO. By comparison, the emissions of older automobiles of all makes contained on average 4 to 8% CO.

21. The correct classification and systematic name for CO is given in row

Row	Type of Compound	Systematic Name
A.	Ionic	Carbon monoxide
B.	Molecular	Carbon monoxide
C.	Ionic	Carbon oxide
D.	Molecular	Carbon dioxide

Use the following information to answer the next question.

Aluminum is the second most abundant metal in Earth's crust. When exposed to oxygen, aluminum can react to form aluminum oxide.

Numerical Response

2. If the chemical formula for aluminum oxide is Al_xO_y, the numerical values of x and y respectively are ____ and ____.

Use the following information to answer the next question.

Both the United States and Canada are trying to decrease their production of sulfur dioxide gas, a byproduct of some common industrial processes and a principal cause of acid rain. Sulfur dioxide is produced along with zinc oxide when zinc sulfide undergoes combustion.

22. Which of the following chemical equations describes the given reaction?

A. $2ZnS_{(s)} + 3O_{2(g)} \rightarrow 2ZnO_{(s)} + 2SO_{2(g)}$

B. $2ZnS_{(s)} + 3O_{2(g)} \rightarrow 2ZnO_{2(s)} + 2SO_{(g)}$

C. $3ZnS_{(s)} + 4O_{2(g)} \rightarrow 3ZnO_{(s)} + 3SO_{2(g)}$

D. $2ZnS_{(s)} + 3O_{2(s)} \rightarrow 2ZnO_{(s)} + 2SO_{2(s)}$

Use the following information to answer the next two questions.

Edmonton's Clover Bar Landfill has recently received international acclaim for its system of capturing waste methane gas. Methane is produced when garbage is decomposed by bacteria. Once in the atmosphere, methane has a significant effect on global warming. The Clover Bar Landfill has developed a way to recover methane (the main component of natural gas) and use it as fuel to produce heat. An unbalanced equation for the combustion of methane is shown here.

$$\_\_CH_{4(g)} + \_\_O_{2(g)} \rightarrow \_\_CO_{2(g)} + \_\_H_2O_{(g)}$$

23. Which of the following sets of coefficients balances the given equation when inserted from left to right?

A. 2, 1, 1, 2 **B.** 2, 2, 1, 1

C. 1, 1, 2, 2 **D.** 1, 2, 1, 2

24. In the given reaction, the reactant or product that can be defined as a molecular element is

A. O_2 **B.** CH_4

C. CO_2 **D.** H_2O

Use the following information to answer the next question.

Butane, $C_4H_{10(g)}$, is commonly used in lighters that people use to light barbecues or candles. When the lighter is ignited, the following reaction takes place:

$$2C_4H_{10(g)} + 13O_{2(g)} \rightarrow 8CO_{2(g)} + 10H_2O_{(g)}$$

1. Physical change
2. Chemical change
3. Endothermic reaction
4. Exothermic reaction
5. Formation reaction
6. Decomposition reaction
7. Single replacement reaction
8. Double replacement reaction
9. Combustion reaction

Numerical Response

3. When listed in ascending numerical order, the descriptions that can be used to classify the butane reaction are _____, _____, and _____.

25. The exhaust that can be seen coming from the chimneys of homes during the winter is

A. water vapour that has condensed

B. methane that has not yet been burned

C. the pollutants of combustion (often called smog)

D. carbon dioxide combined with other greenhouse gases

Use the following information to answer the next question.

Many gases, including carbon dioxide, contribute to the effects of global warming. Photosynthesis is a process that removes carbon dioxide gas from the atmosphere. Photosynthesis can be represented by the following balanced equation:
$6H_2O + 6CO_2 \rightarrow C_6H_{12}O_6 + 6O_2$

26. Photosynthesis can be described as which of the following types of reactions?

A. Formation

B. Exothermic

C. Endothermic

D. Decomposition

Use the following information to answer the next question.

$$NaOH_{(aq)} + HCl_{(aq)} \rightarrow NaCl_{(aq)} + H_2O_{(l)}$$

27. The given reaction is an example of which of the following types of chemical reactions?

A. Combustion

B. Decomposition

C. Single replacement

D. Double replacement

28. If 18 mol of carbon dioxide and an unlimited supply of water and sunlight were available to a plant, how many moles of glucose would it produce?

A. 1 mol

B. 3 mol

C. 6 mol

D. 9 mol

Use the following information to answer the next question.

A mole is the amount of a substance that contains particles equal to Avogadro's number, 6.02×10^{23}. In simpler terms, one mole of any compound is equal to its molecular weight in grams. To calculate the molar mass of a compound, refer to the periodic table for the atomic mass in grams of each of the elements that make up the compound. Adding these atomic masses together gives the molar mass of the entire compound. For example, the molar mass of CO_2 is equal to the atomic masses (in grams) of carbon + oxygen + oxygen.

Numerical Response

4. To the nearest whole number, the molar mass of water is _______ g.

Use the following information to answer the next question.

Frost forms when moisture in the air condenses onto surfaces such as windows. The condensation then freezes as a result of cold air temperatures, and white crystals form. During the formation of frost, heat is released into the air.

29. The formation of frost is an example of an

A. exothermic physical change

B. exothermic chemical change

C. endothermic physical change

D. endothermic chemical change

Use the following information to answer the next question.

During the fractionation phase of the refining process, crude oil is separated into several useful parts. Some of these parts are gasoline, kerosene, light gas oil, and heavy gas oil. During fractionation, the temperature of the crude oil mixture is raised until one of these components becomes a gas and separates from the rest of the mixture. This component is removed, and the temperature of the crude oil is again raised until the next component separates.

30. The fractionation process functions by relying upon the

A. chemical properties of the components

B. physical properties of the components

C. products of hydrocarbon combustion

D. decomposition of crude oil

Use the following information to answer the next two questions.

Two important components of insecticides are copper(II) nitrate and copper(II) sulfate. To test for the presence of copper(II) ions in a solution of insecticide, sodium hydroxide is added. When sodium hydroxide reacts with copper(II) nitrate, the products are sodium nitrate and copper(II) hydroxide.

31. Evidence that this reaction has occurred would be the

A. formation of gas bubbles

B. appearance of a precipitate

C. increasing pH of the solution

D. ability of the resulting solution to conduct electricity

32. It is possible to extract pure silver from a silver nitrate solution by adding pure copper(II) to the solution. The balanced chemical equation that describes this process is

A. $2Cu_{(s)} + Ag(NO_3)_{2(aq)} \rightarrow 2CuNO_{3(aq)} + Ag_{(s)}$

B. $2Cu_{(s)} + Ag(NO_3)_{2(s)} \rightarrow 2CuNO_{3(s)} + Ag_{(s)}$

C. $Cu_{(s)} + 2AgNO_{3(aq)} \rightarrow Cu(NO_3)_{2(s)} + 2Ag_{(s)}$

D. $Cu_{(aq)} + 2AgNO_{3(aq)} \rightarrow Cu(NO_3)_{2(aq)} + 2Ag_{(aq)}$

33. A chemist mixes a solution of potassium iodide ($KI_{(aq)}$) and lead nitrate ($Pb(NO_3)_2$). According to a solubility chart, what precipitate will form?

A. $Pb(NO_3)_2$

B. KNO_3

C. PbI_2

D. KI

Written Response

Use the following information to answer the next three questions.

Many frying pans and cooking utensils that have non-stick coatings are coated with a type of plastic called Teflon. Teflon is a soft, waxy, opaque material that is 90% crystalline and has a molar mass of between 500 000 g/mol and 2 000 000 g/mol. This material is made up of a polymer chain of repeated units of a simple organic molecule of carbon and fluorine atoms, which are covalently bonded to one another (C_2F_4). One of the advantages of Teflon is that it is strongly resistant to chemical changes and high temperatures.

1. **a)** A chemical engineer who wanted to make 1 mol of Teflon ended up with 1 000 kg of Teflon. Explain whether or not she made a mistake.

b) If the molecular mass of a single unit of C_2F_4 is 60 amu, how many units are there in a Teflon molecule with a mass of 500 000 amu? Give your answer to the nearest whole number.

c) Why does Teflon have a range of molecular masses (500 000 g/mol to 2 000 000 g/mol)?

Use this additional information to answer the next two questions.

Although Teflon is very resistant to high temperatures (and can therefore be used in cooking and industrial applications), at temperatures above 600°C, the bonds between the carbon and fluorine atoms begin to break down and Teflon depolymerizes. Even at 400°C, some Teflon particles can become airborne, causing people exposed to them to develop a flu-like condition known as polymer fume fever.

d) Is depolymerization a physical change or a chemical change? Explain your answer.

e) Since Teflon is used to protect cooking utensils, should people be worried about developing polymer fume fever? Provide some guidelines that could be printed on the packaging for Teflon-coated cooking utensils.

Use the following information to answer the next three questions.

Ms. Francic, a science teacher, entered her room one morning and saw that a beaker containing clear liquid had been left on one of the lab benches. The day before, the students had been carrying out a number of chemistry experiments, and she did not know who had left the beaker or what it may have contained. When the students entered the classroom, Ms. Francic asked the students if they knew what was in the beaker. "I think that is the hydrochloric acid I was using," said Maria. "It could be the sodium sulfate solution I was using," said Jordan. "I think it is a butanol solution," said Tracy.

"How will we be able to figure out what is in this beaker?" asked Ms. Francic. "Tasting it is not an option."

2. **a)** Describe a diagnostic test that could be performed to determine if the solution is the hydrochloric acid that Maria was using.

b) To determine if the solution is the sodium sulfate solution that Jordan was using, he needs to find out if it contains an ionic compound. Describe a diagnostic test he could perform to find out if the solution contains an ionic compound.

c) The students determine that the solution is a butanol solution. However, they are not sure if butanol is poisonous or could damage the school's plumbing, so they are not sure if it can be poured down the drain. Describe the reference material they should consult to determine the correct disposal procedure for butanol.

ANSWERS AND SOLUTIONS—PRACTICE QUESTIONS

1. A	9. A	16. D	23. D	29. A
2. A	10. B	17. C	24. A	30. B
3. A	11. C	18. C	NR3. 2 4 9	31. B
4. C	12. A	19. A	25. A	32. C
5. D	13. B	20. A	26. C	33. C
6. B	14. B	21. B	27. D	WR1. See Solution
7. D	15. C	NR2. 2 3	28. B	WR2. See Solution
8. C	NR1. 2 1 3 4	22. A	NR4. 18	

1. A

A photon is not a subatomic particle; it is a quantity of light energy. The others are subatomic particles. Protons and neutrons are in the nucleus. A proton has a charge of +1; a neutron has no charge. An electron has a charge of –1 and exists outside the nucleus.

2. A

Almost all the mass of the atom is in the nucleus, which is occupied by protons and neutrons. The electrons that exist outside the nucleus have almost no mass. The nucleus contains very little of the volume of the atom. Most of the volume is the space occupied by the electrons.

3. A

Ice floats on water because ice is less dense than water. Water has a unique quality in that its solid form is less dense than its liquid form. As with all substances, the denser form (water) sinks and the less dense substance (ice) floats. Water has its greatest density at 4°C. Both ice and water are composed of molecules containing an oxygen atom with a charge of –2 and two hydrogen atoms each with a charge of +1.

Therefore, both ice and water are electrically neutral: $(-2 + 1 + 1 = 0)$.

4. C

The high surface tension of water is created by its hydrogen bonds. Hydrogen bonding exists between the hydrogen and oxygen atoms of adjacent molecules in water. Thus, it is a bond that exists between molecules, not within a molecule of water. The hydrogen bonds are also responsible for the high specific heat capacity and relatively high boiling point of water. However, neither the specific heat capacity nor the boiling point is responsible for the surface tension of water.

5. D

Diagrams A and B depict hydrogen as having either a positive or a negative charge and oxygen as neutral, which is incorrect. Diagram C depicts hydrogen as negative and oxygen as positive. Since the reverse is true, alternative C is incorrect. Diagrams A, B, and C also indicate that there is bonding between similar atoms of different molecules; i.e., H–H or O–O, which is also incorrect.

6. B

During a chemical change, new substances are formed. When metal rusts, a chemical reaction (oxidation) that creates a new substance (rust) occurs. This is a chemical change.

During a physical change no new substances are formed. A change of state, such as Popsicle melting or iodine vaporising are physical changes. Pulling copper into a wire is also a physical change.

7. D

Lithium and sodium are both members of the alkali metal group (Group 1) on the periodic table. In a group, all elements have similar properties. If lithium and sodium react with water, it is reasonable to assume that the other elements in this group will as well. In Group 1, the reactivity of the elements increases from top to bottom. Cesium (Cs) is near the bottom of Group 1, and therefore you can predict that it is the most reactive of the given elements and would react the most vigorously with water.

8. C

The only difference among the four compounds $RhPtF_6$, $KPtF_6$, $XePtF_6$, and $SePtF_6$, is the first element in each. Therefore, analyze the relative reactivities of the elements Rh, K, Xe, and Se.

On the periodic table, locate the group that each element belongs to.

Rh—Group 9
K—Group 1
Xe—Group 18
Se—Group 16

Since Xe belongs to Group 18 (noble gases), it would be the least reactive of the elements. Therefore, the compound that contains Xe (xenon) is the compound that Bartlett most likely synthesized.

9. A

The roman numerals in brackets are derived from the Stock system. The Stock system is useful for most transition metals (Group 3 to the non-metals), which can have more than one ion charge. The Stock system indicates the charge, as seen in the following examples:

Nickel(II)—Ni^{2+}
Nickel(III)—Ni^{3+}
Copper(II)—Cu^{2+}
Copper(I)—Cu^{+}
Iron(II)—Fe^{2+}
Iron(III)—Fe^{3+}

10. B

Earth's atmosphere is 70% nitrogen gas and 21% oxygen gas. The remaining 9% is composed of neon, argon, and other gases. Therefore, the element that makes up the major portion of air that humans breathe is nitrogen. Nitrogen (N) is located in Group 15.

11. C

Elements in Group 1 lose one electron to form ions with a +1 charge.

Elements in Group 2 lose two electrons to form ions with a +2 charge.

Elements in Group 17 gain one electron to form ions with a –1 charge.

Elements in Group 18 do not normally form ions, because they have filled valence electron shells and therefore are most stable in their elemental form.

12. A

Hydrogen gas makes up 75% of the atoms in the universe. Because hydrogen has only one proton, its atomic number is 1.

13. B

Initially, each atom of tungsten had an equal number of protons and electrons. When electrons were emitted from the atoms of tungsten, there were more positively charged protons in the atoms than negatively charged electrons. The result is a net positive charge on the tungsten surface.

14. B

Carbon-14 and carbon-12 are isotopes of carbon. Isotopes are elements that have the same atomic number (and therefore the same number of protons) but different atomic masses. The atomic mass depends on the number of protons, neutrons, and electrons in the atom. Since isotopes are not ions, the number of electrons is also the same as the number of protons. Therefore, since the number of protons and electrons does not change, the only difference between isotopes of an element is the number of neutrons that are contained in the nucleus of the atom.

15. C

Recall the relative masses of the three fundamental particles found in an atom. The masses of protons, neutrons, and electrons are shown here.

Particle	Relative Mass	Mass (g)
Proton	1 836	1.67×10^{-24}
Neutron	1 839	1.67×10^{-24}
Electron	1	9.11×10^{-28}

Protons and neutrons have approximately the same mass, and both have a larger mass than electrons.

NR 1 2 1 3 4

Molecular mass is a reflection of the number of atoms in a molecule and their atomic masses. Each of the molecules in the question contains a hydrogen atom and a halide. Since each hydrogen halide molecule has one atom of hydrogen, the difference in molecular mass is a result of the difference in atomic mass of the four halogens: chlorine, fluorine, bromine, and iodine. In Group 17 on the periodic table, the order of these elements from top to bottom is F, Cl, Br, and I.

On the periodic table, elements that are in the same group increase in atomic mass from the top to the bottom of the group. Therefore, in order of their masses, the four elements are F, Cl, Br, and I. Therefore, the four hydrogen halides listed in order of increasing molecular mass are HF, HCl, HBr, and HI (2, 1, 3, and 4).

16. D

The atom consists of a tiny nucleus containing positively charged protons and uncharged neutral neutrons. Negatively charged electrons occupy a large space surrounding the nucleus, which is sometimes referred to as an electron cloud.

17. C

The maximum number of electrons that can exist at each energy level, starting at the lowest energy level, is 2, 8, and 8. Lower energy levels are filled first. Therefore, potassium's 19 electrons are arranged in the order 2, 8, 8, and 1.

18. C

Metals, such as potassium, retain their names when they become ions. Potassium loses one electron to become a 1^+ ion, so the symbol is K^+.

	Atom	Ion
Electrons in each energy level	1e	0e
	8e	8e
	8e	8e
	2e	2e
Symbol	K	K+
Protons and electrons	19p(+) 19e(–)	19p(+) 18e(–)
Charge	0	1+

19. A

In a correct ionic formula, the positive charge equals the negative charge, making the formula balanced. The ions with their charges are shown here.

Al^{3+}, N^{3-}, Cl^{-}, S^{2-}

A. K_2^{2+} S^{2-} Balanced

B. K^+ N_3^{9-} Not balanced

C. K^+ Cl_2^{2-} Not balanced

D. K_3^{3+} Al^{3+} Not balanced

20. A

To answer this question, first use the Stock system to find the ion charges.
Iron(II): Fe^{2+}
Iron(III): Fe^{3+}

In a balanced ionic formula, the positive and negative charges are balanced.

A. Fe^{2+} O^{2-}, $Fe_2^{6+}O_3^{6-}$ Balanced

B. Fe_2^{4+} O^{2-}, $Fe_3^{9+}O_2^{4-}$ Not balanced

C. Fe^{2+} O_2^{4-}, $Fe_2^{6+}O_4^{8-}$ Not balanced

D. Fe_2^{4+} O_2^{4-}, $Fe_2^{6+}O_3^{6-}$ Balanced, but without the lowest possible coefficients

21. B

The molecule CO is composed of two non-metals: carbon (C) and oxygen (O). A compound that is composed entirely of non-metals is called a molecular compound because the non-metals form covalent bonds through the sharing of electrons.

Molecular compounds are named systematically by using the following rules (CO is shown as an example):

1. Write the entire name of the first element in the compound.
carbon

2. Write the name of the second element, changing its ending to –ide.
oxide

3. Use prefixes to indicate the number of each type of atom in the formula. Normally, the prefix mono- is not used when there is only one atom of the first element.
carbon monoxide

1	mono-	6	hexa-
2	di-	7	hepta-
3	tri-	8	octa-
4	tetra-	9	nona-
5	penta-	10	deca-

NR 2 2 3

Aluminum oxide is an ionic compound because it contains a metal (aluminum) and a non-metal (oxygen). Each molecule in an ionic compound is held together by an ionic bond, which is a bond formed from the attraction between two oppositely charged ions. In this case, the ions are aluminum ions (Al^{3+}) and oxygen ions (O^{2-}).

In an ionic compound, the total number of positive and negative charges must be equal. In other words, the sum of the ionic charges must be equal to zero.

Each Al atom loses three electrons to become an Al^{3+} ion. Each O atom gains two electrons to become an O^{2-} ion. Two Al^{3+} ions balance three O^{2-} ions.

$$2(+3)+3(-2)$$
$$6+(-6)=0$$

Therefore, the formula for aluminum oxide is Al_2O_3. The values of *x* and *y* respectively are 2 and 3.

22. A

The balanced chemical reaction formula for the production of sulfur dioxide is as follows:

$$2ZnS_{(s)}+3O_{2(g)}\rightarrow 2ZnO_{(s)}+2SO_{2(g)}$$

A. This is the correct formula for the reaction, which includes the correct states, the correct chemical formulas for each compound, and balanced coefficients for each reactant and product.

B. This response is incorrect because the formula for sulfur dioxide is incorrectly stated as $SO_{(g)}$, not $SO_{2(g)}$. Sulfur dioxide must have two oxygen atoms in it, as the prefix di- in the name indicates.

C. This reaction is incorrect because the equation is improperly balanced. On the left side of the reaction, there are eight oxygen atoms, and on the right side of the reaction, there are nine oxygen atoms.

D. This reaction is incorrect because all the states in the reaction are listed as solids. Oxygen (O_2) and sulfur dioxide are both gases.

23. D

According to the law of conservation of mass, the number of atoms of each element on the reactant side must be the same as the number of atoms of each element on the product side.

Count the atoms in the picture below.

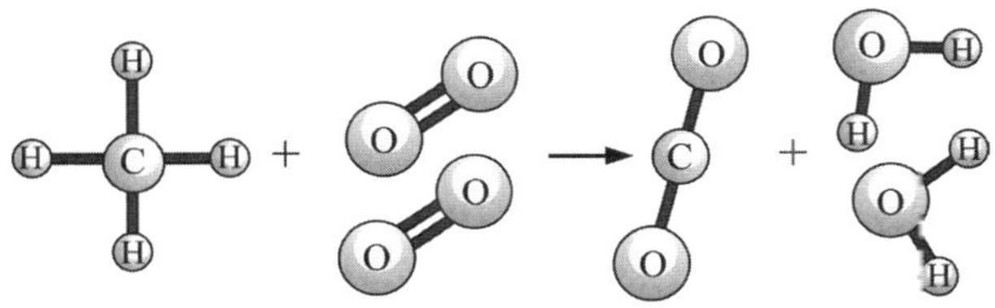

1 C	1 C
4 H	4 H
4 O	4 O

$CH_4 + 2O_2 \rightarrow CO_2 + 2H_2O$

Thus, the correct coefficients are 1, 2, 1, 2.

24. A

An element is composed of only one kind of atom. In contrast, a compound is composed of two or more kinds of atoms. Oxygen is called a molecular element because, in a pure form, two oxygen atoms join through covalent bonds to make O_2.

NR 3 2 4 9

Recall the definitions for the given descriptions:

1. A physical change is one in which no new substances are formed.
2. A chemical change is one in which new substances are produced. The new substances in reaction of butane are CO_2 and H_2O.
3. An endothermic reaction is one that absorbs energy from its surroundings.
4. An exothermic reaction is one that releases energy to its surroundings. Burning (as in the butane reaction) releases heat energy.
5. A formation reaction is one in which simple elements combine to form larger, more complex compounds.
6. A decomposition reaction is one that produces products that are simpler than the reactants.
7. A single replacement reaction is one in which there is an exchange of one ion between the reactants to form products that are neither more nor less complex than the reactants.
8. A double replacement reaction is one in which there is a simultaneous exchange of two ions between the reactants to form products that are neither more nor less complex than the reactants.
9. A combustion reaction is a chemical reaction of a substance with oxygen that produces energy. The given reaction is a combustion reaction.

Therefore, the reaction of butane with oxygen, which produces new substances (carbon dioxide and water) and releases heat to its surroundings, can be described as a chemical change, an exothermic reaction, and a combustion reaction, which are items 2, 4, and 9, respectively.

25. A

Normally, water produced during combustion is hot and disperses as invisible vapour. However, as this vapour leaves a chimney in winter, it cools quickly, thereby producing a cloud of liquid water. Car exhaust is visible in winter for the same reason.

26. C

Photosynthesis can be described as an endothermic reaction because energy enters the reaction in the form of light.

27. D

This is a double replacement reaction because the cations of NaOH and HCl exchange places to form two new compounds: NaCl and H_2O.

28. B

Plants produce glucose through a photosynthetic reaction.

$6H_2O + 6CO_2 \rightarrow C_6H_{12}O_6 + 6O_2$

It takes 6 mol of CO_2 to make 1 mol of glucose. Therefore, 18 mol of CO_2 ($6 \times 3 = 18$) can make 3 mol of glucose ($1 \times 3 = 3$).

NR 4 18

Molar mass is the mass of 1 mol of a substance. The molar mass of any element is equal to the atomic mass of that element, in grams.

1 mol of H = 1.01 g
1 mol of O = 16.00 g

Since water is H_2O, the combined mass of the elements can be found as follows:

$$\begin{aligned} H_2 &= 1.01 \times 2 = 2.02\,\text{g} \\ O &= 16.00 \times 1 = \underline{16.00\,\text{g}} \\ & \qquad\qquad\quad 18.02\,\text{g} \end{aligned}$$

Correct to the nearest whole number, the molar mass of water is 18 g.

29. A

A physical change is one in which no new substances are formed.

A chemical change is one in which matter changes to produce new substances.

An endothermic reaction is one that absorbs energy from its surroundings.

An exothermic reaction is one that releases energy to its surroundings.

Therefore, the formation of frost, which produces no new substances (frost is only another form of the moisture in air) and releases heat to its surroundings, is an exothermic physical change.

30. B

The fractionation of crude oil into its components takes advantage of the different boiling points that the components have. As each component evaporates, it separates from the crude oil and is then piped into a separate container for further purification.

Because the boiling point of a substance is one of its physical properties, the fractionation process uses the physical properties of the components.

31. B

In the given reaction, a precipitate, copper(II) hydroxide, will form. However, no gas will form.

Since all ionic solutions conduct electricity, the reactants and products would both conduct electricity.

The base, sodium hydroxide, is broken down, so the pH will decrease.

32. C

Silver nitrate is $AgNO_{3,}$ and copper (II) nitrate is $Cu(NO_3)_2$.Both should be listed as being in an (aq) state. All compounds containing nitrate have high solubilities.

Cu and Ag are pure metals. Their states should be (s), not (aq).

33. C

Mixing a solution of $KI_{(aq)}$ and $Pb(NO_3)_{2(aq)}$ will result in the following ions in solution: K^+, I^-, Pb^{2+}, and NO_3^-. The possible compounds that could form from these ions are KI, KNO_3, $Pb(NO_3)_2$, and PbI_2. Referring to the solubility chart, ionic compounds containing the NO_3^- ion are soluble since these compounds were initially in solution. Most ionic compounds containing an I^- ion are soluble except when the compound contains the Pb^{2+} ion. Therefore, PbI_2 is insoluble, which means it is the precipitate.

1. **a)** *A chemical engineer who wanted to make 1 mol of Teflon ended up with 1 000 kg of Teflon. Explain whether or not she made a mistake.*

She did not make a mistake, because the molecular weight of Teflon can be between 500 000 g/mol and 2 000 000 g/mol. That is, 1 mol of Teflon could have a mass of between 500 000 g and 2 000 000 g, which is about 500 kg to 2 000 kg. Thus, 1 000 kg fits in that range.

b) *If the molecular mass of a single unit of C_2F_4 is 60 amu, how many units are there in a Teflon molecule with a mass of 500 000 amu? Give your answer to the nearest whole number.*

If each C_2F_4 unit has a molecular weight of 60, then about 8 333 units would be contained in one molecule that had a molecular weight of 500 000 g/mol.

This is because $\frac{500\ 000}{60} = 8\ 333$.

c) *Why does Teflon have a range of molecular masses (500 000 g/mol to 2 000 000 g/mol)?*

Teflon can have a range of molecular weights because the number of C_2F_4 units can change. The length of the polymer chain can be short or long.

d) *Is depolymerization a physical change or a chemical change? Explain your answer.*

Depolymerization is a chemical change because it is a change in the covalent bonds between the carbon and fluorine atoms.

e) *Since Teflon is used to protect cooking utensils, should people be worried about developing polymer fume fever? Provide some guidelines that could be printed on the packaging for Teflon-coated cooking utensils.*

People should not be worried, because normal cooking temperatures do not reach 400°C or above. For example, oven temperatures for cooking rarely go over 500°F, which is 260°C. Answers may vary for guidelines, but they should include suggestions to avoid using Teflon-coated materials for unintended uses that involve high heat, or to use protective equipment in the case of high-temperature Teflon exposure.

2. **a)** *Describe a diagnostic test that could be performed to determine if the solution is the hydrochloric acid that Maria was using.*

If the solution is hydrochloric acid, it will have a pH lower than 7. A number of tests can be performed to see if this solution is an acid.

A pH meter can be used. A pH meter is an electronic instrument that measures the acidity or alkalinity of a liquid with a measuring probe that is placed in the liquid. The probe is connected to an electronic meter that measures and displays the pH reading.

Another method is to use indicator paper that changes colour to show an approximate pH. Dip the paper in the solution, and then match the colour the paper becomes with a colour chart to determine the pH.

Litmus paper could also be used. In an acid, red litmus remains red, and blue litmus turns red.

Another way to determine if the solution is an acid is to put a small piece of an active metal, such as magnesium, into it. In the presence of an active metal, a reaction will occur that will release hydrogen gas, and bubbles will be observable.

b) *To determine if the solution is the sodium sulfate solution that Jordan was using, he needs to find out if it contains an ionic compound. Describe a diagnostic test he could perform to find out if the solution contains an ionic compound.*

With knowledge of the physical properties of ionic compounds, you can perform diagnostic tests to confirm whether the solution contains an ionic compound.

Physical Property		**Test**
State at room temperature	Solid	Allow water to evaporate to determine state
Boiling/melting point	High	Heat to melting and boiling points if possible
Solubility in water	High	Dissolve sample in water
Electrical conductivity	Solid-no Liquid-yes	Measure using an ohmmeter

c) *The students determine that the solution is a butanol solution. However, they are not sure if butanol is poisonous or could damage the school's plumbing, so they are not sure if it can be poured down the drain. Describe the reference material they should consult to determine the correct disposal procedure for butanol.*

All chemical containers, including those containing butanol, will have a WHMIS label. WHMIS stands for Workplace Hazardous Materials Information System. The label will show one or more warning symbols relating to the substance. As well, each substance is accompanied by an MSDS data sheet.
The MSDS sheet provides information on the hazards of the substance, including safe and environmentally responsible ways to dispose of the chemical.

UNIT TEST—ENERGY AND MATTER IN CHEMICAL CHANGE

1. According to the model proposed by John Dalton, the atom

A. is like a plum pudding

B. is solid and indivisible

C. has electrons existing in energy levels

D. has electrons spinning in circular orbits

2. Current scientific understanding of the atom suggests that

A. most of the volume is taken up by the nucleus

B. the nucleus contains only neutrons

C. most of the mass is in the nucleus

D. the nucleus contains only protons

3. The atomic number of an atom refers to how many

A. protons it has

B. neutrons it has

C. protons and neutrons it has

D. protons, neutrons, and electrons it has

4. The region around the nucleus of an atom, which makes up most of the atom's volume, is occupied by

A. protons

B. electrons

C. protons and neutrons

D. neutrons and electrons

Use the following information to answer the next question.

The three labels shown here are all from bottles of hydrogen peroxide. The percentage of hydrogen peroxide in water varies among the bottles.

H_2O_2 in H_2O:	H_2O_2 in H_2O:	H_2O_2 in H_2O:
50%	6%	3%

5. As the percentage of hydrogen peroxide (H_2O_2) in water decreases, the solution becomes

A. more corrosive

B. non-oxidizing

C. more toxic

D. less toxic

6. The correct formula for ammonium phosphate is

A. $NH_4PO_{4(s)}$

B. $NH_4(PO_4)_{3(s)}$

C. $(NH_4)_3PO_{4(s)}$

D. $(NH_4)_3(PO_4)_{4(s)}$

7. Which of the following substances is a binary molecular compound?
   A. $Cl_{2(aq)}$
   B. $NO_{2(g)}$
   C. $NaCl_{(s)}$
   D. $CuZn_{3(s)}$

8. Which of the following statements is **not** part of the empirical definition of an acid?
   A. Acids are soluble in water.
   B. Acids turn red litmus paper blue.
   C. Acids form solutions that conduct electricity.
   D. Acids can be solids, liquids, or gases at room temperature.

9. Fertilizer contains NH_4^+ and SO_4^{2-} ions. The compound formed when these ions come together would have the formula
   A. $NH_4SO_{4(s)}$
   B. $NH_4(SO_4)_{2(s)}$
   C. $(NH_4)_2SO_{4(s)}$
   D. $(NH_4)_2(SO_4)_{3(s)}$

10. The presence of an acid can be indicated by
    A. red litmus paper turning blue
    B. red litmus paper remaining red
    C. bromothymol blue remaining blue
    D. bromothymol blue becoming colourless

11. The presence of a strong base can be indicated by
    A. phenolphthalein turning pink
    B. bromothymol blue turning yellow
    C. bromothymol blue turning colourless
    D. phenolphthalein remaining colourless

12. Which of the following compounds is **not** molecular?
    A. CO_2
    B. $BaCl_2$
    C. SF_6
    D. PCl_5

13. Which of the following statements would **not** be part of an empirical definition of a molecular compound?
    A. Molecular compounds dissolve in water.
    B. Molecular compounds are composed of a metal and a non-metal.
    C. At room temperature, molecular compounds can be solids, liquids, or gases.
    D. Aqueous solutions containing molecular compounds do not conduct electricity.

14. In the unbalanced chemical equation $Ca(NO_3)_2 + Na_3PO_4 \rightarrow Ca_3(PO_4)_2 + NaNO_3$, the precipitate is
    A. calcium phosphate
    B. sodium phosphate
    C. calcium nitrate
    D. sodium nitrate

15. The molar mass of oxygen gas is
    A. 4.00 g/mol
    B. 8.00 g/mol
    C. 16.00 g/mol
    D. 32.00 g/mol

16. The molar mass of copper(II) chloride is
    A. 116.55 g/mol
    B. 134.45 g/mol
    C. 162.55 g/mol
    D. 198.45 g/mol

17. What mass of solid sodium carbonate is contained in 2 mol of the compound?

A. 127.46 g

B. 153.81 g

C. 211.98 g

D. 261.43 g

18. What mass of liquid carbon tetrachloride is contained in 6 mol of the compound?

A. 412.01 g

B. 547.46 g

C. 853.81 g

D. 922.86 g

19. Oxygen has an atomic number of 8 because each oxygen atom has eight

A. protons

B. neutrons

C. electrons

D. energy levels

Use the following information to answer the next question.

> Glucose, a carbohydrate that is produced by plants during photosynthesis, can be used by animals for energy. During cellular respiration, glucose enters into a series of reactions called the Krebs cycle. The Krebs cycle, which occurs in mitochondria, results in the release of energy from glucose.

20. The balanced equation for the aerobic respiration of glucose is

A. $C_6H_{12}O_{6(s)} + H_2O_{(g)} \rightarrow C_6H_{14}O_{7(s)}$

B. $C_6H_{12}O_{6(s)} + 3O_{2(g)} \rightarrow 12H^+ + 6CO_{2(g)}$

C. $C_6H_{12}O_{6(s)} + 6O_{2(g)} \rightarrow 6H_2O_{(g)} + 6CO_{2(g)}$

D. $C_6H_{12}O_{6(s)} + 6CO_{2(g)} \rightarrow C_{12}H_6O_{3(s)} + 3H_2O_{(g)} + 6O_{2(g)}$

Written Response

Use the following information to answer the following questions.

> A common chemical reaction that can be demonstrated in high school involves placing a piece of copper wire (copper(II)) in a solution of silver nitrate. Copper(II) has a stronger attraction for the nitrate ions than silver does, so the nitrate joins the copper, leaving silver by itself.

1. **a)** For the given chemical reaction, write a balanced equation that includes the states of matter.

b) Describe how you would be able to observe that the given reaction took place.

c) Suppose that the copper wire you used had a mass at the start of the experiment of 1.3 g and that the mass of the wire was 0.8 g when the reaction was complete. Explain why the mass of the copper wire decreased.

d) The periodic table shows that the molar mass of copper is 63.55 g/mol. How many moles of copper were consumed during this reaction?

e) The coefficients in the balanced equation represent a mole ratio. How many moles of silver would be produced for every 1 mol of copper consumed?

f) In part **d)**, the exact number of moles of copper consumed was determined. Using this value and the mole ratio from the balanced equation, predict the exact number of moles of silver produced in this reaction.

g) The periodic table shows that the molar mass of silver is 107.87 g, which means 1 mol of silver has a mass of 107.87 g. Predict the mass of silver that would be produced in the given reaction.

ANSWERS AND SOLUTIONS—UNIT TEST

1. B	6. C	11. A	16. B	WR1. See Solution
2. C	7. B	12. B	17. C	
3. A	8. B	13. B	18. D	
4. B	9. C	14. A	19. A	
5. D	10. B	15. D	20. C	

1. B

John Dalton proposed that an atom is like a billiard ball—solid and indivisible. It was Thomson who proposed that the atom was like a plum pudding, with electrons stuck on the nucleus. Rutherford proposed that electrons spin around the nucleus. Bohr proposed that electrons exist in certain energy levels.

2. C

More than 99% of the mass of the atom is taken up by the nucleus, which is composed of protons and neutrons. However, less than 1% of the volume is in the nucleus. Most of the volume is the space occupied only by electrons. Atomic mass can vary greatly, from the lightest atom, hydrogen, to very heavy atoms, such as uranium.

3. A

The atomic number indicates the number of protons each atom has.

4. B

The space around the nucleus is not all empty space. It is occupied by electrons. The nucleus, which takes up very little space in an atom, contains protons and neutrons.

5. D

From left to right, the labels show that the percentage of hydrogen peroxide in water is decreasing. The safety precautions displayed indicate that at 3% the solution is still oxidizing, but it is no longer corrosive or toxic. In comparison with the higher-concentration solutions, the 3% solution is less toxic.

6. C

Ammonium (NH_4^+) is a polyatomic ion that has a charge of +1. Phosphate (PO_4^{3-}) is a polyatomic ion that has a charge of –3. Three ammonium ions (total charge +3) are needed to balance one phosphate ion. To indicate that the 3 refers to both the nitrogen and the hydrogen of the ammonium, the ammonium ion must be in brackets followed by a 3 as a subscript.

7. B

A molecular substance is composed of non-metals joined by covalent bonds. Sodium and copper are metals. A binary molecular compound is composed of two different elements. Chlorine, being composed of only one non-metal element, is called a molecular element. $NO_{2(g)}$ contains oxygen and nitrogen (two non-metals), so it is a binary molecular compound.

8. B

An empirical definition provides information about properties that are observable. Each of the statements could be part of an empirical definition because they all provide information about observable properties, but acids do not turn red litmus paper blue. Acids turn blue litmus paper red, and red litmus paper remains red when placed in an acid.

9. C

Ammonium (NH_4^+) is a polyatomic ion that has a charge of +1. Sulfate (SO_4^{2-}) is a polyatomic ion with a charge of –2. It takes two ammonium ions (total charge +2) to balance one sulfate ion. The brackets are needed to indicate that the 2 refers to both the nitrogen and the hydrogen of the ammonium.

10. B

In an acid, red litmus paper stays red and blue litmus paper turns red. The opposite is true in a base. In an acid, bromothymol blue turns yellow. In a base, bromothymol blue remains blue.

11. A

The indicator phenolphthalein turns pink in a base and remains colourless in an acid. Bromothymol blue remains blue in a base and becomes yellow in an acid.

12. B

A molecular compound contains only non-metals. CO_2, SF_6, and PCl_5 are compounds that are composed of all non-metals. Barium is a metal, so $BaCl_2$ is an ionic compound.

13. B

An empirical definition provides information about properties that are observable. The statements all provide information about observable properties, but molecular compounds are made entirely of non-metals.

14. A

A solubility chart should be consulted to determine if an ionic compound has high or low solubility in water. However, you should memorize the following generalization: any compound containing ammonium, nitrate, or any Group 1 ion will have high solubility. Sodium is in Group 1, and since any compound containing nitrate has high solubility, that leaves only calcium phosphate as the precipitate. Checking a solubility chart would confirm that calcium phosphate has low solubility in water.

15. D

The molar mass is the mass of 1 mol of the substance. Oxygen gas has the formula O_2. The mass of 1 mol oxygen atoms is 16.00 g. Since the formula for oxygen gas is O_2, its molar mass is $16.00 \times 2 = 32.00$ g/mol.

16. B

The formula for copper(II) chloride is $CuCl_2$. The molar mass of a compound is found by adding the molar masses of the elements it contains. The molar mass of copper is 63.55 g, and the molar mass of chloride is 35.45 g. Therefore, the molar mass of the entire compound is $63.55 + 35.45 + 35.45 = 134.45$ g/mol.

17. C

First, determine the molar mass of sodium carbonate. The molar mass of a compound is found by adding the molar masses of the elements it contains. The formula for sodium carbonate is Na_2CO_3. The molar mass of sodium is 22.99 g, the molar mass of carbon is 12.01, and the molar mass of oxygen is 16.00 g. Therefore, the molar mass of sodium carbonate is

$2(22.99)+12.01+3(16.00)=105.99$ g/mol.

Since the question asked for the mass of 2 mol of sodium carbonate, the answer is $105.99 \times 2 = 211.98$ g.

18. D

First, determine the molar mass of carbon tetrachloride. The molar mass of a compound is found by adding the molar masses of the elements it contains. The formula for carbon tetrachloride is CCl_4. The molar mass of carbon is 12.01 g, and the molar mass of chlorine is 35.45 g. Therefore, the molar mass of carbon tetrachloride is $12.01 + 4(35.45) = 153.81$ g/mol.

Since the question asked for the mass of 6 mol of carbon tetrachloride, the answer is $153.81 \times 6 = 922.86$ g.

19. A

The atomic number of an element refers to the number of protons that are in the atom. Oxygen has eight protons in its nucleus.

20. C

The mass of the reactants must equal the mass of the products. In a balanced chemical equation, the total number of atoms of each element on the left side of the equation must equal the number of atoms on the right side. The process of aerobic respiration involves the reaction of glucose with oxygen to produce carbon dioxide, water, and energy. The balanced equation for this reaction is as follows:

$$C_6H_{12}O_{6(s)} + 6O_{2(g)} \rightarrow 6H_2O_{(l)} + 6CO_{2(g)} + \text{energy}$$

1. **a)** *For the given chemical reaction, write a balanced equation that includes the states of matter.*

$$Cu_{(s)} + 2AgNO_{3(aq)} \rightarrow Cu(NO_3)_2 + 2Ag_{(s)}$$

b) *Describe how you would be able to observe that the given reaction took place.*

You may see some of the copper dissolve as it reacts with the nitrate. You certainly will see solid silver appear as a precipitate.

c) *Suppose that the copper wire you used had a mass at the start of the experiment of 1.3 g and that the mass of the wire was 0.8 g when the reaction was complete. Explain why the mass of the copper wire decreased.*

As the reaction progressed, some of the copper joined the nitrate ions to become copper(II) nitrate. This would cause a reduction in the amount of copper in the copper wire.

d) *The periodic table shows that the molar mass of copper is 63.55 g/mol. How many moles of copper were consumed during this reaction?*

If 0.5 g of copper was lost from the wire, then that is the amount of copper consumed in the reaction.
$0.5 \text{ g} \times 1 \text{ mol}/63.55 \text{ g} = 0.0079 \text{ mol}$

Thus, 0.0079 mol of copper was consumed.

e) *The coefficients in the balanced equation represent a mole ratio. How many moles of silver would be produced for every 1 mol of copper consumed?*

For every 1 mol of copper consumed, 2 mol of silver will be produced.

f) *In part (d), the exact number of moles of copper consumed was determined. Using this value and the mole ratio from the balanced equation, predict the exact number of moles of silver produced in this reaction.*

In this case, 0.0079 mol of copper was consumed. For every 1 mol of copper consumed, 2 mol of silver will be produced.
$0.0079 \text{ mol} \times 2 = 0.0158 \text{ mol}$

Therefore, 0.0158 mol of silver will be produced.

g) *The periodic table shows that the molar mass of silver is 107.87 g, which means that 1 mol of silver has a mass of 107.87 g. Predict the mass of silver that would be produced in the given reaction.*

Since 0.0158 mol of silver will be produced and each mole of silver has a mass of 107.87 g, the mass of the silver that will be produced can be calculated as follows:
$107.87 \text{ g/mol} \times 0.0158 \text{ mol} = 1.70 \text{ g}$.

NOTES

Energy Flow in Technological Systems

ENERGY FLOW IN TECHNOLOGICAL SYSTEMS

Table of Correlations				
Specific Expectation	**Practice Questions**	**Unit Test Questions**	**Practice Test 1**	**Practice Test 2**
By the end of this course, students will:				
B1 Analyze and illustrate how technologies based on thermodynamics were formulated.				
B1.1 illustrate, by use of examples from natural and technological systems, that energy exists in a variety of forms	9, WR1	1, NR2, 5, 9	NR4, 16, 17	18, 19
B1.2 describe, qualitatively, current and past technologies used to transform energy from one form to another, and describe that energy transfer technologies produce measurable changes in motion, shape, or temperature		NR1, 10, 11, 12	14, 18	15
B1.3 identify the processes of trial and error that led to the invention of the engine, and relate the principles of thermodynamics to the development of more efficient engine designs				
B2 Explain and apply concepts used in theoretical and practical measures in mechanical systems.				
B2.1 describe evidence for the presence of energy; i.e., observable physical and chemical changes, and changes in motion, shape, or temperature			36	
B2.2 define kinetic energy as energy due to motion, and define potential energy as energy due to relative position or condition	23, 27, 31, WR2d	6	19	16
B2.3 describe chemical energy as a form of potential energy	25			
B2.4 define, compare, and contrast scalar and vector quantities		2		
B2.5 describe displacement and velocity quantitatively	NR1, NR2, 10, 12, 20, WR2b	3	NR7	
B2.6 define acceleration quantitatively as a change in velocity during a time interval: $\vec{a} = \frac{\Delta\vec{v}}{\Delta t}$	WR2c			WR2a
B2.7 explain that, in the absence of restive forces, motion at constant speed requires no energy input				
B2.8 recall from previous studies the operational definition of force as a push or a pull and the operational definition of work as energy expended when the speed of an object is increased or when an object is moved against the influence of on opposing force	6			
B2.9 define gravitational potential energy as the work against gravity			15	
B2.10 relate gravitational potential energy to work done using $E_p = mgh$ *and* $W = fd$*, and show that a change in energy is equal to work done on a system:* $\Delta E = W$	NR3, 11, 16, 17, 18, 19, 22, 26	8	NR6	NR3, WR2c
B2.11 quantify kinetic energy using $E_k = \frac{1}{2} mv^2$*, and relate this concept to energy conservation in transformations*	15, 21, 24	7	NR5	17, 22

B2.12 derive the SI unit of energy and work, the joule, from fundamental units				
B2.13 investigate and analyze one-dimensional scalar motion and work done on an object or system using algebraic and graphical techniques	7, 8, 14	NR3		WR2b
B3 Apply the principles of energy conservation and thermodynamics to investigate, describe, and predict the efficiency of energy transformation in technological systems.				
B3.1 describe, qualitatively and in terms of thermodynamic laws, the energy transformations occurring in devices and systems	1, WR2d	13		
B3.2 describe how the first and second laws of thermodynamics have changed scientists' understanding of energy conversions	2, 3, 13, 28	4		21
B3.3 define, operationally, useful energy from a technological perspective, and analyze the stages of useful energy transformations in technological systems		14		
B3.4 recognize that there are limits to the amount of useful energy that can be derived from the conversion of potential energy to other forms in a technological device		WR1a, WR1c		
B3.5 explain, quantitatively, efficiency as a measure of the useful work compared to the total energy put into an energy conversion process or device	29	NR4, WR1b		20, 23
B3.6 apply the concepts related to efficiency of thermal energy conversion to analyze the design of a thermal device	5			
B3.7 compare the energy content of fuels used in thermal power plants in Alberta, in terms of costs, benefits, efficiency, and sustainability				
B3.8 explain the need for efficient energy conversions to protect the environment and to make judicious use of natural resources				

ENERGY FLOW IN TECHNOLOGICAL SYSTEMS

B2.4 *define, compare, and contrast scalar and vector quantities*

B2.5 *describe displacement and velocity quantitatively*

B2.6 *define acceleration quantitatively as a change in velocity during a time interval:*

$$\vec{a} = \frac{\Delta \vec{v}}{\Delta t}$$

MOTION

Speed and velocity both describe motion, but speed is a **scalar** quantity (describes the magnitude of the motion only) and velocity is a **vector** quantity (describes the magnitude and direction of the motion). Distance travelled is a scalar quantity. Displacement is a vector quantity, because along with the distance travelled, it includes the direction.

Example

A teacher is pacing her classroom. She walks 5 m toward the east wall, then 3 m toward the west wall.

The distance the teacher travelled is a scalar quantity, so direction is not important—only her total motion is.

The total distance travelled can therefore be calculated as follows:
5 m + 3 m = 8 m

The teacher's displacement is a vector quantity, so direction is important.
5 m (east) + 3 m (west) = 2 m (east)

5 m (E) + 3 m (W) = 2 m (E)

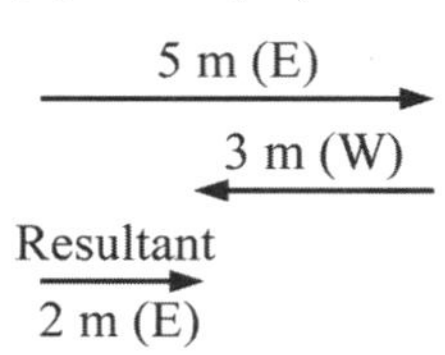

Her displacement is 2 m east.

The **velocity** of a car is generally thought of in terms of kilometres per hour; that is, the change in the distance travelled over the change in time. Velocity can be determined by using the following equation:

$$\vec{v} = \frac{\Delta \vec{d}}{\Delta t}$$

$\vec{v}$ = the velocity of the object.

The units must be indicated and should be shown as a change in a displacement unit over a time unit, such as metres per second (m/s) or kilometres per hour (km/h). Velocity is a vector quantity, so its magnitude and direction must be stated.

$\Delta \vec{d}$ = change in displacement of the object in units such as metres (m) or kilometres (km)

Displacement is a vector quantity, so the direction of motion must be included.

Δt = the change in time, or the time taken, in units such as seconds (s) or hours (h)

A **position-time graph** can be used to show velocity. The slope of the graph's line represents velocity. The slope can be determined by calculating the rise over the run. The rise is the change in position (displacement), and the run is the change in time.

$$v = \frac{\Delta y}{\Delta x}, \text{ or } \vec{v} = \frac{\Delta \vec{d}}{\Delta t}$$

The steeper the slope, the faster the velocity. A horizontal line means that the distance is not changing, or that the speed is 0. The graph below with the curved line represents an object that is accelerating. A slope that begins steep and then levels off represents an object that is slowing to a stop.

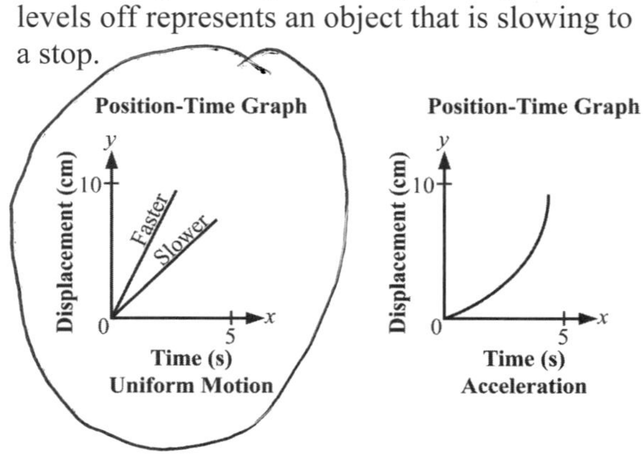

Acceleration can be thought of in terms of a change in velocity over a change in time (m/s^2) in a given direction. A **velocity-time graph** can be used to show acceleration. The graph shown here indicates that as time changes, the change in velocity becomes greater. The steeper the slope of a velocity-time graph, the greater the rate of acceleration.

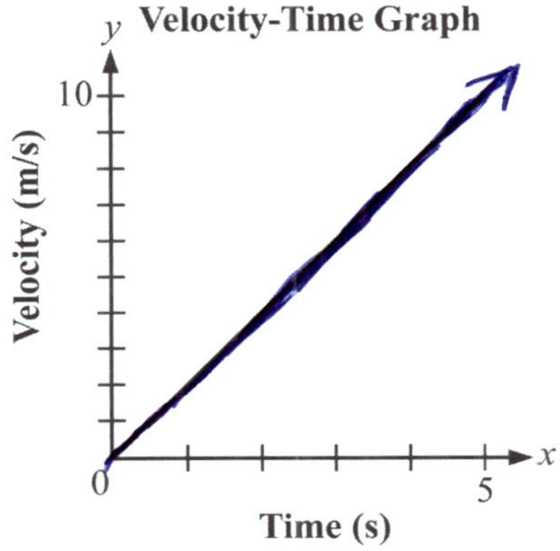

Acceleration can also be determined by using the following equation:

$$\vec{a} = \frac{\Delta \vec{v}}{\Delta t}$$

$\vec{a}$ = acceleration of the object in units such as m/s^2 or km/h^2
$\Delta \vec{v}$ = change in velocity in units like m/s or km/h
Δt = change in time in units such as seconds or hours

When you calculate the area under a velocity-time graph, you have determined the distance travelled. To do that, use the following equation:

$$d = \frac{1}{2} \times \Delta v \times \Delta t$$

On the given velocity-time graph, the distance travelled in 4 s can be determined as follows:

$$d = \frac{1}{2} \times \Delta v \times \Delta t$$
$$d = \frac{1}{2} \times 8 \text{ m/s} \times 4 \text{ s}$$
$$d = 16 \text{ m}$$

Practice Questions: NR1, NR2, 10, 12, 20, WR2b, WR2c

B2.7 *explain that, in the absence of restive forces, motion at constant speed requires no energy input*

B2.8 *recall from previous studies the operational definition of force as a push or a pull and the operational definition of work as energy expended when the speed of an object is increased or when an object is moved against the influence of on opposing force*

B2.12 *derive the SI unit of energy and work, the joule, from fundamental units*

B2.13 *investigate and analyze one-dimensional scalar motion and work done on an object or system using algebraic and graphical techniques*

FORCE AND WORK

A **force** is any push or pull on an object. If a force causes an object to move, energy has been transferred to the object.

Inertia is a term that means that if an object is not moving, it will remain motionless unless a force is applied to it. As well, if an object is moving, the law of inertia states that the object will continue to move until a force is applied to it.

To calculate the force that has been applied to an object, use the equation $F = ma$.

F = force
m = mass of the object in kilograms (kg)
a = acceleration of the object in metres per second squared (m/s^2)

The units for force are $kg{\bullet}m/s^2$, which can also be expressed as N (for newtons).

N = kg•m/s²

Work is done when a force is applied to an object and the object moves over a distance. When the object is moved, energy has been transferred to the object. The greater the force that is required, the greater the amount of work that has been done. The greater the distance the object is moved, the greater the amount of work that has been done. To calculate work, multiply the force by the distance.

$W = F \times d$
W = work done in $\text{N} \cdot \text{m}$ or J (joules)
F = force in newtons (N)
d = distance the object moved in metres (m)

If you push on an object (exert a force) but the object does not move, no energy has been transferred to the object and no work has been done.

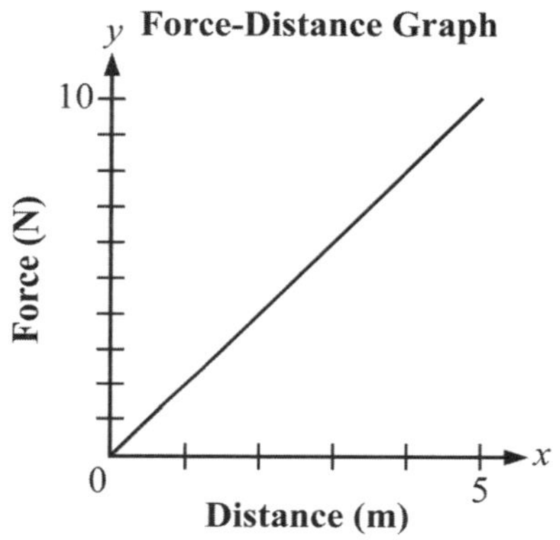

The given force-distance graph shows that force is increasing as an object moves over a certain distance. The area under the line represents the work done. You can calculate the area under the line this way: one-half of the maximum force multiplied by the total distance moved equals the area under the line.

$$W = \frac{1}{2} \times F \times d$$

$$\frac{1}{2} \times 10 \text{ N} \times 5 \text{ m} = 50 \text{ N} \cdot \text{m}$$
$$= 50 \text{ J}$$

Practice Questions: 6, 7, 8, 14

B2.2 *define kinetic energy as energy due to motion, and define potential energy as energy due to relative position or condition*

B2.10 *relate gravitational potential energy to work done using $E_p = mgh$ and $W = fd$, and show that a change in energy is equal to work done on a system: $\Delta E = W$*

B2.11 *quantify kinetic energy using $E_k = \frac{1}{2} mv^2$, and relate this concept to energy conservation in transformations*

ENERGY

Energy is the capacity to do work. Energy is normally measured in **joules**. Work and energy are closely related; when an energy transfer occurs, work has been done.

$\Delta E = W$
ΔE = change in energy measured in joules
W = work measured in joules

KINETIC ENERGY

The movement of an object represents its **kinetic energy**. The faster an object moves, the more kinetic energy it has. The greater an object's mass, the more kinetic energy it has.

The equation for calculating the kinetic energy of an object is $E_k = \frac{1}{2} mv^2$.

E_k = kinetic energy in joules (J)
m = object's mass in kilograms (kg)
v = object's speed in metres per second (m/s)

Practice Questions: NR3, 11, 15, 16, 17, 18, 19, 21, 22, 23, 26, 27, 31, WR2d

B2.3 describe chemical energy as a form of potential energy

B2.9 define gravitational potential energy as the work against gravity

POTENTIAL ENERGY

Potential energy is energy derived from the position of objects or particles, rather than their motion. If you are holding a stone, the stone is not moving, so it does not have kinetic energy. However, there are still forces acting on it. For example, a stone being held above the ground has **gravitational potential energy**. Gravitational potential energy can be calculated by using the equation $E_p = mgh$.

E_p = gravitational potential energy in joules (J)
m = object's mass in kilograms (kg)
g = the acceleration of the object due to the force of gravity (on Earth, that force is 9.81 m/s^2)
h = the object's height in metres (m)

Thus, a heavier stone, or one being held higher up, has more potential energy.

There are other kinds of potential energy. The food that we eat has **chemical potential energy.** The process of cellular respiration releases the energy from food. The human body uses this energy in the form of glucose. The gasoline used in cars also has chemical potential energy. A battery has **electrical potential energy**.

Practice Question: 25

B1.1 illustrate, by use of examples from natural and technological systems, that energy exists in a variety of forms

B3.4 recognize that there are limits to the amount of useful energy that can be derived from the conversion of potential energy to other forms in a technological device

OTHER FORMS OF ENERGY

Energy can exist in many forms. It can be heat or **electricity**. It can be kinetic (mechanical or movement) or chemical, as in gasoline or food. Light is energy. The nuclei of atoms contain nuclear energy.

Energy can be converted from one form to another, and there are many technologies that can perform this conversion. For example, electricity can be produced from the movement of water flowing through a hydroelectric dam and from the heat released during the burning of coal or other fuels. Electricity can also be produced when moving air turns a windmill or when the sunlight contacts a solar cell.

A steam engine was an early technology that functioned on the conversion of energy. The chemical energy of coal was converted to heat as it burned. The heat was used to create movement in the engine's mechanism. The first steam engines were used as water pumps, but soon after they were used in trains.

Unfortunately, the first steam engines were very inefficient. Most of the heat released from the burning of coal was lost. Very little of that heat energy was converted to a usable form.

Practice Questions: 9, WR1

B2.1 *describe evidence for the presence of energy; i.e., observable physical and chemical changes, and changes in motion, shape, or temperature*

B3.1 *describe, qualitatively and in terms of thermodynamic laws, the energy transformations occurring in devices and systems*

B3.2 *describe how the first and second laws of thermodynamics have changed scientists' understanding of energy conversions*

B3.3 *define, operationally, useful energy from a technological perspective, and analyze the stages of useful energy transformations in technological systems*

B3.5 *explain, quantitatively, efficiency as a measure of the useful work compared to the total energy put into an energy conversion process or device*

Energy Conversions

Energy is defined as the ability to do work. Energy comes from light, heat, chemicals, electricity, mechanical devices, or nuclear fission. It is possible to convert one form of energy into another form.

Energy that is stored (potential energy) is generally converted into energy of motion (kinetic energy). For example, the water behind the wall of a dam has stored energy. This energy has the potential to be changed into energy of motion. When the gate of the dam is opened, the stored energy in the water becomes energy of motion. The running water rotates the turbine and generator to produce electricity.

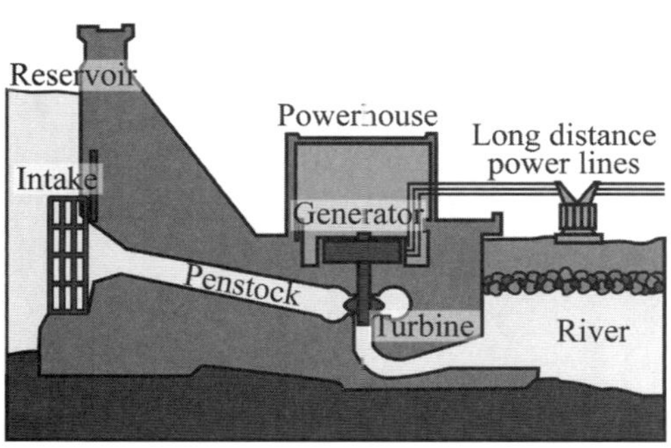

Conservation Laws

The **first law of thermodynamics** states that energy cannot be created or destroyed, although it may be converted from one form to another. For example, if you hold a stone above your head, the stone has gravitational potential energy, but because it is not moving, the stone has no kinetic energy. If you drop the stone, gravity will cause the stone to move toward the ground. The closer the stone gets to the ground, the lower its height, so the less potential energy it has. Just as the stone is reaching the ground, its potential energy is 0 J. However, as the stone is falling, it is accelerating as a result of the force of gravity. The faster the stone moves, the more kinetic energy it has. It is reaching its maximum kinetic energy just as it is reaching the ground. Throughout the fall, potential energy is converted to kinetic energy.

The Conversion of Potential Energy to Kinetic Energy as an Object Falls

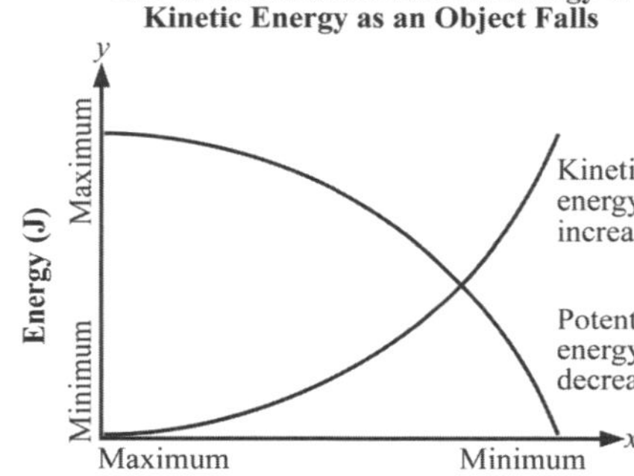

The **second law of thermodynamics** states that during an energy transfer, some of the energy is lost as heat. Consider the example of a pendulum. The bob swings back and forth because potential energy is converted to kinetic energy and then back to potential energy. If all of these conversions were 100% efficient, the bob would swing forever. However, the bob will eventually stop. This is because some energy is lost as friction from the air or within the bending string. The friction generates heat energy that is lost from the system.

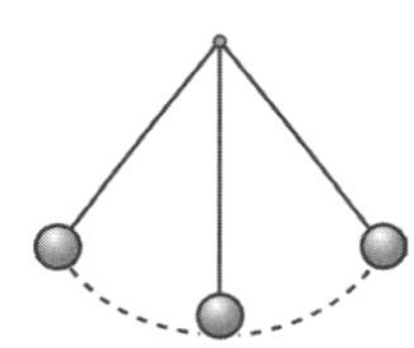

The second law also states that heat will always flow from a hot object to a cold object.
Heat pumps and heat engines make use of the second law of thermodynamics. Heat pumps remove unwanted heat from an area (for example, a refrigerator is a heat pump), while heat engines convert thermal energy into electric or mechanical energy.

Another example of energy conversion involves the consumption of gasoline by a car. The intention is to convert the chemical energy in the gas to useful kinetic energy to make the car move. However, only a small amount of the chemical energy consumed becomes movement. Most of the energy is converted into heat and is lost from the system. Inefficiency is always present to some degree in any energy conversion system.

The **efficiency** of an energy conversion system can be calculated with the following equation:

$$\%\text{ efficiency} = \frac{\text{useful energy output}}{\text{total energy input}} \times 100$$

Practice Questions: 1, 2, 3, 13, 28, 29, WR2d

B1.2 *describe, qualitatively, current and past technologies used to transform energy from one form to another, and that energy transfer technologies produce measurable changes in motion, shape or temperature*

B1.3 *identify the processes of trial and error that led to the invention of the engine, and relate the principles of thermodynamics to the development of more efficient engine designs*

B3.6 *apply the concepts related to efficiency of thermal energy conversion to analyze the design of a thermal device*

WORK DONE BY A HEAT ENGINE

A heat engine in the real world is not able to convert all of its thermal energy into work, because of the second law of thermodynamics. Some of the energy will be lost as waste heat in the cold reservoir. The given diagram shows a real heat engine.

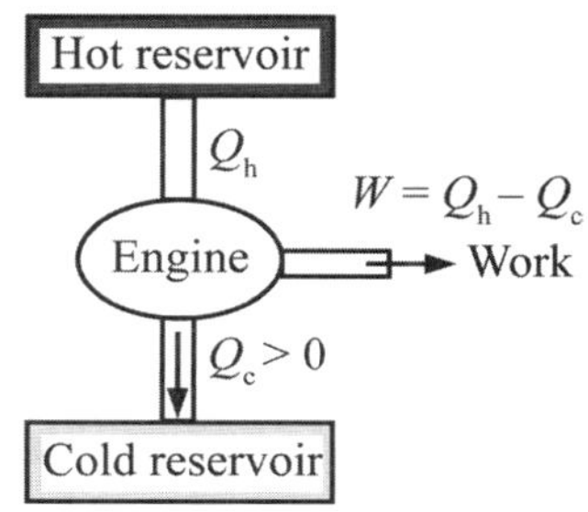

The amount of work that is done by a heat engine can be calculated by using the formula $W = Q_h - Q_c$, in which Q_h is the thermal energy added to the system by the hot reservoir and Q_c is the heat lost to the cold reservoir.

The efficiency of the engine can be calculated by using the formula $e = \frac{Q_h - Q_c}{Q_h}$ or $e = 1 - \frac{Q_c}{Q_h}$.

Example

What is the efficiency of a heat engine that does 500 J of work when 700 J of thermal energy leaves the hot reservoir?

This problem can be solved by combining the two formulas $W = Q_h - Q_c$ and $e = \frac{Q_h - Q_c}{Q_h}$ to form $e = \frac{W}{Q_h}$.

$$e = \frac{W}{Q_h}$$
$$e = \frac{500\text{ J}}{700\text{ J}}$$
$$e = 0.714 \text{ or } 71.4\%$$

DEVELOPMENT OF THE ENGINE

The development of the engine was driven by a need to increase efficiency.

In 1712, **Thomas Newcomen** (1664–1729) used a boiler to produce steam to move a piston upward within a cylinder. Cold water was used to condense the steam so that the piston would move back down. The process was very inefficient because constantly heating and cooling the piston required too much energy.

In 1763, **James Watt** (1736–1819) developed an engine that had a separate condenser that cooled the steam so that the boiler cylinder would not have to cool down. It still required a lot of heat to run since so much heat was lost to the surroundings.

In 1801, **Phillipe Lebon** (1767–1804) invented the internal combustion engine. This engine was still very inefficient and could not produce much force.

Nikolaus A. Otto (1832–1891) and **Eugen Langen** (1833–1895) improved the efficiency of the internal combustion engine. In 1867, they mixed coal gas and air and exploded it under pressure to create enough force to move pistons.

In 1885, **Gottlieb Daimler** (1834–1900) invented a petroleum-fuelled engine that was powerful enough to run an automobile.

Practice Question: 5

B3.7 *compare the energy content of fuels used in thermal power plants in Alberta, in terms of costs, benefits, efficiency, and sustainability*

B3.8 *explain the need for efficient energy conversions to protect the environment and to make judicious use of natural resources*

ENERGY IN ALBERTA

The world's population is increasing, which has led to an increase in the demand for energy. In Alberta, the majority of electrical energy generation is from coal-burning plants. Coal-burning plants tend to be inefficient, losing more than half the energy from the coal as waste heat. In recent years, therefore, scientists and engineers have worked to develop more efficient and environmentally sound ways of producing energy. For example, special scrubbers can eliminate emissions that cause acid rain. Zero-emissions coal (ZEC) processes are highly efficient and do not generate pollution.

There has also been a shift toward more efficient power plants, like hydroelectric plants, which do not contribute to global warming or acid rain production. Future energy sources will have to be efficient and have a low impact on the environment in order for people to have a sustainable future.

PRACTICE QUESTIONS—ENERGY FLOW IN TECHNOLOGICAL SYSTEMS

Use the following information to answer the next question.

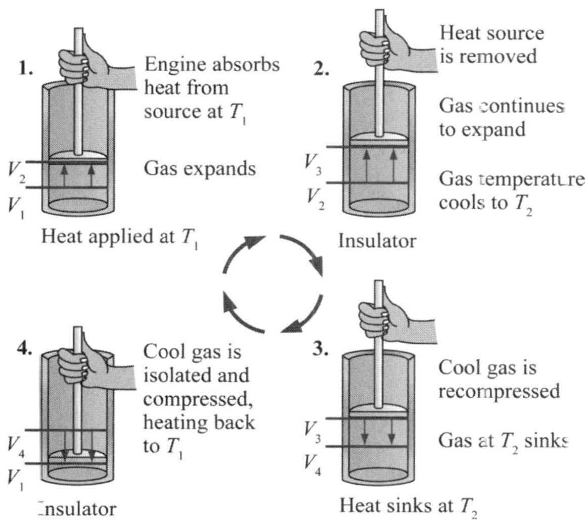

In order to study the laws of thermodynamics, scientists make use of the Carnot engine. As shown in the diagram, heat from a metal source, at a temperature (T_1), is absorbed by a gas that has a significantly lower temperature (T_2). The gas expands, driving a piston upward. Soon, the gas cools and is recompressed by the falling piston, which generates heat that is reabsorbed by the metal beneath. This is a nearly perfect energy transfer system because very little energy is lost from it.

1. What other law can this system be used to study?
   - **A.** The law of conservation of momentum
   - **B.** The law of conservation of energy
   - **C.** Newton's second law
   - **D.** Newton's first law

Use the following information to answer the next two questions.

The vacuum flask, invented by Scottish scientist Sir James Dewar in the 1890s, was first used to store liquid gases at very low temperatures. A vacuum flask can also be used to carry and insulate hot liquids. However, it is not able to maintain liquids at a constant temperature indefinitely.

2. A vacuum flask is unable to maintain a hot liquid at a constant high temperature indefinitely **mainly** because the
   - **A.** heat is slowly but invariably lost to the external environment
   - **B.** lid cannot be sealed tightly enough to prevent heat loss, so it is the only place from which heat escapes
   - **C.** heat from the liquid transfers to the air in the flask
   - **D.** temperature of the liquid declines even though heat energy is not lost

Use this additional information to answer the next question.

The structure of most vacuum flasks is very simple. The flask is a double-walled (1, 2) glass vessel sealed at the neck with a plastic cap (4). A vacuum (3) exists between the two glass walls. This vacuum hinders the flow of heat to and from the flask. Also, reflective material inside the container reduces heat loss by radiation.

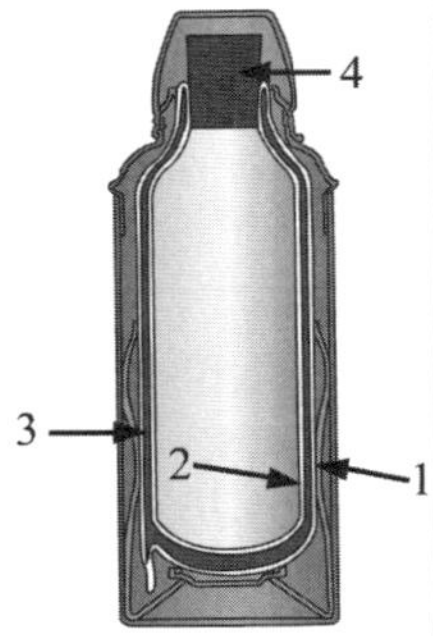

3. It is recommended that a vacuaum flask be kept upright so that no fluid comes in contact with the plastic cap, because the

A. loss of heat would be greatly accelerated through the neck of the flask since no vacuum exists there

B. fluid can diffuse out of the flask through the neck

C. diffusion of liquid through the sides of the flask is greater than through the lid

D. diffusion of liquid through the lid is greater than through the sides of the flask

Use the following information to answer the next question.

The Steel Phantom roller-coaster in the United States has the steepest and longest drop of any roller-coaster in the world. It drops 68.55 m down the side of a ravine. There are also several sections where the track loops. There is an energy transfer as the roller-coaster moves through a loop, as shown in the given diagram.

1. Into the loop
2. Top of the loop
3. Out of the loop

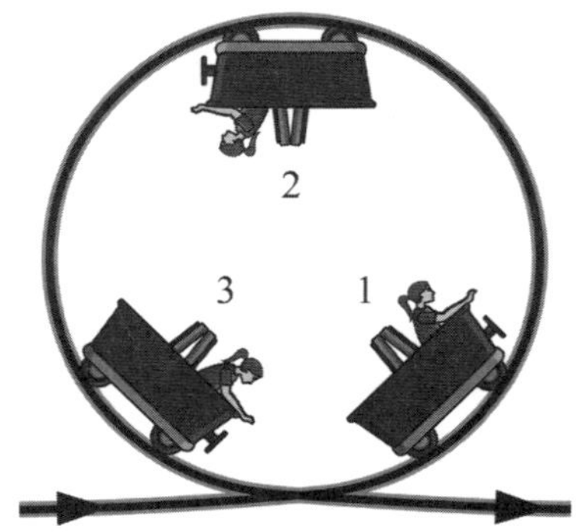

4. Which of the following rows indicates the energy transfer that occurs at each of the three points on the diagram?

Row	Point 1	Point 2	Point 3
A.	Kinetic	Potential	Potential
B.	Potential	Kinetic	Potential
C.	Kinetic	Potential	Kinetic
D.	Potential	Kinetic	Kinetic

Use the following information to answer the next question.

A student listed some advantages that electric cars have over cars powered by fossil fuels.

I. Electric cars reduce pollution in cities.

II. Electric cars regain energy while braking.

III. Electric motors consume no energy while at rest.

IV. Electric motors are quieter than internal combustion engines.

V. Electric cars do not need to be recharged at gas stations; they can be recharged at home.

VI. Electric cars can be charged with renewable sources of energy, such as wind power.

VII. Electric motors give off less heat.

5. Of these advantages, the ones that indicate that electric cars are more efficient than cars powered by fossil fuels are

A. I, II, III, and VII

B. II, III, IV, and VII

C. I, II, III, IV, VI, and VII

D. II, III, IV, V, VI, and VII

6. If $\vec{F} = ma$, which of the following equations could also define $\vec{F}$?

A. $\vec{F} = \dfrac{\Delta\vec{v} \times \Delta t}{m}$

B. $\vec{F} = \dfrac{m \times \Delta\vec{v}}{\Delta t}$

C. $\vec{F} = m \times \Delta\vec{v} \times \Delta t$

D. $\vec{F} = \dfrac{\Delta\vec{v}}{m \times \Delta t}$

Use the following graph to answer the next two questions.

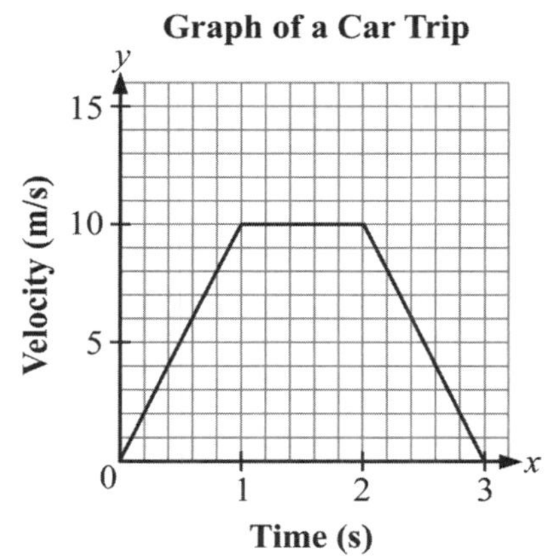

7. From $t = 1$ s until $t = 2$ s, the car is

A. stopped

B. accelerating uniformly

C. decelerating uniformly

D. travelling at uniform speed

8. The distances that the car travelled from $t = 0$ s to $t = 1$ s and from $t = 1$ s to $t = 2$ s, respectively, are

A. 5.0 m and 0 m

B. 5.0 m and 10.0 m

C. 10.0 m and 5.0 m

D. 10.0 m and 10.0 m

Use the following information to answer the next question.

The Galileo spacecraft that reached Jupiter in 1995 sent back a wealth of information about the giant planet. Galileo launched a probe into the atmosphere of Jupiter. Before it was eventually crushed by the immense pressure of Jupiter's lower atmospheric layers, the probe relayed information back to Earth. Galileo used the gravitational forces between Venus and Earth to accelerate to a speed of 39 km/s.

Numerical Response

1. The distance the Galileo spacecraft travelled in 1 min at a speed of 39 km/s, expressed in scientific notation, is $b \times 10^{w}$ m. The value of b to the nearest hundredth is __________.

Use the following information to answer the next question

I. The strongest earthquake ever recorded occurred in 1964 in Alaska; it measured 9.2 on the Richter scale.

II. The highest wind speed ever recorded, 372 km/h, was measured on Mt. Washington on April 12, 1934.

III. Photosynthesis allows a young sapling to grow into a giant redwood tree.

IV. Pacific Ocean currents make the climate of British Columbia milder than the climate of Manitoba.

9. Energy from the sun was **not** required by the phenomenon described in statement

A. I

B. II

C. III

D. IV

Numerical Response

2. If a hockey player shoots the puck at a speed of 90 km/h from the top of the offensive faceoff circle, which is 15 m from the net, how long, to the nearest hundredth of a second, will it take the puck to reach the net? __________ s

Use the following information to answer the next question.

One of the fastest-moving arachnids is the long-legged sun spider (genus *Solpuga*). These spiders are capable of moving up to 16 km/h.

10. If it is moving at its maximum speed, what is the **least** amount of time it would take a sun spider to run between two fig trees that are 3.6 m apart?

A. 0.23 s **B.** 0.81 s

C. 1.50 s **D.** 14.0 s

Use the following information to answer the next three questions.

Pierre Lueders from Edmonton, Alberta, is an Olympic champion in the two-man bobsled event. Lueders trains at one of the world's most challenging runs, located in Calgary, Alberta. The bobsled run at Calgary Olympic Park has a length of 1 500 m and a height of 121 m.

11. If Lueders' bobsled, including the riders, has a mass of 250 kg, how much potential energy does the bobsled have as it is about to start its run?

A. 297 MJ **B.** 29.7 MJ

C. 297 kJ **D.** 297 J

12. If all the potential energy is converted to kinetic energy as the bobsled speeds past the finish line, what is the bobsled's velocity?

A. 2 374.0 m/s

B. 1 187.0 m/s

C. 97.4 m/s

D. 48.7 m/s

13. Although the potential energy is converted into kinetic energy, some of the potential energy is

A. conserved as potential energy

B. lost to the atmosphere

C. lost through friction

D. converted to mass

Use the following graph to answer the next question.

Force-Distance Graph for a Spring Pushing a Block

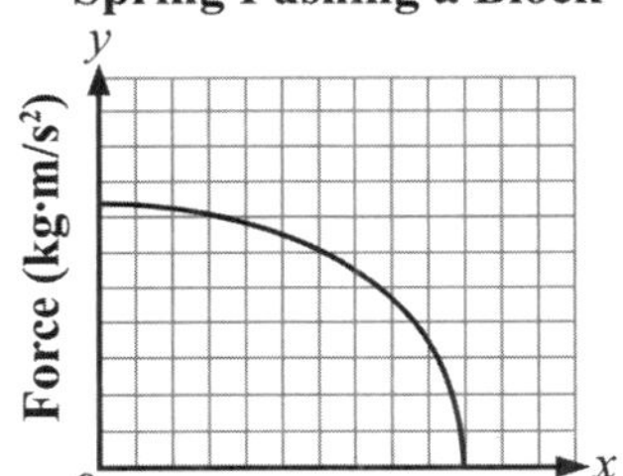

14. A person could calculate the work done on the block by finding the

A. area under the curve

B. x-intercept of the curve

C. y-intercept of the curve

D. average slope of the curve

Use the following information to answer the next question.

When skydivers free-fall, gravity causes them to accelerate toward Earth until they reach a maximum speed of 50 m/s. This velocity is called the terminal velocity.

15. How much kinetic energy does a 60 kg skydiver have at terminal velocity?

A. 1.5×10^5 J

B. 7.5×10^4 J

C. 3.5×10^4 J

D. 2.5×10^3 J

16. From the top of an 80 m hill, a 60 kg downhill skier starts from rest and then skis down to the base. Assuming there is no friction, how fast is the skier travelling when he is 40 m from the base of the hill?

A. 14.0 m/s

B. 28.0 m/s

C. 39.0 m/s

D. 78.0 m/s

Use the following information to answer the next question.

The highest point on Earth is the peak of Mount Everest, which is 8 848 m above sea level. The deepest point on Earth is the floor of the Mariana Trench, which is 10 924 m below sea level.

Numerical Response

3. The potential energy gained as a person with a mass of 75.0 kg travels from the bottom of the Mariana Trench to the top of Mount Everest, expressed in scientific notation, is $b\times10^{w}$ J. What is the value of b to the nearest hundredth? __________

17. The tallest structure ever built is a steel radio mast in Plock, Poland, that is 646 m tall. If an antenna at the top of the mast has gravitational potential energy of 31.7 kJ, then the mass of the antenna is

A. 0.50 g

B. 5.00 g

C. 0.50 kg

D. 5.00 kg

Use the following information to answer the next question.

The tallest freestanding structure in the world is the CN Tower in Toronto, Ontario. The tallest mountain in the world is Mount Everest, with a height of approximately 8 848 m. It is estimated that a 68 kg man has 5 533 428.6 J more potential energy while standing at the top of Mount Everest than while standing at the top of the CN Tower.

18. How tall is the CN Tower?

A. 553.0 m

B. 830.0 m

C. 5 530 m

D. 8 300 m

Use the following information to answer the next question.

Helicopters usually have two types of rotors. The main rotor is mounted horizontally above the body, and a second rotor is usually mounted vertically on the tail. The horizontal rotor gives the helicopter lift and forward thrust. The vertical rotor is used to keep the helicopter from spinning uncontrollably as a result of the motion of the main rotor.

19. If a helicopter has a mass of 1 000 kg, how much work against gravity is done by the main rotor to move the helicopter up 10 m at a constant velocity?

A. 9.81 kJ

B. 10.0 kJ

C. 98.1 kJ

D. 100 kJ

Use the following information to answer the next question.

On July 16, 1994, 21 pieces of the comet Shoemaker-Levy 9 collided with Jupiter. Scientists estimated that some fragments nearly 2 km in diameter struck the planet's surface at speeds of approximately 60 km/s. The fragments then exploded with a force that was estimated to be greater than the potential force contained within all the nuclear weapons on Earth.

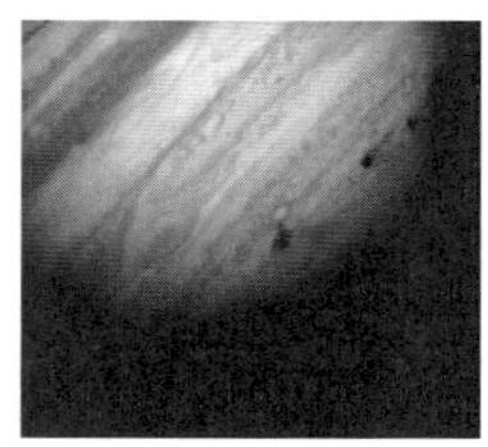

20. The kinetic energy of a fragment with a mass of 8.33×10^{12} kg was

A. 1.16×10^{15} J

B. 2.50×10^{17} J

C. 1.50×10^{22} J

D. 3.10×10^{25} J

Use the following information to answer the next question.

The cheetah is the fastest land animal on Earth over short distances. It can reach a maximum speed of 100 km/h.

21. If a cheetah has 31 kJ of kinetic energy while running at maximum speed, what is its mass?

A. 40 kg **B.** 80 kg

C. 100 kg **D.** 120 kg

Use the following information to answer the next question.

The Waimangu Geyser in New Zealand erupted every 26 to 30 hours from 1903 to 1904. Water from this geyser reached heights of over 460 m.

22. If a jet of water travelled 460 m upward and had a mass of 123 kg, how much energy did the geyser release during this eruption?

A. 452 kJ **B.** 555 kJ

C. 832 kJ **D.** 167 MJ

23. Bamboo can grow to a height of 30 m in less than three months. Glucose produced at the top of the plant must be transported down to the roots for storage. During this process, the glucose

A. gains gravitational potential energy

B. loses gravitational potential energy

C. gains kinetic energy

D. loses kinetic energy

24. A prototype for an electric car has a mass of 1 400 kg. It converts electrical energy into kinetic energy with an efficiency of 90%. The approximate amount of energy its battery expends to accelerate the car from rest to 25 m/s is

A. 240 kJ **B.** 390 kJ

C. 440 kJ **D.** 490 kJ

Use the following information to answer the next question.

Phosphocreatine is a chemical compound that is found in the human body. During times of high energy demand, phosphocreatine reacts with adenosine diphosphate (ADP) to form adenosine triphosphate (ATP). ATP is then used by cells as an energy source. Stores of phosphocreatine can provide a person with up to 8 s worth of energy. The reaction between phosphocreatine and adenosine diphosphate is as follows:

phosphocreatine + ADP → creatine + ATP

25. Energy is stored in phosphocreatine as

A. chemical energy and potential energy

B. chemical energy and thermal energy

C. potential energy and thermal energy

D. potential energy and kinetic energy

Use the following information to answer the next question.

NASA's space shuttles achieve their orbits by using rocket engines to gain significant amounts of potential and kinetic energy. During re-entry into the atmosphere, a shuttle sheds all of its energy as heat. The space shuttle usually re-enters at a height of 122 km above Earth and at a velocity of 7.22 km/s. The heat energy released is equal to the potential and kinetic energy lost as the shuttle plummets to Earth.

26. If the mass of the shuttle is 1.02×10^5 kg, how much energy does the shuttle lose as heat during re-entry?

A. 1.25×10^8 J **B.** 1.22×10^{11} J

C. 2.54×10^{12} J **D.** 2.77×10^{12} J

Use the following information to answer the next question.

The combustion engines used in the Acura RL automobile convert chemical energy into mechanical energy. When gasoline is ignited, it explodes, producing a force that is used to move the pistons in the engine. Within the transmission, this mechanical energy is then used to move the car, creating kinetic energy.

27. In 38 L of gasoline, there is 1.52×10^9 J of energy. When 57 L of gas is burned in an internal combustion engine that is 25% efficient, the amount of kinetic energy produced is

A. 2.28×10^9 J

B. 1.52×10^9 J

C. 5.7×10^8 J

D. 0 J

28. Which of the following laws contradicts the claim that some modern cars can convert chemical energy to kinetic energy at an efficiency of 100%?

A. First law of thermodynamics

B. Newton's first law of motion

C. Second law of thermodynamics

D. Law of conservation of momentum

Use the following information to answer the next question.

Since 3000 BC, when the Sumerians used furnaces for baking pottery, furnaces have been used for many purposes. Traditional fuels for furnaces have been coal and coke. During burning, the total amount of potential energy stored in coal and coke cannot be completely converted into useful energy.

29. The fraction of energy lost as unused heat in the process of burning the fuel is called

A. mechanical energy

B. an inefficiency

C. an efficiency

D. waste energy

Use the following information to answer the next question.

The air inside a hot-air balloon is heated by a flame at the balloon's opening. The hot air exerts pressure on the walls of the balloon, keeping it inflated and causing it to rise toward the less dense, cooler upper atmosphere. At higher altitudes, the temperature both outside and inside the balloon drops, and the balloon begins to collapse as a result of a lack of internal air pressure. Using these principles, Per Lindstrand achieved an altitude record of 19 811 m in a Colt 600 hot-air balloon over Laredo, Texas, on June 6, 1988.

30. When the air within a hot-air balloon is heated, the average kinetic energy of the air molecules within the balloon

A. increases

B. decreases

C. remains constant

D. matches that of the outside air

Use the following information to answer the next question.

Absolute zero is –273.15°C. At this theoretical temperature, the molecules within a system do not move.

31. At which of the following temperatures would a substance have the **most** kinetic energy?

A. –272°C

B. –81°C

C. –40°C

D. 0°C

Written Response

Use the following information to answer the next question.

Nuclear power plants produce huge amounts of electrical energy, thousands of megawatts per station. Unfortunately, they are not very efficient. The given table provides the efficiencies of three types of power stations.

Type of Station	Efficiency (%)
Hydroelectric	70
Fossil fuels	36
Nuclear	30

1. In a unified and organized essay, discuss the types of energy conversions in each of the given types of power stations. Also, discuss where energy is lost in each type of power station.

Use the following information to answer the next question.

The given diagram shows the track of a toy roller-coaster. The car has a mass of 1.20 kg.

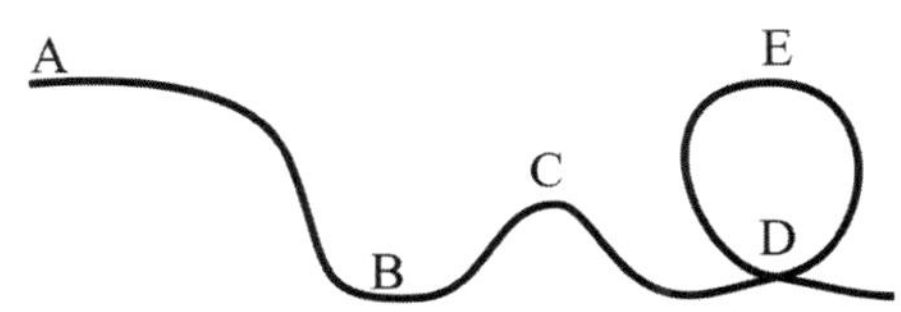

2. **a)** If point A on the track is 1.00 m higher than point B, how much potential energy does the car have at point A?

b) If there is no friction slowing the car, what is the velocity of the car when it arrives at point B?

c) The car ascends the loop, coming almost to a stop at point E before hurtling down toward point D. The velocity at point E was 0 m/s, and at point D it was 2.3 m/s. If the time taken to get from point E back to point D was 1.3 s, what was the car's acceleration?

d) The roller-coaster car had no kinetic energy at the top of the loop and a lot of kinetic energy at the bottom. Energy cannot be created or destroyed, so how did the car gain kinetic energy?

ANSWERS AND SOLUTIONS—PRACTICE QUESTIONS

1. B	NR1. 2.34	15. B	22. B	30. A
2. A	9. A	16. B	23. B	31. D
3. A	NR2. 0.60	NR3. 1.45	24. D	WR1. See Solution
4. C	10. B	17. D	25. A	WR2. See Solution
5. B	11. C	18. A	26. D	
6. B	12. D	19. C	27. C	
7. D	13. C	20. C	28. C	
8. B	14. A	21. B	29. B	

1. **B**

The Carnot engine can also be used to study the law of conservation of energy. Energy that is not used to pump the piston or to change the temperature of the gas is converted to heat energy that escapes to the surroundings. The amount of useful energy lost in each cycle of the engine can be determined in order to calculate the engine's efficiency. Conservation of momentum; Newton's first law (a body at rest tends to stay at rest, and a body in motion tends to stay in motion); and Newton's second law (changing the magnitude or direction of an external force on a body will cause a change in acceleration of the body relative to its mass; $F = ma$) are not clearly demonstrated by the Carnot engine, because velocity, momentum, and acceleration are not described.

2. **A**

The second law of thermodynamics states that heat will flow from matter at a high temperature (liquid) to matter at a lower temperature (the flask and trapped air). The flask in turn will lose heat to the surrounding cooler air.

3. **A**

A vacuum (empty space) prevents heat loss because heat requires some form of matter (a conductor) to flow from one area to another. The plastic cap consists of only one layer of material without an intervening vacuum and, therefore, conducts heat from the hot liquid to the outside air. The loss of heat from the liquid through the lid causes the temperature of the liquid to drop.

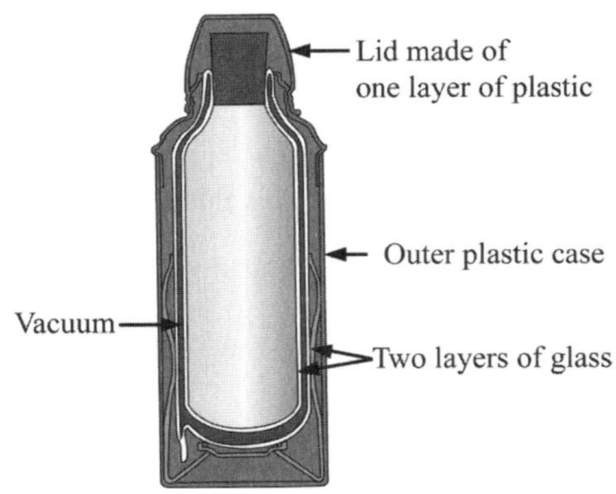

4. **C**

As the roller-coaster car approaches the loop, it is moving with a high velocity and therefore possesses kinetic energy. As the car moves up the loop, it loses some velocity and kinetic energy, but it gains height and therefore potential energy. At point 2, the car has the greatest amount of potential energy because it is at its highest altitude. As the car moves down the loop, this potential energy is converted back into kinetic energy.

5. B

Statement I—Reduced pollution is a result of the type of energy used, not the efficiency.

Statement II—The electric car regains energy that can be used again, making it more efficient.

Statement III—Gas-powered cars lose energy while at rest, but electric cars do not. Therefore, electric cars are more efficient.

Statement IV—Since electric cars lose less energy because of noise pollution, they are more efficient.

Statement V—This has nothing to do with the efficiency of the car, only the convenience of the car.

Statement VI—This has nothing to do with the efficiency of the car, just the nature of the fuel.

Statement VII—Since electric cars lose less energy as heat, they are more efficient.

Statements II, III, IV, and VII all show that the total energy lost is less for electric cars than cars that run on fossil fuels, making electric cars more efficient.

6. B

F = force (any push or pull)
m = mass
a = acceleration.

Acceleration is a change in velocity over time.

If $\vec{F} = m\vec{a}$ and $\vec{a} = \dfrac{\Delta\vec{v}}{\Delta t}$, substituting for a gives

$$\vec{F} = \frac{m \times \Delta\vec{v}}{\Delta t}.$$

7. D

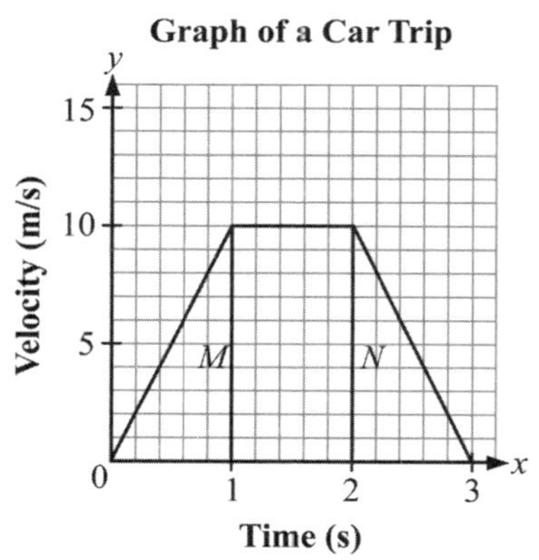

According to the graph, at t = 1s the velocity is 10 m/s, and at t = 2s the velocity is 10 m/s.

Since there is no change in velocity from t = 1 s to t = 2 s, the car is travelling at a uniform speed of 10 m/s.

8. B

In a velocity-time graph, the area under the line represents the distance travelled.

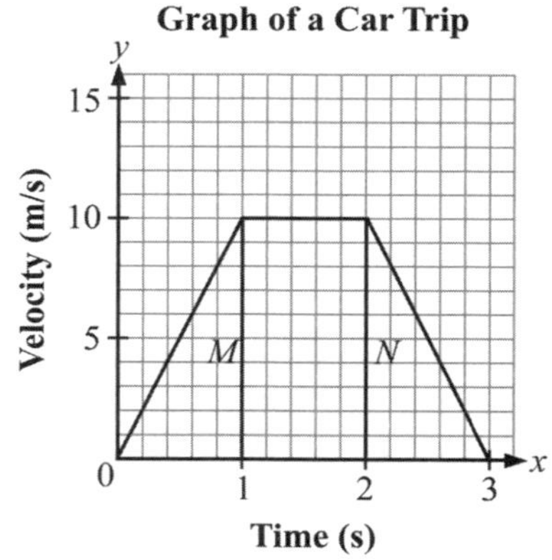

In the graph, the area of region M is equal to the distance travelled from t = 0 s to t = 1 s. The area of region N is equal to the distance travelled from t = 2 s to t = 3 s. In M *or* N, the formula for the area of a triangle is $A = \frac{1}{2}bh$.

Substitute b = 1 s and h = 10 m/s.

$$A = \frac{1}{2}(1\ \text{s})(10\ \text{m/s})$$
$$A = 5\ \text{m}$$

Between triangles M and N is a rectangular space corresponding to the time interval between one second and two seconds. The formula for the area of a rectangle is $A = lw$.

Substitute l = 10 m/s and w = 1 s.
A = (1 s)(10 m/s) = 10 m

NR 1 2.34

The formula $vt = d$ can be used to calculate the distance travelled. Substitute v = 39 km/s = 39 000 m/s and t = 60 s.

$$(39\ 000\ \text{m/s})(60\ s) = d$$
$$d = 2\ 340\ 000\ \text{m}$$
$$= 2.34 \times 10^6\ \text{m}$$

The value of b to the nearest hundredth is 2.34.

9. A

Earthquakes are caused by the movement of tectonic plates in Earth's crust. Movement of the plates is not caused by energy from the sun. Winds are created by convection currents—the sun heats Earth's surface, which in turn heats the surrounding air. Warm air rises and is replaced by cooler air, creating an air current. In photosynthesis, plants use the energy of the sun to create carbohydrates and water. Ocean currents are caused by solar heating and gravity.

NR 2 0.60

The player shoots the puck at 90 km/h. Convert the speed of the shot into metres per second, so the units match and calculate how long it will take for the shot to travel 15 m.

$$\frac{90 \text{ km}}{\text{h}} = \frac{90 \text{ km} \times 1\ 000 \text{ m/km}}{1 \text{ h} \times 60 \text{ min/h} \times 60 \text{ s/min}} = 25.0 \text{ m/s}$$

Given that $t = \frac{d}{v}$, where t = time, d = distance, and v = velocity, substitute $d = 15$ and $v = 25.0$ into the formula.

$$t = \frac{d}{v}$$
$$t = \frac{15}{25}$$
$$t = 0.6$$

The answer, correct to the nearest hundredth of a second, is 0.60 s.

10. B

The spider moves at a speed of 16 km/h. Convert this speed into metres per second to match the units and calculate the time it takes to travel 3.6 m.

$$\frac{16 \text{ km}}{1 \text{ h}} = \frac{16 \text{ km} \times 1\ 000 \text{ m/km}}{1 \text{ h} \times 60 \text{ min/h} \times 60 \text{ s/min}} = 4.44 \text{ m/s}$$

Since time equals distance divided by velocity, substitute $d = 3.6$ m and $v = 4.44$ m/s into the formula $t = \frac{d}{v}$.

$$t = \frac{3.6 \text{ m}}{4.44 \text{ m/s}}$$
$$t = 0.81 \text{ s}$$

11. C

Calculate the potential energy by using the formula $E_p = mgh$.

$$\begin{aligned} E_p &= mgh \\ &= 250 \text{ kg} \times 9.81 \text{ m/s}^2 \times 121 \text{ m} \\ &= 296\ 752 \text{ J} \\ &= 297 \text{ kJ} \end{aligned}$$

12. D

Calculate the velocity by using the formula for kinetic energy. Divide both sides by $\frac{1}{2}m$.

$$E_k = \frac{1}{2}mv^2$$
$$v^2 = \frac{E_k}{\frac{1}{2}m}$$
$$v = \sqrt{\frac{E_k}{\frac{1}{2}m}}$$

Substitute E_k = 296 752 J and m = 250 kg.

$$v = \sqrt{\frac{296\ 752}{\frac{1}{2} \times 250}} = \sqrt{2\ 374}$$
$$v = 48.7 \text{ m/s}$$

13. C

A moving object loses energy as heat because of friction.

14. A

Work is force × distance ($W = Fd$). In a force-distance graph, force × distance is equal to the area under the curve.

The x-intercept (where $y = 0$) is the total distance travelled. The y-intercept (where $x = 0$) is the maximum force applied. The slope of the graph is unrelated.

15. B

Kinetic energy is energy due to motion. At terminal velocity, the jumper is moving at a velocity of 50 m/s.

$$E_k = \frac{1}{2}mv^2$$
$$E_k = \frac{1}{2}(60\ \text{kg})(50\ \text{m/s})^2$$
$$E_k = 75\ 000\ \text{J}$$
$$E_k = 7.5\times10^4\ \text{J}$$

16. B

The skier has potential energy at the top of the hill. This energy is converted to kinetic energy as he moves down the hill. Using the law of conservation of energy, calculate how much E_p is converted into E_k. The potential energy possessed by the skier at the top of the hill, at a height of 40 m above the tree, will be equal to the total gain in kinetic energy by the time the skier reaches the tree.

The total potential energy the skier has at the top can be found by using the formula $E_p = mgh$.

$$\begin{aligned} E_p &= mgh \\ &= (60\ \text{kg})(9.81\ \text{m/s}^2)(40\ \text{m}) \\ &= 2.35\times10^4\ \text{J} \end{aligned}$$

Therefore, 2.35×10^4 J of E_p is converted to kinetic energy, E_k. Substitute 2.35×10^4 J for E_k, 60 kg for m, and then solve for v.

$$E_k = \frac{1}{2}mv^2$$
$$v^2 = \frac{E_k}{\frac{1}{2}m}$$
$$v = \sqrt{\frac{E_k}{\frac{1}{2}m}}$$
$$v = \sqrt{\frac{2\ 350\ \text{J}}{\frac{1}{2}(60\ \text{kg})}}$$
$$v = 28.0\ \text{m/s}$$

NR 3 1.45

To calculate the potential energy, first determine the total distance that the person travels.
$h = 8\ 848\ \text{m} + 10\ 924\ \text{m} = 19\ 772\ \text{m}$

The person's potential energy at the bottom of the trench is equal to 0. Calculate how much energy is gained by climbing 19 772 m.

$$\begin{aligned} E_p &= mgh = (75\ \text{kg})(9.81\ \text{m/s}^2)(19\ 772\ \text{m}) \\ &= 1.45\times10^7\ \text{J} \end{aligned}$$

Therefore, the value of b to the nearest hundredth is 1.45.

17. D

Use the equation for gravitational potential energy, $E_p = mgh$, and solve for mass.

$$m = \frac{E_p}{gh}$$
$$m = \frac{31.7\times10^3\ \text{J}}{(9.81\ \text{m/s}^2)(646\ \text{m})}$$
$$m = 5.0\ \text{kg}$$

18. A

This question can be solved in three steps.

First, calculate the man's potential energy at the top of Mount Everest.

$$\begin{aligned} E_p &= mgh \\ &= 68\ kg\times9.81\ \text{m/s}^2\times8\ 848\ \text{m} \\ &= 5\ 902\ 323.8\ \text{J} \end{aligned}$$

Next, find the difference in E_p between Mount Everest and the CN Tower.

$$\begin{array}{r} 5\ 902\ 323.8\ \text{J} \\ \underline{-5\ 533\ 428.8\ \text{J}} \\ 368\ 895.2\ \text{J} \end{array}$$

The answer will be the man's E_p at the top of the CN Tower.

Finally, use this information to determine the height of the CN Tower.

$$E_p = mgh$$
$$h = \frac{E_p}{mg}$$
$$h = \frac{368\ 895\ \text{J}}{68\ \text{kg}\times9.81\ \text{m/s}^2}$$
$$h = 553\ \text{m}$$

19. C

The amount of work done to lift the helicopter 10 m is equal to the change in energy the helicopter undergoes. On the ground, the helicopter has zero potential energy. Use the formula $E_p = mgh$ to calculate the amount of energy the helicopter has at 10 m above the ground.

$E_p = mgh$
$E_p = (1\ 000 \text{ kg})(9.81 \text{ m/s}^2)(10 \text{ m})$
$E_p = 98.1 \text{ kJ}$

Therefore, the amount of work done to move the helicopter 10 m is 98.1 kJ.

20. C

First, change the velocity of the pieces from km/s to m/s.
60 km/s = 60 × 1 000 m/s = 60 000 m/s

Next, substitute this velocity into the equation for kinetic energy.

$E_k = \frac{1}{2}mv^2$
$E_k = \frac{1}{2}(8.33 \times 10^{12} \text{ kg})(60\ 000 \text{ m/s})^2$
$E_k = 1.5 \times 10^{22} \text{ J}$

21. B

Use the formula for kinetic energy to determine the mass of the cheetah.

First, determine the velocity in m/s.

$$\frac{100 \text{ km}}{1 \text{ h}} = \frac{100 \text{ km} \times 1\ 000 \text{ m/km}}{1 \text{ h} \times 3\ 600 \text{ s/h}} = 27.8 \text{ m/s}$$

Next, substitute this value into $E_k = \frac{1}{2}mv^2$.

$$31\ 000 \text{ J} = \frac{1}{2} m(27.8 \text{ m/s})^2$$
$$m = \frac{2(31\ 000 \text{ J})}{(27.8 \text{ m/s})^2}$$
$$m = 80 \text{ kg}$$

22. B

Assuming that all 123 kg of water reached a height of 460 m, calculate how much potential energy this mass has at this height. The law of conservation of energy states that the potential energy at this height is equal to the energy released at the bottom to propel the water upward. Given that $E_p = mgh$, where m is the mass, g is the acceleration due to gravity, and h is the height, substitute m = 123 kg, $g = 9.81 \text{ m/s}^2$, and h = 460 m into the formula.

$E_p = mgh$
$E_p = (123 \text{kg})(9.81 \text{m/s}^2)(460 \text{m})$
$E_p = 555 \text{kJ}$

23. B

Gravitational potential energy is energy possessed by a body because of its height above, or distance from, a body of mass possessing a gravitational force of attraction.

$E_p = mgh$

The glucose loses gravitational potential energy because of the loss in height when it travels from the leaves at the top to the roots at the bottom.

24. D

At rest, the car has no kinetic energy. The amount of energy the car will have used at 25 m/s can be calculated as follows:

$$E_{\text{used}} = E_k = \frac{1}{2}mv^2$$
$$= \frac{1}{2}(1\ 400 \text{ kg})(25 \text{ m/s})^2$$
$$= 4.38 \times 10^5 \text{ J}$$

The battery must expend more energy than 4.38×10^5 J because the car is only 90% efficient. Therefore, the total amount of energy expended can be found as follows:

$$90\% = \frac{90}{100} = \frac{4.38 \times 10^5 \text{ J}}{E_{\text{battery}}}$$
$$E_{\text{battery}} = \frac{4.38 \times 10^5 \text{ J}}{90} \times 100$$
$$= 486 \text{ kJ}$$
$$= 4.9 \times 10^2 \text{ kJ}$$

25. A

Chemical energy is energy stored in the chemical bonds of a substance. Because the energy is stored until the bonds are broken, bond energy is also potential energy. Therefore, the phosphocreatine is a form of chemical potential energy that is released when needed. Kinetic energy is energy as a result of the motion of a body. Thermal energy is heat energy, which is released only if the chemical bonds are broken.

26. D

The total amount of energy that the shuttle possesses just before re-entry is equal to the amount of energy that it must lose. Before it re-enters the atmosphere, it has both kinetic and potential energy.

$$E_{\text{total}} = E_{\text{P}} + E_{\text{k}}$$
$$E_{\text{p}} = mgh$$
$$= \left(1.02\times10^{5}\ \text{kg}\right)\left(9.81\ \text{m/s}^{2}\right)\left(122\times10^{3}\ \text{m}\right)$$
$$E_{\text{p}} = 1.22\times10^{11}\ \text{J}$$
$$E_{\text{k}} = \frac{1}{2}mv^{2}$$
$$= \frac{1}{2}\left(1.02\times10^{5}\ \text{kg}\right)\left(7.22\times10^{3}\ \text{m/s}\right)^{2}$$
$$E_{\text{k}} = 2.65\times10^{12}\ \text{J}$$
$$E_{\text{total}} = 2.65\times10^{12}\ \text{J} + 1.22\times10^{11}\ \text{J}$$
$$E_{\text{total}} = 2.77\times10^{12}\ \text{J}$$

27. C

The energy stored in the chemical bonds of gasoline is called chemical potential energy. When fuel is burned in an internal combustion engine (e.g., a car engine), this potential energy is converted to kinetic energy as pistons are moved and gears are turned. As stated in the question, the conversion of chemical potential energy to kinetic energy is not 100% efficient, since some energy is lost as heat, noise, friction, and other less useful forms of energy.

Let x be the total amount of energy in 57 L of gasoline.

$$\frac{1.52\times10^{9}\ \text{J}}{38\ \text{L}} = \frac{x}{57\ \text{L}}$$
$$38x = \left(1.52\times10^{9}\ \text{J}\right)57\ \text{L}$$
$$x = \frac{\left(1.52\times10^{9}\ \text{J}\right)57\ \text{L}}{38}$$
$$x = 2.28\times10^{9}\ \text{J}$$

The engine is only 25% efficient in converting this potential energy into useful kinetic energy.

$$\left(2.28\times10^{9}\ \text{J}\right)\times0.25 = 5.7\times10^{8}\ \text{J}$$

28. C

The second law of thermodynamics states that useful energy is lost during any energy conversion. Newton's laws of motion and the law of conservation of momentum deal with motion and not energy efficiency. The first law of thermodynamics states that energy cannot be created or destroyed; it can only be converted from one form to another. The first law of thermodynamics does not include a statement about the efficiency of energy conversion.

29. B

Inefficiency is the fraction of energy lost during an energy conversion process. Mechanical energy is the energy of an object in motion. The total energy lost is called the waste energy.

30. A

When a substance (in this case, air) undergoes an increase in temperature, the kinetic energy (speed of the movement of molecules) of that substance increases. The increased kinetic energy increases the frequency with which the air molecules collide with the inside of the balloon. This increases the air pressure placed on the inner walls of the balloon. As the altitude increases, the air temperature drops, which causes the kinetic energy of the air molecules outside the balloon to decrease.

31. D

Higher temperatures result in greater random movement of the molecules within a substance. This increase in the velocity of the molecules results in an increase in kinetic energy.

The formula for the kinetic energy is $E_{\text{k}} = \frac{1}{2}mv^{2}$.

As velocity (v) increases, the kinetic energy (E_{k}) will also increase. Therefore, a substance at 0°C would have more kinetic energy than at any of the other given temperatures.

1. *In a unified and organized essay, discuss the types of energy conversions in each of the given types of power stations. Also, discuss where energy is lost in each type of power station.*

Your essay should include some of the following information:

- Hydroelectric—A hydroelectric power station uses moving water to turn a generator, which produces electrical energy. The water has velocity and therefore kinetic energy. This kinetic energy is used to turn the generator, giving it mechanical kinetic energy. The generator then produces electrical energy. Most of the energy lost will be as a result of friction, heat, and sound produced in the generator.
- Fossil fuels—In this type of power station, natural gas or coal is burned in a furnace to turn water into steam. The steam is then used to turn a generator, which produces electrical energy. The natural gas or coal is chemical potential energy that is burned and converted into thermal energy, which is then used to heat water and turn it into steam. The steam is then used to turn a generator, giving it mechanical kinetic energy, which then produces electrical energy. Most of the energy is lost as heat up the smokestacks, but some is lost as friction, heat, and sound in the generator.
- Nuclear—In a nuclear reactor, the energy stored in an atom of uranium is released to give heat that is used to turn water into steam. The steam is then used to turn a generator, creating electricity. The energy in the uranium is released from the nucleus and is therefore nuclear energy. It is converted into thermal energy, which is used to turn the water into steam. The steam is then used to turn a generator, giving it mechanical kinetic energy, which produces electrical energy. Some energy is lost as heat exhaust, while some energy is lost in the generator as friction, heat, and sound energy.

2. **a)** *If point A on the track is 1.00 m higher than point B, how much potential energy does the car have at point A?*

Mass of car: 1.20 kg
Force of gravity: 9.81 m/s^2
Height: 1.00 m

$$E_p = mgh$$
$$= 1.20 \text{ kg} \times 9.81 \text{ m/s}^2 \times 1.00 \text{ m}$$
$$= 11.8 \text{ J}$$

The answer should have three significant digits because each of the numbers in the formula has three significant digits.

b) *If there is no friction slowing down the car, what is the velocity of the car when it arrives at B?*

If there is no friction slowing the roller-coaster car, all the potential energy has been converted to kinetic energy at point B.

$$E_k = \frac{1}{2}mv^2$$
$$v = \sqrt{\frac{2E_k}{m}}$$
$$v = \sqrt{\frac{2(11.8 \text{ J})}{1.2 \text{ kg}}}$$
$$v = 4.44 \text{ m/s}$$

c) *The car ascends the loop, coming almost to a stop at point E before hurtling down toward point D. The velocity at point E was 0 m/s, and at point D it was 2.3 m/s. If the time taken to get from point E back to point D was 1.3 s, what was the car's acceleration?*

$$a = \frac{\Delta v}{\Delta t}$$
$$a = \frac{2.3 \text{ m/s}}{1.3 \text{ s}}$$
$$a = 1.8 \text{ m/s}^2$$

d) *The roller-coaster car had no kinetic energy at the top of the loop and a lot of kinetic energy at the bottom. Energy cannot be created or destroyed, so how did the car gain kinetic energy?*

Although energy cannot be created or destroyed, it can be converted from one form to another. The potential energy that the car had at the top of the loop was converted to kinetic energy at the bottom of the loop.

At the bottom, there was no potential energy—it had all been converted to kinetic energy.

UNIT TEST—ENERGY FLOW IN TECHNOLOGICAL SYSTEMS

Use the following information to answer the next question.

To power a wind turbine with energy from the sun, energy is converted to the following forms:

1.	Kinetic	**2.**	Heat
3.	Electrical	**4.**	Solar

Numerical Response

1. The correct sequence of the energy forms from the sun to the turbine is ____, ____, ____, and ____.

1. Compared with electricity generated by nuclear, wind, or solar plants, the generation of electricity in coal-burning plants

A. relies on a cheaper source of energy

B. produces much more electricity

C. makes use of renewable energy

D. generates greenhouse gases

Use the following information to answer the next question.

1. Chemical
2. Thermal
3. Current
4. Static
5. Solar

Numerical Response

2. Listed from lowest to highest, the forms of energy above that represent stored forms of energy are ____ and ____.

2. Which of the following statements about scalar and vector quantities is **true**?

A. Scalar quantities, such as speed, include direction.

B. Vector quantities, such as speed, include direction.

C. Scalar quantities, such as velocity, include direction.

D. Vector quantities, such as velocity, include direction.

3. Which of the following definitions is **true**?

A. Speed represents the distance travelled over a period of time.

B. Speed represents the distance travelled at a constant rate.

C. Velocity represents the distance travelled over a period of time.

D. Velocity represents the distance travelled at a constant rate.

4. When people say "The cold went right through me," they are **not** scientifically correct, because

A. heat flows from a warm object to a cooler object, whereas cold does not flow

B. cold temperatures move from a body that is colder to a body that is warmer

C. cold temperatures stop molecules, so people would die if the cold went through them

D. moving molecules that account for heat move randomly and do not flow in one direction

5. What type of energy is passed from plants to animals?

A. Light

B. Kinetic

C. Thermal

D. Chemical

Use the following information to answer the next two questions.

Angel Falls, the longest free-falling waterfall in the world, is located in Venezuela. It was named after the pilot Jimmy Angel, who spotted it from his plane in 1933. Water falls 800 m from the top of the falls.

6. When water initially travelling at 1.00 m/s falls to the bottom of Angel Falls, it reaches a speed of 10 m/s. As it falls, the water undergoes

A. a decrease in both potential and kinetic energy

B. an increase in both potential and kinetic energy

C. an increase in kinetic energy and a decrease in potential energy

D. an increase in potential energy and a decrease in kinetic energy

7. If the potential energy of 1 000 kg of water at the top of the falls is converted with an efficiency of 37% to electrical energy, how much electrical energy is produced?

A. 7.8×10^6 J

B. 5.2×10^6 J

C. 2.9×10^6 J

D. 1.3×10^6 J

Use the following information to answer the next question.

At the 1996 Summer Olympics in Atlanta, Canadian sprinter Donovan Bailey ran the 100 m sprint in a (then) world record time of 9.84 s.

Numerical Response

3. What was Donovan Bailey's average velocity in m/s to the nearest tenth? __________ m/s

Use the following information to answer the next question.

The world's longest crude oil pipeline connects Edmonton, Alberta, to Buffalo, New York. The pipeline requires 13 pumping stations to maintain the flow of over 31 million L of oil per day over a distance of 2 856 km.

8. If the total force of the pumps is $1.12\ \text{kg} \cdot \text{m/s}^2$, then the amount of energy needed to pump the oil from Edmonton to Buffalo along this pipeline is

A. 1.10 MJ

B. 2.85 MJ

C. 3.20 MJ

D. 4.92 MJ

Use the following information to answer the next question.

The two Voyager spacecraft launched in 1977 to explore the outer planets of the solar system took advantage of a rare planetary alignment that occurs once every 175 years. This alignment allowed these spacecraft to use the gravitational force of one planet to propel them to the next, thus eliminating the need for large onboard propulsion systems.

9. These spacecraft converted gravitational potential energy into what other type of energy?

A. Solar

B. Kinetic

C. Electrical

D. Mechanical

Use the following information to answer the next question.

Photovoltaic cells, such as those used to power satellites, consist of two layers of material. One layer is positively charged, and the other is negatively charged. Sunlight passes through these charged layers and causes electrons to move from the negatively charged layer to the positively charged layer, thus creating an electric current.

10. Photovoltaic cells convert

A. solar energy into thermal energy

B. solar energy into electrical energy

C. thermal energy into potential energy

D. electrical energy into potential energy

Use the following information to answer the next question.

The Clover Bar Generating Station near Edmonton, Alberta, burns natural gas at a temperature of approximately 1 000°C. The resulting heat is used to convert water into steam, which turns a generator at 3 600 rpm, producing 600 MW of power.

11. Which of the following energy-conversion sequences describes what takes place at this power station?

A. Mechanical → kinetic → electrical

B. Potential → kinetic → electrical

C. Chemical → thermal → kinetic

D. Potential → kinetic → nuclear

Use the following diagram to answer the next question.

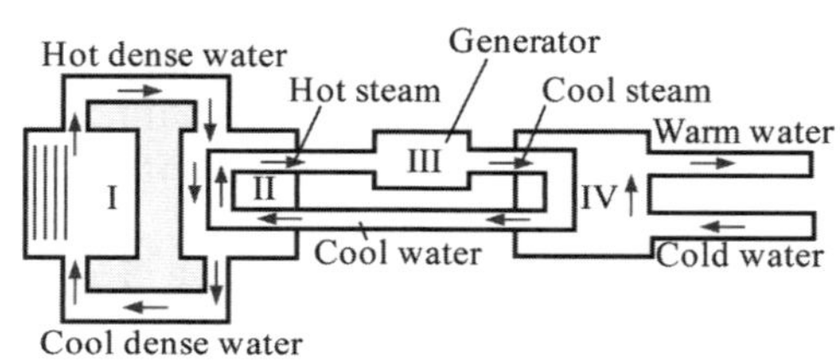

12. In the given system, kinetic energy is produced at

A. I

B. III

C. I, II, and III

D. I, II, III, and IV

Use the following information to answer the next question.

Modern household refrigerators operate on the principle that gases heat up under high pressure and cool down under low pressure. Pipes running through a refrigerator carry Freon gas at low pressure, causing the boiling point of Freon to drop below freezing. When the Freon boils, it absorbs heat from the contents of the refrigerator, thereby cooling the interior.

13. In a refrigerator, the flow of heat from a warmer object to a colder one is an example of

A. the first law of thermodynamics

B. the second law of thermodynamics

C. the law of conservation of energy

D. the law of conservation of mass

Use the following information to answer the next question.

Plants use glucose produced through photosynthesis for energy. From 1 mol of glucose, 2 874 kJ of energy can theoretically be extracted. On average, however, only 1 149 kJ of useful energy is extracted from 1 mol of glucose. The rest of the energy is lost as heat.

Numerical Response

4. Correct to two significant digits, the efficiency of glucose metabolism is approximately what percentage?
__________%

Use the following information to answer the next question.

At the 1998 Winter Olympics in Nagano, Japan, Catriona Le May Doan captured a gold medal and a bronze medal for Canada, in the 500 m and 1 000 m speedskating events respectively. In both events, she expended a significant amount of energy over a short period of time. Her total energy input, however, was greater than her net useful energy output.

14. The ratio of energy input to energy output is **best** described as

A. efficiency

B. inefficiency

C. waste energy

D. mechanical energy

Written Response

Use the following information to answer the next question.

Early steam engines, such as Newcomen's engine (shown here), were used to pump water out of coal mines. At these places, there was an ample supply of coal for the engines to use as fuel.

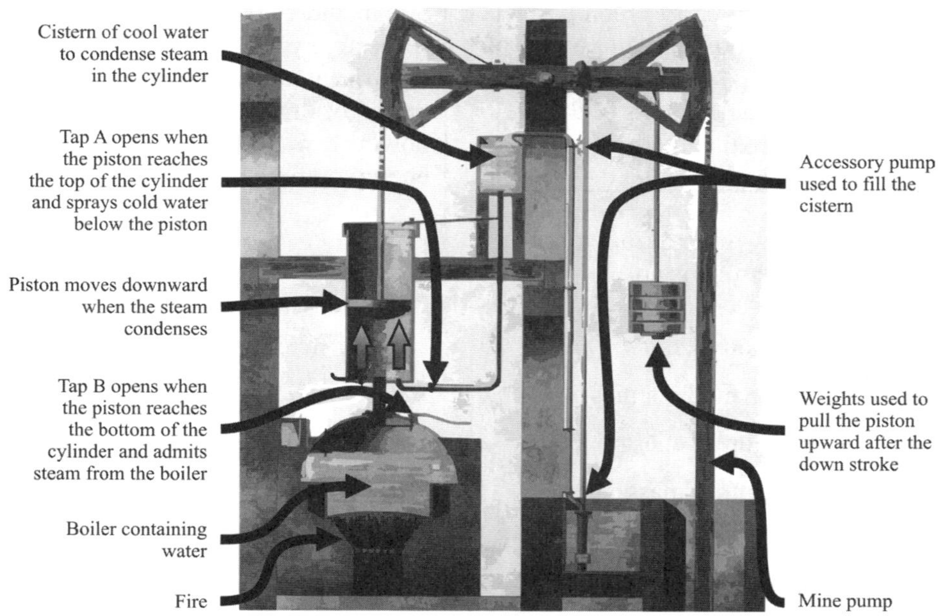

1. **a)** For an engine like the one shown, what type of energy is the input energy and what type is the output energy?

b) One problem with these early engines is that they were only about 1% efficient. If 1.0 kJ of energy was put into one of these engines, what would the output energy be? Show your work by writing the correct formula for calculating efficiency and then substituting the appropriate numbers into it.

c) Using the diagram, explain what happens to the energy that does not become output energy.

d) If the piston moves up and down, what makes the piston go up?

e) What makes the piston go down?

ANSWERS AND SOLUTIONS—UNIT TEST

NR1. 4 2 1 3	4. A	8. C	13. B
1. D	5. D	9. B	NR4. 40
NR2. 1 4	6. C	10. B	14. A
2. D	7. C	11. B	WR1. See Solution
3. A	NR3. 10.2	12. B	

NR 1 4 2 1 3

The sun produces solar energy. Upon hitting Earth, the solar energy is converted to heat energy. Differential heating of Earth results in weather patterns, including wind. The wind contains kinetic energy. It is this kinetic energy that turns a wind turbine, which produces electricity.

1. D

Unlike nuclear, wind, or solar plants, coal-burning plants rely on the combustion of fossil fuels. When these fuels burn, carbon gases are produced as waste. These carbon gases are greenhouse gases. They cause heat energy to get trapped in the atmosphere.

NR 2 1 4

Chemical energy is energy stored in chemical bonds. The energy can be released when the chemical bonds are broken. Food is an example. A potato has stored energy, but after you digest it, the glucose it contains can be split to release the energy your body needs. As well, a piece of wood contains stored energy. When you light it on fire, chemical bonds are broken and energy is released in the form of heat and light. The chemical reactions that involve the release of energy are called exothermic.

Static electricity is also stored energy. The energy is stored as a result of the position of electrons. A lot of electrons piled up on one side of a gap will result in a difference in charge. If allowed, the electrons will jump from a place where there is more of them (negative charge) to a place where there are fewer of them (positive charge). In this movement of electrons, the stored energy is released.

2. D

In physics, movement can be described as scalar or vector. Scalar quantities include speed, distance, and time. However, scalar quantities do not include direction. Vector quantities include velocity, displacement, and changes in position, and must include direction.

3. A

If you travel down a curvy road, your velocity is your displacement (a straight line between your starting and finishing points) divided by the time it took to travel the road. Your speed is the actual distance you travelled through all the curves divided by the time. Velocity does not take into account every turn you took, only your overall change in position.

4. A

It is more correct to say that heat flows rather than to say that cold flows. Since heat is the energy of the movement of molecules, that movement can spread from an area where there is more movement to one where there is less movement. Therefore, we can say that heat flows from an area of more heat to one where there is less heat.

5. D

Animals gain energy when they eat. If they eat plants, animals gain the energy that is stored in the plants. That type of energy is chemical. It is the energy stored in the plants' chemical bonds. When animals make use of food molecules, they break those bonds and release energy. Animals use this energy to move, synthesize molecules, and carry out all other activities that occur inside their cells.

6. C

Potential energy is energy as a result of position or condition. The potential energy of a system increases as its height increases, and decreases as its height decreases.

Kinetic energy is energy as a result of motion. Kinetic energy increases as velocity increases, and decreases as velocity decreases.

The velocity of the water that travels from the top of Angel Falls to the bottom increases from 1.0 m/s to 10.0 m/s, which means the kinetic energy increases.

The water falls a distance of 800 m, so it loses height and therefore potential energy.

7. C

First, calculate the potential energy of the water at the top of the falls.

$$E_p = mgh$$
$$= (1\ 000 \text{ kg})(9.81 \text{ m/s}^2)(800 \text{ m})$$
$$E_p = 7.8 \times 10^6 \text{ J}$$

Given that the power station is 37% efficient, only 37% of the 7.8×10^6 J will be converted into electrical energy.

$$\% \text{ efficiency} = \frac{\text{useful energy output}}{\text{total energy input}} \times 100$$
$$\text{useful energy output} = \frac{\% \text{ energy}}{100} \times \text{total energy input}$$
$$E = (0.37)(7.8 \times 10^6 \text{ J})$$
$$= 2.9 \times 10^6 \text{ J}$$

NR 3 10.2

The average velocity is calculated by dividing the distance Bailey ran (100 m) by the time he ran it in (9.84 s).

$$v_{\text{ave}} = \frac{d}{t}$$
$$= \frac{100 \text{ m}}{9.84 \text{ s}}$$
$$= 10.2 \text{ m/s}$$

Therefore, Donovan Bailey's average velocity was 10.2 m/s.

8. C

The amount of energy needed to pump oil from Edmonton to Buffalo will be equal to the amount of work done to pump the oil.

To calculate how much work is done to pump the oil over this distance, recall that work is equal to force multiplied by distance.

$$Work = Force \times distance$$
$$W = Fd$$
$$= (1.12 \text{ N})(2\ 856 \times 10^3 \text{ m})$$
$$= 3.20 \times 10^6 \text{ J}$$

Note: In order to calculate an answer in joules, the distance the oil travels must be in metres, not kilometres.

Therefore, the energy needed to pump the oil from Edmonton to Buffalo is 3.20×10^6 J, or 3.20 MJ.

9. B

The spacecraft used the gravitational potential energy of the planets to gain velocity. Therefore, by increasing their velocities (v), each spacecraft increased its kinetic energy, E_k (motion).

10. B

Solar energy that strikes photovoltaic cells is eventually converted into electrical energy. Thermal energy (heat energy) is the total energy of all the particles of a substance. Potential energy is energy that is stored as a result of position or condition.

11. B

The natural gas represents chemical potential energy because energy is released as the chemical bonds in natural gas molecules are broken during combustion reactions. The heat that is released converts water into steam, which subsequently turns a generator, giving the generator kinetic energy. The generator then produces power in the form of electrical energy. Therefore, during the entire process, potential energy is converted to kinetic energy, which is then converted to electrical energy.

12. B

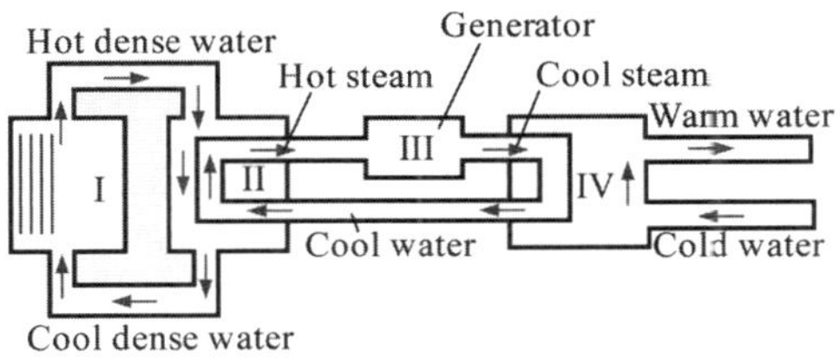

Kinetic energy is energy as a result of motion. The only moving part in the reactor shown is the generator at III. All the remaining areas of energy transfer involve thermal energy. This thermal energy causes phase changes of water at II and IV.

13. B

The operation of a refrigerator demonstrates a part of the second law of thermodynamics: heat always flows from matter at a higher temperature to matter at a lower temperature. The first law of thermodynamics and the law of conservation of energy are terms for the same concept: energy is never destroyed or created, only converted to different forms. The law of conservation of matter states that in ordinary chemical reactions matter is neither created nor destroyed.

NR 4 40

Efficiency is the amount of useful work gained divided by the amount of energy entered into a system.

$$\%\ \text{efficiency} = \frac{\text{useful energy output}}{\text{total energy input}} \times 100\%$$

$$\%\ \text{efficiency} = \frac{1\ 149\ \text{kJ}}{2\ 874\ \text{kJ}} \times 100\%$$
$$= 40\%$$

14. A

The relationship between energy input and energy output is called efficiency. A system is more efficient (has a greater value of efficiency) if more useful energy is gained from a given energy input.

Mechanical energy is the energy of an object in motion. Waste energy is the amount of energy lost. Inefficiency is the fraction of energy lost.

1. **a)** *For an engine like the one shown, what type of energy is the input energy and what type is the output energy?*

The burning of coal generates heat. Heat energy is the input energy. The output is movement, or kinetic energy.

b) *One problem with these early engines is that they were only about 1% efficient. If 1.0 kJ of energy was put into one of these engines, what would the output energy be? Show your work by writing the correct formula for calculating efficiency and then substituting the appropriate numbers into it.*

$$\%\ \text{efficiency} = \frac{\text{useful energy output}}{\text{total energy input}} \times 100\%$$

The question asks for the output energy. Let x = useful output energy.

$$1\% = \frac{x}{1\ 000\ \text{J}} \times 100\%$$

Convert the percentages to fractions.

$$1\% = \frac{1}{100},\ 100\% = \frac{100}{100} = 1$$

$$\frac{1}{100} = \frac{x}{1\ 000\ \text{J}} \times 1$$

$$100x = 1\ 000\ \text{J}$$
$$= 10\ \text{J}$$

If 1 kJ of energy is put into the engine and the engine works at 1% efficiency, the useful output energy is 10 J.

c) *Using the diagram, explain what happens to the energy that does not become output energy.*

Heat energy is used to heat the water and convert liquid water to gas. However, quite a bit of the heat energy will be lost from the system by heating the machine components and the cooling water not just the water in the boiler. It is possible that some of the steam will slip past the piston because it would be hard to make the seal between the piston and the cylinder completely watertight. A loss of steam will be a further loss of heat energy.

d) *If the piston moves up and down, what makes the piston go up?*

When liquid water becomes steam, it expands. This expansion pushes the piston up.

e) *What makes the piston go down?*

When the piston is at the top of the cylinder, a spray of cold water is injected into the cylinder causing the steam to cool and condense. This removes the pressure of the steam that forces the piston up and gravity pulls the piston down.

Cycling of Matter in Living Systems

CYCLING OF MATTER IN LIVING SYSTEMS

Table of Correlations				
Specific Expectation	**Practice Questions**	**Unit Test Questions**	**Practice Test 1**	**Practice Test 2**
By the end of this course, students will:				
C1 Explain the relationship between developments in imaging technology and the current understanding of the cell.				
C1.1 trace the development of the cell theory: all living things are made up of one or more cells and the materials produces by these, cells are functional units of life, and all cells come from pre-existing cells	2, 3	1, 2	20	
C1.2 describe how advancements in knowledge of cell structure and function have been enhanced and are increasing as a direct result of developments in microscope technology and staining techniques	1, 5, 6, 7, 8, NR1	3, 4, 5	NR8	
C1.3 identify areas of cell research at the molecular level	4			24
C2 Describe the function of cell organelles and structures in a cell, in terms of life processes, and use models to explain these processes and their applications.				
C2.1 compare passive transport of matter by diffusion and osmosis with active transport in terms of the particle model of matter, concentration gradients, equilibrium and protein carrier molecules	13, 14, 15, 16, 17, 25, 26, 27, 37, 38		24, 25	
C2.2 use models to explain and visualize complex processes like diffusion and osmosis, endo- and exocytosis, and the role of cell membrane in these processes	10, 11, 22, 24	10, 11, 12, 13, 14, 15	22	27
C2.3 describe the cell as a functioning open system that acquires nutrients, excretes waste, and exchanges matter and energy	12, 20, 21		WR1, WR2	30, 33
C2.4 identify the structure and describe, in general terms, the function of the cell membrane, nucleus, lysosome, vacuole, mitochondrion, endoplasmic reticulum, Golgi apparatus, ribosomes, chloroplast and cell wall, where present, of plant and animal cells	9, 18, 19	6, 7, 8, 9	21, 26	26, 28, 29
C2.5 compare the structure, chemical composition and function of plant and animal cells, and describe the complementary nature of the structure and function of plant and animal cells	NR3, 34			WR1a, WR1b
C2.6 describe the role of the cell membrane in maintaining equilibrium while exchanging matter	WR1a, WR1b, WR2b, WR2c, WR2d			
C2.7 describe how knowledge about semi-permeable membranes, diffusion and osmosis is applied in various contexts				25, WR1c
C2.8 describe cell size and shape as they relate to surface area to volume ratio, and explain how that ratio limits cell size	NR2, 23		23	

C3 Analyze plants as an example of a multicellular organism with specialized structures at the cellular, tissue and system levels.				
C3.2 describe how the cells of the leaf system have a variety of specialized structures and functions; i.e., epidermis including guard cells, palisade tissue cells, spongy tissue cells, and phloem and xylem vascular tissue cells to support the process of photosynthesis	NR4, 28, 29, 30, 31, 35, 36	20	29	
C3.3 explain and investigate the transport system in plants; i.e., xylem and phloem tissues and the processes of transpiration, including the cohesion and adhesion properties of water, turgor pressure and osmosis; diffusion, active transport and root pressure in root hairs	WR2a, 40	16, 17, 18, WR1, WR2	27, 28	31
C3.4 explain and investigate the exchange system in plants; i.e., lenticels, guard cells, stomata and the process of diffusion	39			32
C3.5 explain and investigate phototropism and gravitropism as examples of control systems in plants	32, 33	19		

CYCLING OF MATTER IN LIVING SYSTEMS

C1.1 *trace the development of the cell theory: all living things are made up of one or more cells and the materials produces by these, cells are functional units of life, and all cells come from pre-existing cells*

DEVELOPMENT OF CELL THEORY

It was not possible to learn about cell structure until a technology was developed that allowed people to observe cells. That technology was the microscope. During the 1600s, Robert Hooke was able to observe cork through his simple microscope. His microscope was only a magnifying glass, and not a very good one at that. He was able to see the cell walls of the cork. Not long afterward, Anton van Leeuwenhoek discovered the existence of bacteria and other microorganisms that he observed with his simple microscope. In the 1800s, Robert Brown was the first person to identify the nucleus and recognized it as being important to cell functions. In the same century, Matthias Schleiden observed that all plant material was composed of cells. Then, Theodor Schwann observed that all animal material was also composed of cells. Rudolf Virchow concluded that all cells were formed by other cells, and later Louis Pasteur provided evidence that spontaneous generation did not occur. These observations became the **cell theory**, which includes the following ideas:

1. Cells are the smallest functional units of life.

2. All organisms are composed of cells.

3. All cells come from other cells.

It is important to note that subcellular particles like viruses and prions do not fall under the principles of the cell theory.

Cells reproduce through a process known as **mitosis.** During this process, a cell splits into two genetically identical cells. Every generation of cell division results in a doubling of the population of cells.

Practice Questions: 2, 3

C1.2 *describe how advancements in knowledge of cell structure and function have been enhanced and are increasing as a direct result of developments in microscope technology and staining techniques*

C1.3 *identify areas of cell research at the molecular level*

STAINS AND MICROSCOPE DEVELOPMENTS

Developments in microscope technology and staining techniques helped to advance knowledge about the cell. As staining techniques developed, the differences between the structures inside the cell became more noticeable. Fluorescence microscopy gave information about molecules on the surface of the cells, such as blood-type antigens. The electron microscope can magnify objects up to 1 500 000 times and provides three-dimensional views of cells, particles in a cell, cell membranes, and many other structures never seen before.

As a result of improved imaging techniques, research at the molecular level includes DNA sequencing and genome mapping of various organisms.

Two types of stains that are used to distinguish the different parts of cells are iodine and a compound called methylene blue.

Practice Questions: 1, 4, 5, 6, 7, 8, NR1

C2.4 identify the structure and describe, in general terms, the function of the cell membrane, nucleus, lysosome, vacuole, mitochondrion, endoplasmic reticulum, Golgi apparatus, ribosomes, chloroplast and cell wall, where present, of plant and animal cells

C2.5 compare the structure, chemical composition and function of plant and animal cells, and describe the complementary nature of the structure and function of plant and animal cells

Cell Structure

All living things are made of cells. The following diagrams show a typical animal cell and a typical plant cell.

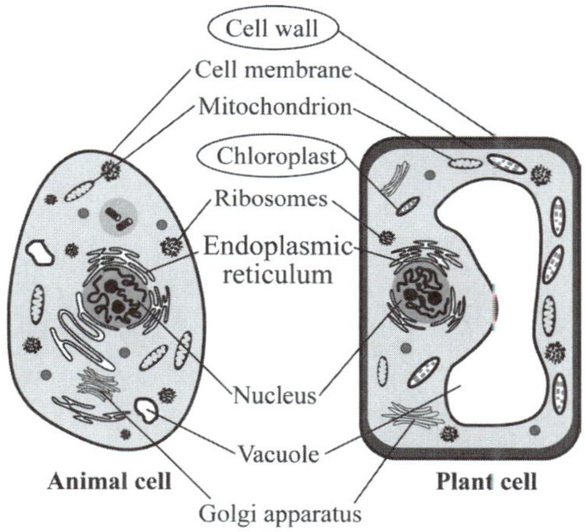

Functions of Cell Organelles

Cell membrane—this serves as a barrier between the cell and its environment. It controls the flow of matter in and out of the cell. A cell membrane is not very strong. The structural support for animal cells comes from the **cytoskeleton**, a three-dimensional network of protein fibres, almost like a 3-D spider's web.

Vacuole—this is a membrane-enclosed storage structure. A **lysosome** is a special kind of vacuole that stores digestive enzymes.

Golgi apparatus—this structure gathers materials and packages them into vacuoles.

Nucleus—this is the cell's control centre. The nucleus contains the **DNA**, the substance that genes are made of. Genes determine the structure of the cell and provide the instructions for what the cell organelles are to do. Gene mapping, which is the process of finding the sequence of DNA, has been completed for many plants and animals, including humans. The technology involved uses chemicals to release the DNA and make copies for computers to analyse.

The Human Genome Project published a complete map of human DNA in 2003.

Nucleolus—this structure plays an important role in the production of RNA.

Endoplasmic reticulum (ER)—this is a network of interconnected tubules. The ER is categorized as either the rough endoplasmic reticulum (RER) which synthesizes proteins, or the smooth endoplasmic reticulum (SER) which synthesis lipids and steroids.

Ribosome—these are structures that make proteins under the direction of the genes.

Mitochondrion—this is the site of **cellular respiration.** Cellular respiration is a chemical process that releases energy from glucose. Both animal and plant cells need energy to perform cell functions, so both kinds of cells perform cellular respiration in their mitochondria. Glucose molecules are combined with oxygen, and the high energy electrons that are in glucose are transferred to the oxygen atoms. This transfer of electrons is used to assemble ATP molecules, which are the rechargeable batteries that all living things run on. Mitochondria therefore serve as "battery chargers" for a cell.

Cytoplasm—this is all of the material outside of the nucleus in which the organelles are suspended.

Plant cells have the same organelles as animal cells, except that they have a few special organelles that animal cells lack.

Cell wall—this is a rigid structure outside of the cell membrane. It provides a framework of support for plant cells. It is composed of **cellulose**.

Chloroplast—this is the site of **photosynthesis**, and like a cell wall, it can only be found when examining plant cells with a microscope. It contains the pigment **chlorophyll**, which absorbs sunlight. The sunlight energizes an electron that the chlorophyll receives from breaking apart a water molecule. The energized electron is added to carbon dioxide molecules and these are used to assemble glucose. Oxygen is released from the chloroplast as waste. Besides light energy, green plants require carbon dioxide from the atmosphere and water from soil to make glucose.

Practice Questions: NR3, 9, 18, 19, 34

C2.1	*compare passive transport of matter by diffusion and osmosis with active transport in terms of the particle model of matter, concentration gradients, equilibrium and protein carrier molecules*
C2.2	*use models to explain and visualize complex processes like diffusion and osmosis, endo- and exocytosis, and the role of cell membrane in these processes*
C2.3	*describe the cell as a functioning open system that acquires nutrients, excretes waste, and exchanges matter and energy*
C2.6	*describe the role of the cell membrane in maintaining equilibrium while exchanging matter*

CELL MEMBRANE

The cell can be thought of as an open system because matter and energy are exchanged across the cell membrane. The **cell membrane** is composed of a double layer of **phospholipid** molecules with **proteins** scattered throughout. The phospholipids form a screen that small molecules (such as oxygen, water, carbon dioxide, and glucose) can readily pass through, while larger molecules (such as proteins and starch) cannot. The model for this membrane is called the **fluid-mosaic model**. Since the membrane allows some things to pass through, but not others, it is described as **semipermeable**. The small molecules move across the membrane by **diffusion**, from an area of high concentration to an area of low concentration.

Such movement across the membrane requires no energy on the part of the cell and is called **passive transport**.

Cell Membrane

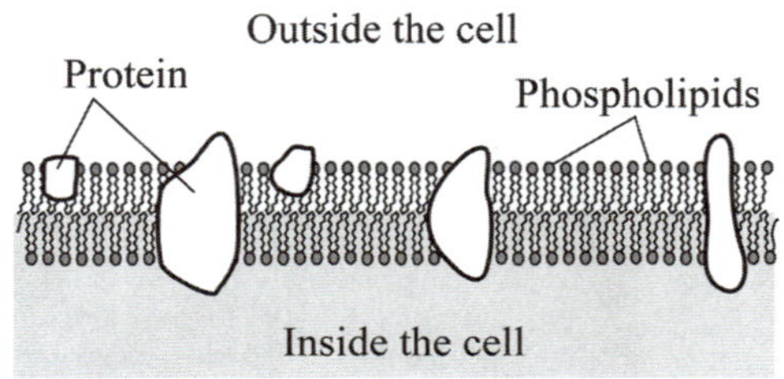

Movement of water across the membrane by diffusion is called **osmosis**. The given diagrams show how osmosis occurs in different cell environments.

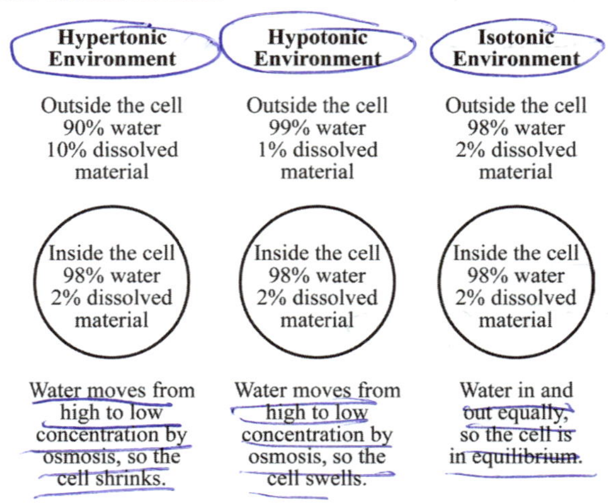

Sometimes, it is necessary to move very large molecules across a membrane or to move molecules across a membrane against the concentration gradient (from a low to a high concentration). Such movement is known as **active transport** and requires energy in the form of ATP. The membrane proteins serve as pumps.

Sometimes, a structure is too large to move across the membrane, even by active transport. In that case, a cell can take it in by forming a vacuole around it. This is called **endocytosis**, or phagocytosis. If the cell expels material in a vacuole, the process is called **exocytosis**. This diagram shows how the cell membrane encloses large molecules that enter the cell.

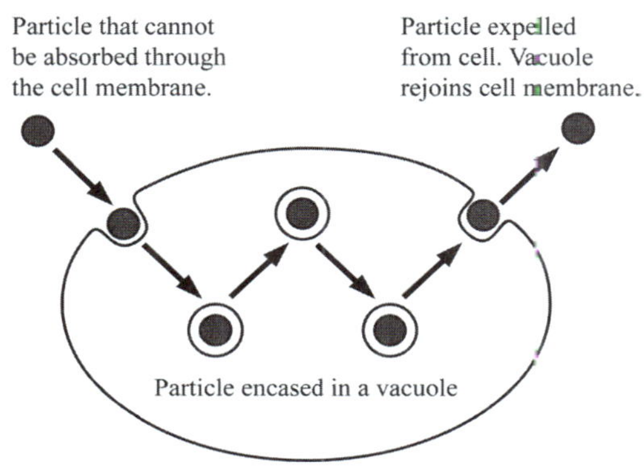

Cell organelles work together. Imagine a cell lining the intestine. It receives a message that there is food to be digested, which means it will have to make certain digestive enzymes (which are proteins). The nucleus sends out a message to the ribosomes to make the enzymes using ATP. ATP is made by the mitochondria. Once assembled, the enzymes are moved through the endoplasmic reticulum to the Golgi bodies, where the enzymes are packaged into vacuoles. The contents of the vacuole are moved out of the cell and into the intestine by the process of exocytosis.

Practice Questions: 10, 11, 12, 13, 14, 15, 16, 17, 20, 21, 22, 24, 25, 26, 27, 37, 38, WR1a

C2.8 *describe cell size and shape as they relate to surface area to volume ratio, and explain how that ratio limits cell size*

C3.1 *explain why, when a single-celled organism or colony of single-celled organisms reaches a certain size, it requires a multicellular level of organization, and relate this to the specialization of cells, tissues and systems in plants*

Surface Area to Volume Ratio

Cell size is limited by two factors. One factor is the amount of nutrients a cell needs to stay alive. The bigger the volume of a cell, the more nutrients it requires. The nutrients from the outside must come through the cell membrane by the processes of diffusion, active transport, or endocytosis. The other factor is the amount of toxic waste the cell produces that must be removed through the cell membrane. The bigger the volume of a cell, the more waste it produces that must be eliminated. Consequently, the surface area of the cell membrane controls the amount of nutrients that can get into a cell and the amount of waste that can get out of a cell. As a cell grows larger, the volume of the cell increases at a faster rate than the surface area. The following graph illustrates the growth of the surface area of a cube relative to its volume.

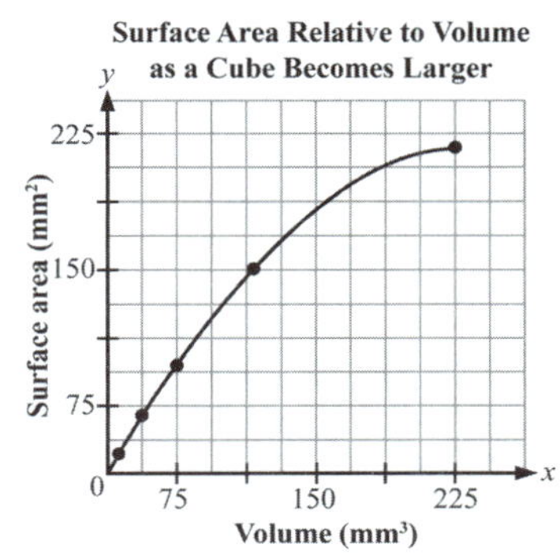

A **multicellular organism** grows by increasing its number of cells. As a result, a human is composed of about 100 trillion very tiny cells. Because a human has so many cells, the cells are **differentiated**. This means that human cells have many different structures and functions. For example, there are muscle cells, nerve cells, and skin cells.

Practice Questions: NR2, 23

C3.2 describe how the cells of the leaf system have a variety of specialized structures and functions; i.e., epidermis including guard cells, palisade tissue cells, spongy tissue cells, and phloem and xylem vascular tissue cells to support the process of photosynthesis

C3.3 explain and investigate the transport system in plants; i.e., xylem and phloem tissues and the processes of transpiration, including the cohesion and adhesion properties of water, turgor pressure and osmosis; diffusion, active transport and root pressure in root hairs

C3.4 explain and investigate the exchange system in plants; i.e., lenticels, guard cells, stomata and the process of diffusion

PHOTOSYNTHESIS IN PLANTS

Photosynthesis occurs in chloroplasts found in the leaf and stem cells of plants. The upper layer of **palisade cells** in a leaf is closely packed and contains many chloroplasts. This arrangement optimizes photosynthesis because sunlight hits this layer of cells directly, thereby increasing glucose production. Stomata are found at the bottom of the leaf, and they open and close to let carbon dioxide into the leaf and oxygen out of the leaf. When the stomata are open, water is lost in a process called **transpiration**. Bundles of xylem within the leaf transport water from the root to the leaf, and bundles of phloem transport glucose made during photosynthesis to the rest of the plant.

WATER TRANSPORT IN PLANTS

In some simple, unicellular organisms, materials move throughout the organism through the process of diffusion. However, plants have complex systems for moving materials. There are three forces that move water in a plant.

First, there is **root pressure**. Water enters a plant through the **root hairs**, which are specialized structures that greatly increase the surface area of the epidermal covering at the end of each root. Because the root cells are hypertonic to the water of the surrounding soil, water enters by osmosis. The force of water moving into the plant by osmosis is called root pressure. Root pressure pushes water up the roots.

Diagram of a Root

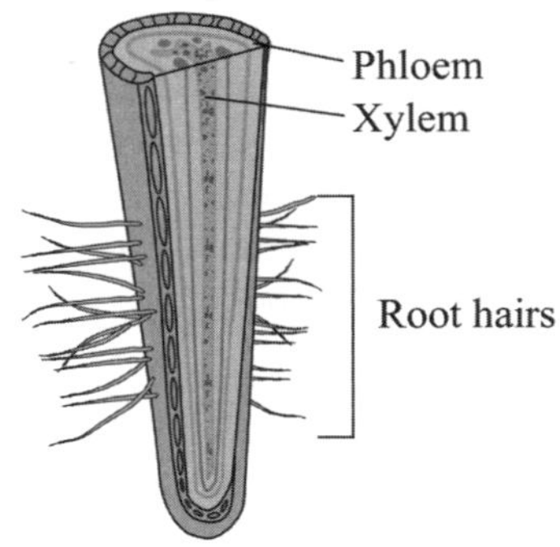

Second, water is pulled inside by the **xylem**. Water and dissolved minerals travel up the roots and stems and through the leaves in tissue called xylem. Xylem is composed of many tiny tubes called **vessel elements**. A force of attraction exists between the water molecules and the surface of the vessel elements. This attraction is called **adhesion**. Adhesion causes water to creep up the vessel elements the way water would creep up the inside of a drinking straw. Because the xylem tubes are so tiny, they have a large surface area when compared to their volume. As a result, the pull of adhesion is quite considerable. Additionally, the force of attraction that exists between water molecules, called **cohesion**, pulls water up through the xylem.

Third, water is pulled to the leaves by the transpiration of water from the **stomata** on the bottom of leaves. Aside from helping to pull up water and minerals, transpiration cools the leaves on hot days. The **guard cells** surrounding the stomata swell to open the stomata on hot, sunny days. The guard cells shrink at night or on cold days to close the stomata and thereby reduce water loss. **Lenticels** are pores on the stems of some plants that serve the same function as the stomata of leaves.

Food is transported throughout plants as well. The **phloem** is a network of sieve tubes that move food from where it is made in the leaves to the other areas of the plant. Unlike vessel elements, which are non-living, the phloem is composed of living cells.

Plants must also transport gases. Plants need to acquire carbon dioxide for photosynthesis and remove the oxygen they produce. The loosely packed, spongy mesophyll layer allows gases to diffuse in and out of cells. In the leaves, the open stomata allow gases to be exchanged. In the stems, small pores called lenticels allow for gas exchange.

Practice Questions: NR4, 28, 29, 30, 31, 35, 36, 39, 40, WR2a

C3.5 *explain and investigate phototropism and gravitropism as examples of control systems in plants*

CONTROL SYSTEMS IN PLANTS

A plant control system is a mechanism that regulates the growth of the plant. Phototropism and gravitropism are two common control systems in plants.

PHOTOTROPISM

You have probably seen a plant grow toward the light or a sunflower turn its face to follow the path of the sun from morning until night. Phototropism provides a plant with maximum exposure to sunlight, which is required for photosynthesis

The growing tip of a plant has a natural growth hormone in it called **auxin**. On the side of the plant that faces the sun, auxin is broken down by sunlight. On the side of the plant that is in shade, auxin does its job and causes the cells on the shaded side to grow and elongate. Because there is more growth on the shady side of the plant than the sunny side, the stem leans or tips toward the sun.

Plant stems are positively phototropic, which means they grow toward the sun. Plant roots are negatively phototropic, which means they grow away from the sun.

GRAVITROPISM

To maximize photosynthesis, the growing tip of a plant stem should grow away from the pull of gravity—upward and toward the sun. Plant roots should be pulled downward by gravity to where they are likely to find water and minerals in the soil. Plant stems are negatively gravitropic, and plant roots are positively gravitropic. Gravitropism is sometimes also called geotropism.

When a plant is put on its side, the stem and leaves will bend away from Earth's core; this is negative gravitropism. The plant's roots will turn to grow toward Earth's core; this is positive gravitropism. Similarly, trees on flat ground grow straight upward, whereas trees on a steep hill grow sideways. Plants in outer space do not show geotropism because there is no gravitational pull.

Practice Questions: 32, 33

PRACTICE QUESTIONS—CYCLING OF MATTER IN LIVING SYSTEMS

1. Which of the following rows correctly identifies an advantage of a light microscope image and an advantage of an electron microscope image?

Row	Light Microscope	Electron Microscope
A.	Has colour	Has high resolution
B.	Can see movement	Has colour
C.	Has high resolution	Has colour
D.	Has colour	Can see movement

2. The first scientist to observe living bacteria in a drop of water was
   - A. Anton van Leeuwenhoek
   - B. Matthias Schleiden
   - C. Robert Hooke
   - D. Louis Pasteur

3. Scientists do not consider viruses to be living organisms. Which of the following statements about viruses is **false**?
   - A. They are not composed of cells.
   - B. Viruses contain DNA and proteins.
   - C. Viruses consume oxygen and food.
   - D. They are reproduced inside of host cells.

4. Which of the following disadvantages of multicellularity occurs because cells are specialized in a division of labour?
   - A. The power of regeneration is lost in some cells.
   - B. Old, injured cells that die cannot be replaced by new cells.
   - C. The outer cells must form a protective layering to protect the internal cells.
   - D. The complexity of the organism increases, and some cells become obsolete.

Use the following information to answer the next question.

The first compound (multiple lens) microscope was invented in 1595 by Zacharias Janssen of Holland. The microscope consisted of two lenses. One lens provided a magnification of 9× and the other provided a magnification of 3×.

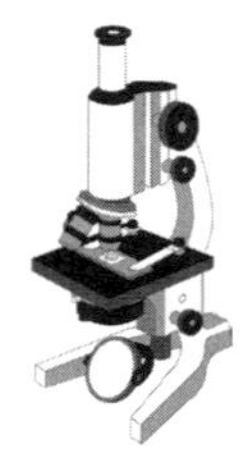

5. The total magnification of Janssen's microscope was
   - A. 9×
   - B. 12×
   - C. 27×
   - D. 90×

6. Modern microscopes are capable of very high magnification, which generally means that their field of view is
   - A. larger than older microscopes
   - B. smaller than older microscopes
   - C. unchanged from older microscopes
   - D. dependent on what is being viewed

Use the following information to answer the next question.

In a technique called fluorescent labelling, a fluorescent molecule is attached to certain structures within a cell. The cell structure is then illuminated using a laser that causes the fluorescent molecule to glow brightly The cell structure that the fluorescent molecule is attached to can be observed under a fluorescent microscope. Biologists at the University of Alberta use this technique to study the structure of plants.

7. If a fluorescent molecule was attached to a mitochondrion in each of the following cell types, the type of cell that would glow **most brightly** under a fluorescent microscope would be
   A. fat
   B. skin
   C. blood
   D. muscle

8. Which of the following definitions **best** describes differential staining?
   A. One type of stain is applied to the tissue, but only structures with specific properties will absorb the stain.
   B. A differential stain is used to stain all nuclei that are negatively charged.
   C. Different stains are applied to different cell structures.
   D. A differential stain is used to dye all cell structures.

Numerical Response

1. A school microscope has a low-power magnification of 40× and high-power magnification of 400×. If the field of view measures 5.0 mm on the low-power magnification, what does the field of view measure on the high-power magnification?
Answer: _____ mm (Record your answer rounded to the nearest **tenth**.)

9. Which of the following organelles are found in plant cells but **not** in animal cells?
   A. Endoplasmic reticulum
   B. Mitochondria
   C. Cell wall
   D. Nuclei

Numerical Response

2. Most cancerous tumours are thought to arise from abnormal cells. The average human cell cycle length (the time it takes a cell to split in two) is about 24 hours. If no cell death occurred, how many cells would there be in a 5-day-old (120 h) tumour that arose from one abnormal cell?
Answer: _____

Use the following information to answer the next two questions.

Cell in Unknown Solution Containing Particles

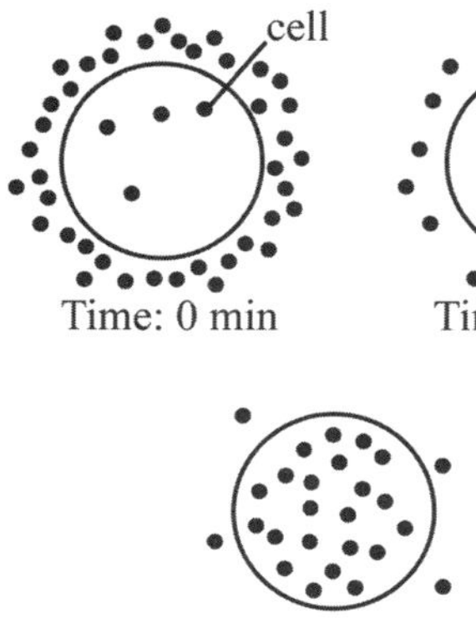

10. What does the given diagram show that suggests that the cell is alive?

A. Osmosis

B. Diffusion

C. Exocytosis

D. Active transport

11. The movement of the particles into the cell requires

A. the release of energy from ATP

B. kinetic energy from the particles

C. energy production by the cell's nucleus

D. energy from the phospholipid molecules to move the particles

12. A cell is considered an open system because

A. the cell membrane contains pores

B. matter can enter a cell, but energy cannot

C. any molecule can pass into and out of a cell

D. molecules that contain chemical energy can enter a cell

Use the following diagram to answer the next four questions.

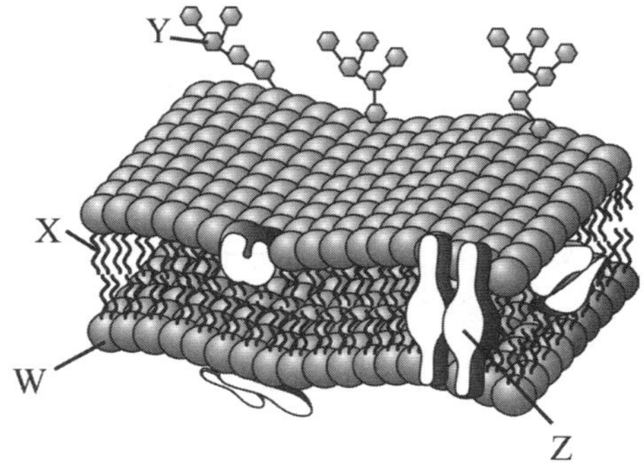

13. Structure Z would be abundant in a cell that

A. lines a blood vessel

B. has a very large nucleus

C. consumes a lot of energy

D. is in contact with other cells

14. Which of the following statements about structures W and X is **true**?

A. These structures are soluble in water.

B. These structures are linked solidly to each other.

C. A lot of the cell's ATP is consumed by these structures.

D. Spaces between these structures allow small molecules to flow through.

15. Which of the following statements about structures W and X is **true**?

A. They are both composed of proteins.

B. They both receive instructions from the nucleus.

C. Together they provide the cell with a semipermeable covering.

D. Together they serve as a passage for large molecules entering the cell.

16. The function of structure Z is to

A. generate ATP for active transport

B. provide structural support for the cell

C. control the cell's activities through the production of DNA

D. move large molecules across the membrane against the concentration gradient

Use the following diagram to answer the next question.

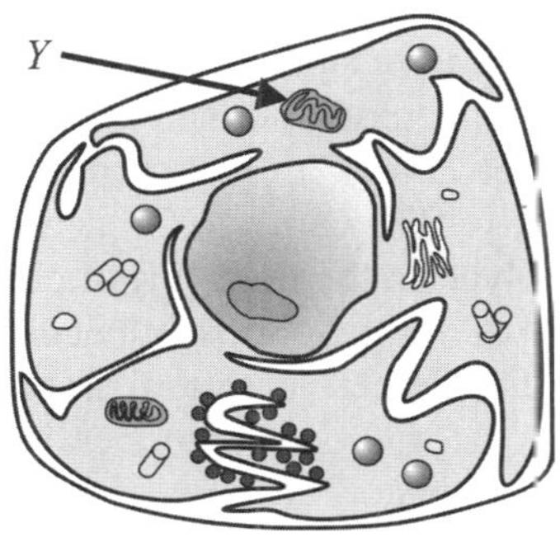

17. Structure Y would be abundant in cells that

A. synthesize proteins

B. store a large amount of fat

C. carry out a lot of active transport

D. have a very permeable membrane

Use the following information to answer the next question.

In 1928, Alexander Fleming observed that a fungal colony growing on a bacteria-covered plate was surrounded by an area with no bacterial growth. The fungus, a member of the Penicillium family, secreted an antibiotic that prevented the growth of bacteria.
This discovery has led to the development of more than 50 clinical antibiotics that are in use today. Some antibiotics act on bacteria by inhibiting the formation of cell walls, while others act by restricting protein synthesis.

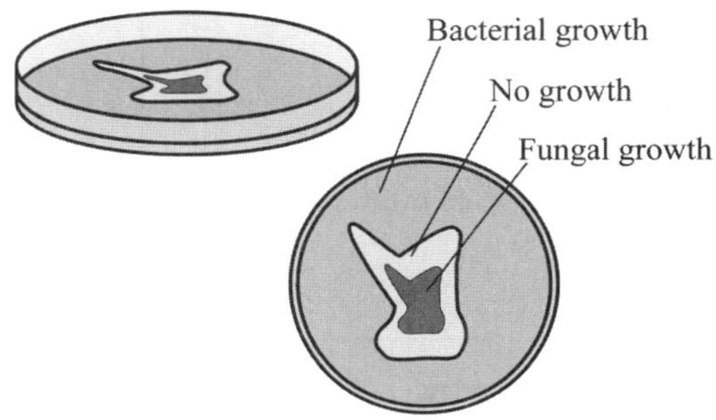

18. Antibiotics that inhibit protein synthesis **most likely** target which of the following cellular organelles?

A. Smooth endoplasmic reticulum

B. Rough endoplasmic reticulum

C. Mitochondrion

D. Nucleus

Use the following diagram to answer the next question.

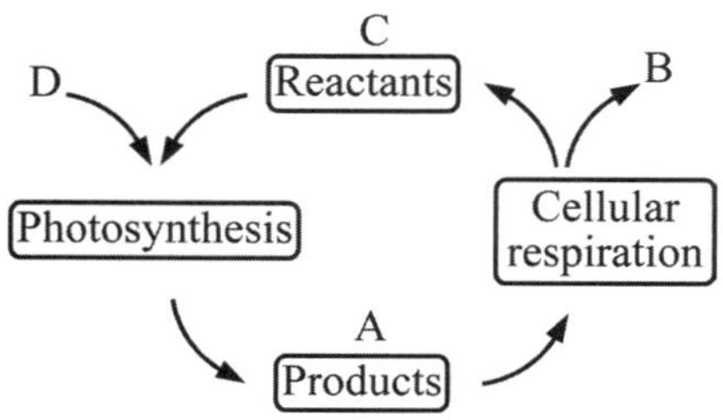

The following terms correspond to the given diagram:

1. Water
2. Carbon dioxide
3. Solar energy
4. Glucose

Numerical Response

3. The numbered terms that correspond with points A, B, C, and D, respectively, are _____, _____, _____, and _____.

Use the following information to answer the next question.

The Microprojectile Bombardment Gun (MBG) is a device used by scientists to introduce foreign DNA into cells. The MBG shoots target cells with tiny high-speed projectiles that are coated with DNA. As these microprojectiles pass through the target cell, the DNA coating is absorbed.

19. Under normal conditions, the entry of foreign DNA molecules into a cell is inhibited by the

A. nuclear membrane

B. plasma membrane

C. Golgi apparatus

D. lysosome

Use the following information to answer the next three questions.

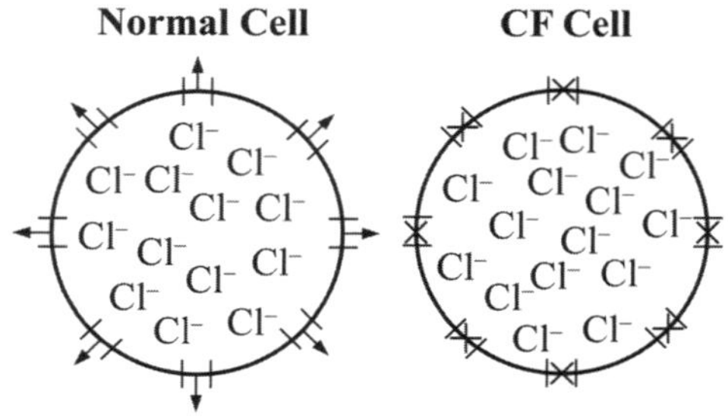

Cystic Fibrosis (CF) is a genetic disorder that affects one in 2 500 children of European descent. It is characterized by high salt concentrations in perspiration and abnormally thick mucous accumulations in the lungs. This mucus can block airways if it is not removed daily. The cause of CF is a defective protein involved in the transport of chloride ions into and out of epithelial cells, the cells that line the lungs. The defective protein is incapable of transporting chloride ions across cell membranes. The normal form of this protein requires energy to transport chloride ions across cell membranes effectively.

20. An inference that can be based on the given information is that chloride is transported across the cell membrane by

A. facilitated diffusion

B. active transport

C. diffusion

D. osmosis

Use the following additional information to answer the next question.

Although the cell membrane is permeable to chloride ions, the regulated transport of chloride ions into and out of cells requires phosphorylation, the addition of a phosphate molecule to the normal CF protein.

21. Which of the following rows lists the name of the molecule that contributes phosphate groups to the phosphorylation of CF proteins and the number of phosphate groups in that molecule?

Row	Molecule	Number of Phosphate Groups
A.	ATP	3
B.	ADP	2
C.	ATP	2
D.	Phosphate	3

Use the following additional information to answer the next question.

Some normal ion concentrations maintained inside and outside a healthy cell are shown in the following table.

Ion	Inside Cell Concentration	Outside Cell Concentration
Na^+	15 mM	145 mM
K^+	140 mM	5 mM
Cl^-	8 mM	110 mM

22. Which of the following rows gives the most likely concentrations of these three ions, inside and outside a CF epithelial cell?

Row	Ion	Inside Cell Concentration	Outside Cell Concentration
A.	Na^+ K^+ Cl^-	80 mM 72.5 mM 59 mM	80 mM 72.5 mM 59 mM
B.	Na^+ K^+ Cl^-	15 mM 140 mM 59 mM	145 mM 5 mM 59 mM
C.	Na^+ K^+ Cl^-	54.3 mM 54.3 mM 54.3 mM	141 mM 141 mM 141 mM
D.	Na^+ K^+ Cl^-	70.5 mM 70.5 mM 70.5 mM	70.5 mM 70.5 mM 70.5 mM

23. If the volume of an animal grows more quickly than its surface area as it develops, it will have

A. an increased risk of overheating

B. a decrease in the amount of energy it requires to move

C. an increase in its metabolic rate

D. a decreased need for nutrients to support its activities

24. The scientific term used to describe the process of development from a single, unspecialized cell to multiple, specialized cells is

A. differentiation

B. fractionation

C. meiosis

D. growth

Use the following diagram to answer the next two questions.

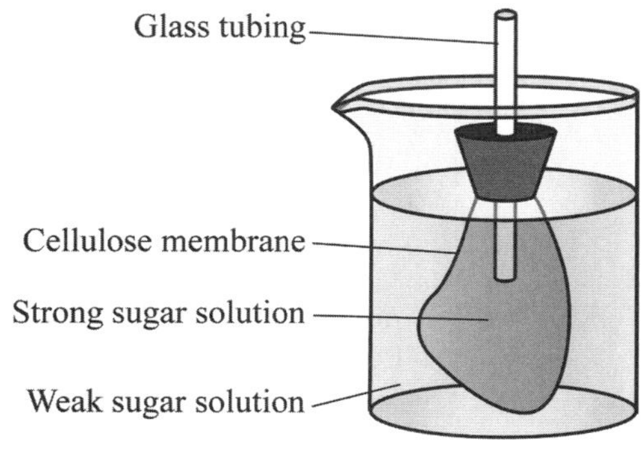

25. The strong sugar solution will rise inside the glass tubing if

A. water moves from inside the membrane to outside the membrane

B. sugar moves from inside the membrane to outside the membrane

C. sugar moves from outside the membrane to inside the membrane

D. water moves from outside the membrane to inside the membrane

26. In the given osmotic system, water molecules will move

A. mostly from the hypertonic environment to the hypotonic environment

B. mostly from the hypotonic environment to the hypertonic environment

C. only from the hypertonic environment to the hypotonic environment

D. only from the hypotonic environment to the hypertonic environment

27. Substances enter cells through different processes. One of the processes that requires energy generated by the cell is called

A. endocytosis

B. diffusion

C. filtration

D. osmosis

Use the following information to answer the next question.

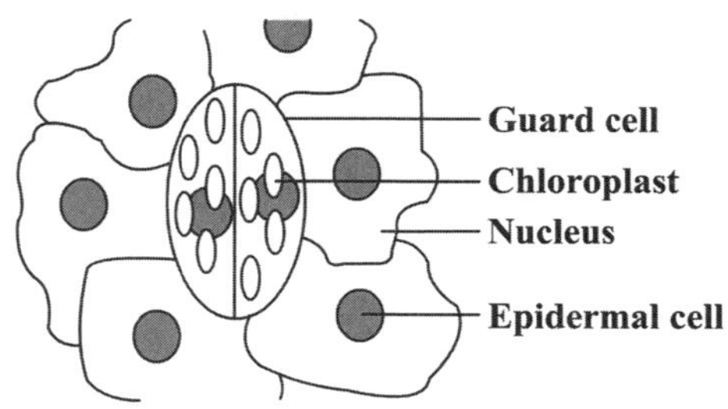

Stomata on the underside of a leaf can open and close depending on the condition of the guard cell that surrounds the stoma. Guard cells contain several chloroplasts, while the neighbouring epidermal cells do not. During the day, the chloroplasts of the guard cells undergo photosynthesis, which causes a concentration of sugar to develop inside the guard cells. No such solution of sugar develops in the neighbouring epidermal cells.

28. The difference in the sugar concentrations between the guard cells and the neighbouring epidermal cells will result in a net flow of water

A. into the guard cells and a decrease in the guard cells' turgor

B. out of the guard cells and a decrease in the guard cells' turgor

C. into the guard cells and an increase in the guard cells' turgor

D. out of the guard cells and an increase in the guard cells' turgor

29. Typically, stomata are open during the day and closed at night. This benefits plants because it allows for

A. gas exchange during the day and a reduction of heat loss during the night

B. gas exchange during the day and a reduction of water loss during the night

C. photosynthesis during the day and a reduction of heat loss during the night

D. photosynthesis during the day and a reduction of water loss during the night

Use the following list to answer the next question.

A list of plant structures is given.

1. Xylem
2. Stomata
3. Root hair
4. Spongy tissue

Numerical Response

4. When the given numbered plant structures are listed in the order in which water moves through them, the order is ____, ____, ____, and ____.

30. Lenticels on the stem of a plant are roughly equivalent to what structures on the leaf?

A. Chloroplasts **B.** Cell Walls

C. Stomata **D.** Veins

31. If the sieve tubes that make up the phloem are clogged, the plant will not be able to transport

A. water

B. mineral nutrients

C. organic nutrients

D. oxygen and carbon dioxide

32. Which of the following rows correctly describes the growth of a germinating seed?

Row	Roots	Shoots
A.	Positive gravitropism	Positive phototropism
B.	Positive gravitropism	Negative phototropism
C.	Negative gravitropism	Positive gravitropism
D.	Negative gravitropism	Negative phototropism

Use the following diagram to answer the next question.

The diagram illustrates a shoot of a plant bending toward light as it grows.

33. The phenomena illustrated occurs because the plant hormone auxin

A. promotes growth on the side closest to the light

B. inhibits growth on the side closest to the light

C. promotes growth on the side opposite the light

D. inhibits growth on the side opposite the light

34. Which of the following statements regarding photosynthesis is **false**?

A. Only green plants carry out the process of photosynthesis.

B. The products of photosynthesis are glucose and oxygen.

C. Aerobic respiration is essentially the reverse of photosynthesis.

D. During photosynthesis, solar energy is converted to chemical energy.

35. Which of the following molecules present in poplar leaves provides the main source of energy for caterpillars that eat the leaves?

A. Oxygen

B. Glucose

C. Water

D. ATP

Use the following information to answer the next question.

The Venus flytrap is one of the rare species of plants that obtain energy from both the insects that they digest and from sunlight. Most other plants obtain their energy only from the sun.

36. As plants grow, they store light energy as what other type of energy?

A. Kinetic

B. Nuclear

C. Potential

D. Chemical

Use the following information to answer the next question.

Four possible cell conditions are given.

I. A semipermeable membrane encloses the cell.

II. The cytoplasm of the cell is hypertonic to moisture in the ground.

III. The cell has energy in the form of ATP.

IV. There is a higher concentration of water inside the cell than outside.

37. Which of the given statements describes the necessary conditions for water to enter the cells of root hairs through the process of osmosis?

A. I and II

B. I and III

C. II and III

D. III and IV

38. Adding too much fertilizer to the ground may cause the soil environment to become hypertonic relative to the cytoplasm in the cells of root hairs. A hypertonic soil environment would cause

A. water to flow from the ground into the cells, providing the plant with additional water

B. water to flow from the cells into the ground, causing the plant to wilt

C. the fertilizer to be absorbed by the plant, stimulating growth

D. the transfer of water between the cells and the soil to stop

Use the following information to answer the next question.

Plants that grow in hot, dry climates have special adaptations to conserve water. By limiting the amount of surface area exposed to the sun, plants can reduce water loss as a result of heat. The pineapple, for example, takes in $CO_{2(g)}$ at night and stores it until daytime, when the $CO_{2(g)}$ can be used for photosynthesis.

In the pineapple, the small openings in leaves called __*i*__ (where gas exchange occurs) are usually __*ii*__ at night and __*iii*__ during the day.

39. The given statement is completed by the information in row

Row	*i*	*ii*	*iii*
A.	stomata	open	closed
B.	lenticels	closed	open
C.	lenticels	open	closed
D.	stomata	closed	open

Use the following information to answer the next question.

One of the largest living organisms on Earth is a Redwood tree that grows in California. It weighs over 2 000 t, measures 25 m around its trunk, and is 84 m tall. Like other plants, this Redwood must transport water and nutrients from its roots to the cells located at the top of the tree.

40. Which of the following events does **not** occur during the transport of water to the top of a tree?

A. Transpiration occurs between plant cells and the atmosphere.

B. Water molecules move by adhesion and cohesion through the xylem.

C. Water molecules repel each other, and thus cause some water to be pushed up the stem.

D. As water molecules enter the roots by osmosis, they push other water molecules up the stem.

41. Which of the following pairs of a plant structure and an animal structure is **most similar** in function?

A. Stomata and the stomach

B. Root hairs and alveoli

C. Phloem and a kidney

D. Xylem and arteries

Written Response

1. **a)** Identify two components of a biological membrane.

b) Describe two advantages of the small size of cells with respect to how cells sense and regulate responses to their environment.

Use the following information to answer the next question.

> As much as 90% of a mature plant cell may be occupied by vacuoles. Vacuoles are filled with "cell sap," which is comprised mainly of water. One of the main roles of the vacuole and the tonoplast (the membrane that encloses the vacuole) is the maintenance of rigid plant tissue (e.g., in stems and leaves), which is accomplished through turgor pressure. Turgor pressure is also used in guard cells to regulate the opening and closing of stomata in leaves.

2. **a)** Define turgor pressure in relation to plant cells and draw a diagram illustrating the concept.

b) Freshwater organisms live in an environment that is hypotonic to their cellular contents. Describe how this affects the movement of substances across the cell membranes of freshwater organisms, and explain how they maintain homeostasis to survive.

c) Describe what would happen in terms of osmosis if a freshwater plant were immersed in salt water, which is a hypertonic solution.

ANSWERS AND SOLUTIONS—PRACTICE QUESTIONS

1. A	**NR2. 32**	**NR3. 4 2 1 3**	**28. C**	**37. A**
2. A	**10. D**	**19. B**	**29. B**	**38. B**
3. C	**11. A**	**20. B**	**NR4. 3 1 4 2**	**39. A**
4. A	**12. D**	**21. A**	**30. C**	**40. C**
5. C	**13. C**	**22. B**	**31. C**	**41. D**
6. B	**14. D**	**23. A**	**32. A**	**WR1. See Solution**
7. D	**15. C**	**24. A**	**33. C**	**WR2. See Solution**
8. A	**16. D**	**25. D**	**34. A**	
NR1. 0.5	**17. C**	**26. B**	**35. B**	
9. C	**18. B**	**27. A**	**36. D**	

1. A

Images from light microscopes show the colour of the specimens since they use visible light. Since light microscopes can observe living specimens, they can also observe movement. In contrast, electron microscopes detect electrons that pass through a specimen. Since there is no light, the image is greyscale. In some cases, the specimen is embedded in plastic and sliced very thin. Since there is no way of observing living matter, it is not possible to observe movement. However, the resolution, or clarity of the image, is excellent.

2. A

Anton van Leeuwenhoek observed living microorganisms in a drop of water. Schleiden observed plant cells later on. Robert Hooke was the first scientist to observe what he called "cells". These were cell walls in a sample of cork. Pasteur did experiments to show how bacteria grow on food.

3. C

Viruses are not considered to be living because they are not metabolically active. That means that all the chemical activities that occur in a living organism do not occur in a virus. It is true that they are not made of cells, and that they contain DNA surrounded by a shell of protein. It is also true that the reproduction of viruses occurs inside host cells.

4. A

When a cell differentiates to form a specialized structure, it loses the power to divide again. Some cells, like neurons, are not replaceable and cannot regenerate themselves. Special cells, called stem cells, are undifferentiated and may be able to replace the specialized cells.

5. C

To determine the magnification of a compound microscope, multiply the magnification of the lenses used.
$9 \times 3 = 27$.

6. B

The field of view is the area that you can see when looking through a microscope. As magnification is increased, the area that you can see is reduced.

7. D

Muscle cells require a large portion of the energy produced by the body (ATP). As a result, cells found in muscles are packed with ATP-generating mitochondria. Relative to other cell types, which also contain mitochondria, muscle cells would glow most brightly.

8. A

An example of a differential stain is the gram stain for bacteria. Bacteria that are stained purple are described as gram-positive and have a different cell wall structure than gram-negative bacteria. This dye stains according to the properties of the cell structure and is used to distinguish between different types of cells. Simple stains are used to stain the whole organism, although the dye may bind to one cell structure more than another. Some pecial dyes, such as red acetocarmine, stain just the nucleus.

NR 1 0.5

$$\frac{\text{Low-power magnification}}{\text{High-power magnification}} = \frac{\text{High-power field of view}}{\text{Low-power field of view}}$$

Let x be the field of view on high-power magnification.

$$\frac{40}{400} = \frac{x}{5.0}$$
$$x = \frac{40 \times 5.0}{400}$$
$$x = \frac{200}{400} = 0.5 \text{ mm}$$

The field of view on the high-power magnification, to the nearest tenth, is 0.5 mm.

9. C

Plant cells can be distinguished from animal cells by the presence of a cell wall. The cell wall is an additional layer surrounding the outer surface of the cell membrane. It is made up of cellulose. Endoplasmic reticulum, the site of protein synthesis, and mitochondria, the site of energy conversion, are found in both plant and animal cells. Plant and animal cells both have nuclei.

NR 2 32

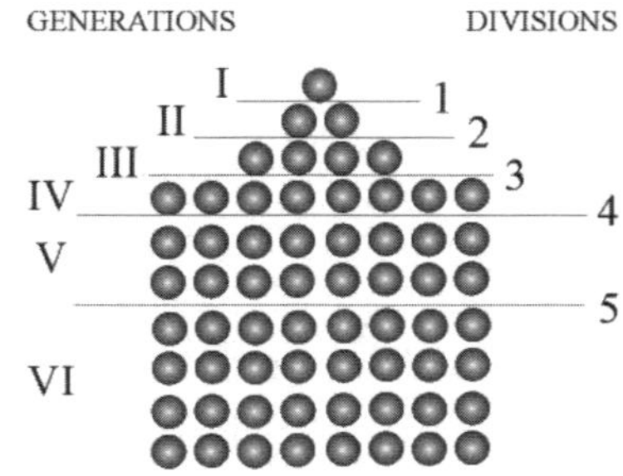

Use a table to calculate the number of cells there would be after 5 divisions.

Start	1 cell
After 1 division	2 cells
After 2 divisions	4 cells
After 3 divisions	8 cells
After 4 divisions	16 cells
After 5 divisions	32 cells

Therefore, there would be 32 cells in a 5-day-old tumour.

10. D

During the first minute, the movement of the particles into the cell could simply be through diffusion. However, by the fifth minute, the particles are moving into the cell against a concentration gradient. That could only happen if the cell membrane was undergoing active transport to draw these particles in. Active transport requires ATP and can only occur in a living cell.

11. A

The movement of the particles into the cell was against the concentration gradient, so it could not happen simply as a result of the kinetic energy of the particles, as with passive transport. Energy in the form of ATP, produced by the mitochondria, is required. It is protein molecules in the membrane, not phospholipids, that move the particles into the cell.

12. D

An open system is one that can exchange matter and energy with its environment. Any molecule that enters a cell is matter. If the molecule contains chemical energy, then the cell is also taking in energy from its environment.

13. C

Structure Z is a protein in the membrane. Proteins are needed to move substances across the membrane by active transport. Since active transport consumes ATP energy, if membrane proteins are abundant, the cell must be consuming a lot of energy.

14. D

Structures W and X are both parts of a phospholipid molecule. W is the glycerol end that is soluble in water. X is the fatty acid end that is insoluble in water. Phospholipids are large molecules, and they have fairly large spaces between them. The phospholipids are like a screen. Small molecules can slip right past them, while larger molecules cannot.

15. C

Labels W and X both point to parts of a phospholipid molecule. W is the glycerol end, and X is the fatty acid end. Phospholipids are the basic covering of the cell membrane. The phospholipids are like a screen. Small molecules can slip right past them, while larger molecules cannot. Therefore, the membrane is described as semipermeable.

16. D

Structure Z is a protein in the membrane. Proteins are needed to move substances across the membrane by active transport. The proteins consume ATP energy and can move large molecules across the membrane against a concentration gradient. Although the proteins use ATP, they do not make it. The ATP is made by mitochondria. Small molecules can move by diffusion with the concentration gradient between the phospholipid molecules of the membrane.

17. C

Structure *Y* is a mitochondrion. Mitochondria are organelles that carry out cellular respiration. In cellular respiration, the mitochondria break down food molecules and use that energy to generate ATP. ATP are high-energy molecules that cells use to carry out metabolic activities, such as active transport.

18. B

Proteins are synthesized by ribosomes, which either float freely in the cytoplasm or are attached to the endoplasmic reticulum (ER). The ibosomes located on the ER are visible under a microscope as small bumps on the surface, giving it a rough appearance, thus they are called the rough ER. Smooth endoplasmic reticulum does not have attached ribosomes and so does not function in protein synthesis. Mitochondria take part in energy production, and the nucleus stores the DNA (genetic material).

NR 3 4 2 1 3

The reactants for photosynthesis are light (solar energy), carbon dioxide, and water. The external ingredient added to the cycle illustrated at point D is solar energy. The products of photosynthesis are energy in the form of glucose and oxygen, making glucose (4) the answer for point A. Cellular respiration gives off carbon dioxide at point B. The products of cellular respiration are carbon dioxide, heat, and water. So, water is the answer for point C, as it is both a product of cellular respiration and a reactant for further photosynthesis.

19. B

The cell is enveloped by the plasma membrane through which all incoming and outgoing molecules must pass. Small molecules such as water or carbon dioxide are able to pass through openings in the membrane, but DNA is too large to cross the plasma membrane. The Golgi apparatus, nuclear membrane, and lysosomes can all be found inside the cell membrane. They do not inhibit the entry of foreign molecules into the cell.

20. B

The information states that in its normal form, the protein uses energy to transport the chloride ions. The only type of transport that uses energy is active transport. Diffusion of molecules occurs from an area of high concentration to one of low concentration, and does not require energy input. When the diffusion of a molecule is aided by proteins embedded in the cell membrane, it is called facilitated diffusion. Osmosis is the diffusion of water.

21. A

In a cell, energy for immediate use is in the form of ATP. ATP stands for adenosine triphosphate. It contains three phosphate groups, which are linked to an adenosine molecule.

22. B

A CF cell is described as having no regulated transport of chloride ions across the cell membrane. Lack of regulated chloride transport renders the CF cell unable to maintain the concentration gradient of chloride ions between the inside and the outside of the cell. The preamble also mentions that the cell membrane is permeable to chloride ions. This means that passive diffusion of chloride ions occurs. In the absence of active transport to maintain the concentration gradient (8 mM versus 110 mM), passive diffusion of chloride ions will lead to the equalization of the chloride ion concentration between the inside and the outside of the cell.
110 mM + 8 mM = 118 mM

The total amount of Cl^- is 118 mM. Dividing the total by 2 results in the number of chloride ions on each side of the membrane 118 ÷ 2 = 59 mM. Because all molecules of one type (e.g., Cl^-) diffuse independently of molecules of all other types (e.g., Na^+ and K^+), the concentrations of potassium and sodium ions should be unaffected in CF cells.

23. A

Heat is generated by an animal's volume and is lost across its surface area. As an animal's heat-generating volume grows faster than its heat-losing surface, animals risk overheating. To avoid overheating, large animals, such as elephants and rhinoceroses, have almost no hair.

Larger animals require more energy to move, tend to have a lower metabolic rate, and require more nutrients to support their activities.

24. A

In the normal development of an organism, the single-cell stage is followed by cell division and cell differentiation. Differentiation produces different cell types that carry out specialized functions. For example, in an adult human, a red blood cell (A) has a different function and structure than a nerve cell (B).

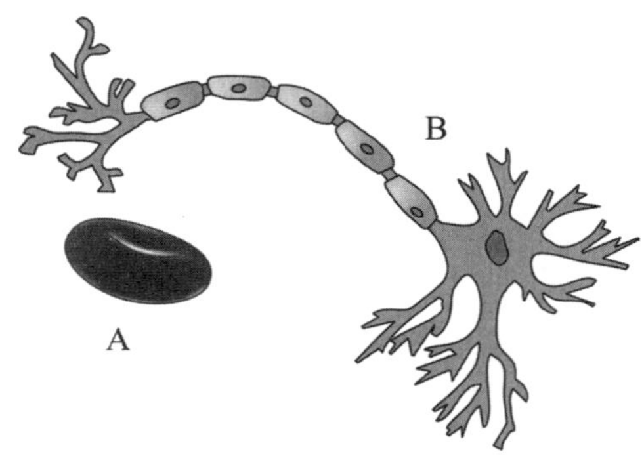

Meiosis is a process of cell division that produces the sex cells (sperm and egg) in multicellular eukaryotes. Fractionation is not a type of cell division.

25. D

The strong sugar solution will rise in the glass tubing if its volume increases. This will occur if water moves from outside the membrane to inside by osmosis. In the strong sugar solution, the concentration of water is lower than in the weak sugar solution, so water will move across the membrane from outside to inside. If sugar were able to pass through the cellulose membrane, it would not directly cause the strong sugar solution to rise up the tubing. If water were able to move from inside the membrane to outside, the level of the solution in the glass tubing would fall.

FACT
90% OF YOUR BONE MASS IS BUILT BY AGE 20.
HELLO
3
BYE
MILK
MILK
SEWER MANHOLE
GET THE FACTS AT NEVERSTOPMILK.CA

Do you have a passion for math or science?
PLAN A GREAT CAREER PATH IN TECHNOLOGY
What are the requirements? Visit:
www.aset.ab.ca/careers
Bioscience
Building
Chemical
Civil
Electrical
Electronics
Forestry
Geomatics
Industrial
Information Technology
Instrumentation
Mechanical
Mineral Resources
Petroleum/Geosciences
ASET
The Association of Science and Engineering Technology Professionals of Alberta
Phone: 780.425.0626 Toll free within Alberta: 1.800.272.5619
or visit www.aset.ab.ca

26. B

Water molecules move randomly in all directions. The terms hypotonic and hypertonic refer to the concentration of molecules in solution. A hypotonic solution has a low concentration of dissolved molecules and a high concentration of water. The opposite is true for a hypertonic solution. More water moves from a hypotonic solution to a hypertonic solution by osmosis than in the opposite direction.

27. A

Both diffusion and osmosis are passive and require no added energy. Filtration is not a mode of transport. Endocytosis involves a cell wrapping itself around an object and taking it in as a vacuole. This process requires added energy.

28. C

The high concentration of glucose inside the guard cells creates a concentration. As a result, there will be a net flow of water into the guard cells. The increase of water inside the guard cells increases the pressure of the water in the cell, pushing on the cell wall. This will increase turgor pressure.

29. B

When the stomata are open, gases can pass in and out of the leaf. During the day, carbon dioxide can enter the leaf to be used in photosynthesis. Oxygen, a waste product of photosynthesis, can pass out of the leaf. As well, during the day, the leaf may be in danger of overheating from sunlight. So, water can transpire from the leaf, which cools it down. When the stomata are closed at night, water cannot be lost through them.

NR 4 **3 1 4 2**

Water enters the plant from the soil through the large surface area of the root hairs (3). Then, water makes its way through the roots, up the stem, and into the leaves through the xylem (1). When the water is in the leaf, it can move into the spaces of the spongy tissue (4). From the spongy tissue, the water molecules can diffuse out of the leaf through the stomata (2).

30. C

Lenticels are pores in the epidermis of a plant's stem. Stomata are pores of the leaf that allow gas exchange between the leaf and the atmosphere. Like stomata, lenticels allow gas exchange between the stem and the atmosphere.

31. C

Sieve tubes make up the vascular tissue known as phloem. The phloem carries food made through photosynthesis to where it is needed or will be stored. Food made by the plant can be thought of as organic nutrients. Mineral nutrients are those that a plant absorbs from the soil. These are transported up the plant with the water of the xylem.

32. A

A tropism is growth in response to a certain stimulus. Gravitropism is growth in response to Earth's gravity. Phototropism is growth in response to light. When a seedling begins to grow, its first root will turn and grow toward Earth (positive gravitropism) and its first shoot will turn and grow toward the light (positive phototropism).

33. C

Auxin is a growth hormone that weakens the cell wall. As a result, turgor pressure forces the cell to enlarge. More auxin is produced on the side of the stem that is shaded. Less auxin is produced on the side of the stem that is close to the light. The result is that auxin promotes growth on the shaded side of the plant.

34. A

Photosynthesis is not restricted to green plants. For example, trees with red leaves are capable of undergoing photosynthesis using pigments other than chlorophyll. Chlorophyll-containing protists, such as euglena and algae, are also capable of producing their own food using sunlight as a source of energy. Many bacteria also carry out photosynthesis. The following reaction shows photosynthesis:

$$6CO_{2(g)} + 6H_2O_{(g)} + \text{light} \rightarrow \underset{\text{glucose}}{C_6H_{12}O_{6(s)}} + \underset{\text{oxygen}}{6O_{2(g)}}$$

This process takes solar energy (i.e., light energy from the sun) and converts it into chemical energy in the form of glucose, $C_6H_{12}O_{6(s)}$.
This reaction is, essentially, the reverse reaction of aerobic respiration.

35. B

The equation for photosynthesis is given.

$$6CO_{2(g)} + 6H_2O_{(g)} + \text{light} \rightarrow \underset{\text{glucose}}{C_6H_{12}O_{6(s)}} + \underset{\text{oxygen}}{6O_{2(g)}}$$

The products of photosynthesis are $C_6H_{12}O_{6(s)}$ (glucose) and $O_{2(g)}$ (oxygen). Sugars, in the form $C_xH_yO_z$, are considered carbohydrates and they store chemical energy. Primary consumers like caterpillars digest carbohydrates. They convert the chemical energy into usable energy in the form of ATP so it can be used for movement, digestion, mating, cellular processes, etc.

36. D

Plants convert light energy into chemical energy in the form of ATP, NADH, sugars (including glucose), proteins, and fat. The main form of stored chemical energy in plants that is used by animals is glucose.

37. A

Osmosis is the diffusion of water from an area with low salt concentration (hypotonic) to an area with high salt concentration (hypertonic). In osmosis, water moves down its concentration gradient.
To enter cells by this method, water must cross the plasma membrane, which is semipermeable (I). The cytoplasm of the cell of the root hair must have a higher salt concentration than the water source—the soil moisture (II). Energy is not required.

38. B

There will be a net flow of water from where there is more of it to where there is less of it. If there is a higher concentration of solute in the water outside of the cells of the root hairs, water will leave those cells to equalize the concentration on both sides of the cell walls.

39. A

To prevent excessive water loss, leaves and stems are covered by cuticle or bark, which are thick protective layers through which water and gases cannot diffuse. Gas exchange is restricted to small air spaces within pores (lenticels in stems and stomata in leaves). In leaves, the major site of photosynthesis, stomata open and close to regulate gas exchange and water loss by transpiration. Normally, plants open the stomata during the day, when sunlight is used for photosynthesis. Photosynthesis requires CO_2 intake and O_2 removal, so gas exchange is crucial. At night, when photosynthesis cannot take place, stomata close to conserve water. Pineapples and other plants in arid climates have special adaptations that allow them to open stomata, capture and store CO_2, and expel O_2 at night, when the risk of H_2O loss is low. Stomata close during the day because of the heat. Photosynthesis in these plants still occurs during the day because it requires sunlight, but it uses the CO_2 stored from the previous night as a reactant.

40. C

Normally water enters a plant through root hairs and leaves via the stomata. Water molecules are attracted to each other by the force of cohesion, allowing water to move upward through the plant.

41. D

Xylem is composed of tubes that carry water and minerals up a plant. Arteries carries blood that contains water, minerals, and other substances throughout the body. Phloem transports food away from leaves, and a kidney filters blood. Stomata exchange gases, and the stomach digests food. Root hairs take in water and minerals, and alveoli exchange gases.

1. **a)** *Identify two components of a biological membrane.*

Two components of a biological membrane are phospholipids and proteins. Phospholipids form the phospholipid bilayer and proteins can be either embedded in the membrane or on one of the surfaces of the membrane. See the given diagram.

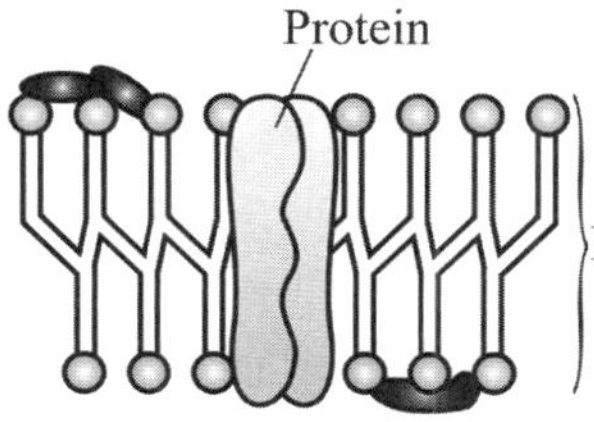

b) *Describe two advantages of the small size of cells with respect to how cells sense and regulate responses to their environment.*

The nucleus that regulates and controls all cellular activity depends on the diffusion of substances from the cytoplasm. The small size of cells is an advantage because a large volume of cytoplasm would slow down the transmission of substances to the nucleus by diffusion.

Movement across the cell membrane is maximized for the proportional volume of the cell. That is, cells sense their external environment by the movement of substances, such as chemical signals (either direct or triggered by bodies such as neighbouring cells), from the environment into the cell. The signal is intensified if the membrane has a large surface area relative to the cell volume, as is present in small cells, which have a large surface area-to-volume ratio.

2. **a)** *Define turgor pressure in relation to plant cells and draw a diagram illustrating the concept..*

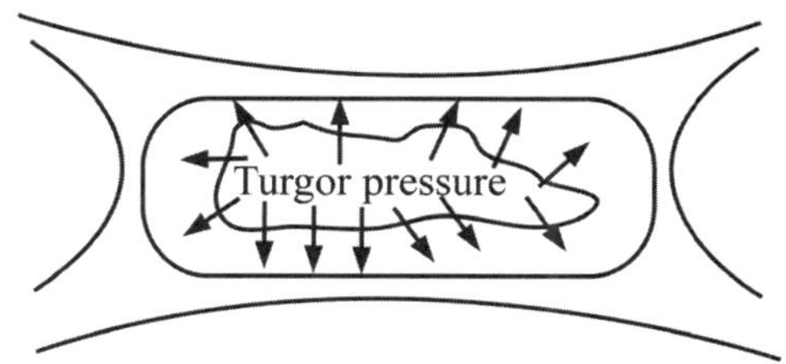

Turgor pressure is the pressure that water exerts outward from the inside of a cell. It maintains the rigidity of a plant cell.

b) *Freshwater organisms live in an environment that is hypotonic to their cellular contents. Describe how this affects the movement of substances across the cell membranes of freshwater organisms, and explain how they maintain homeostasis to survive.*

Because fresh water is hypotonic compared with the inside of a cell, solutes within the cell tend to move out of the cell and water tends to move into the cell. To maintain homeostasis, cells adapted for freshwater survival actively pump excess water out using contractile vacuoles. These special vacuoles collect and expel liquid containing a low concentration of the solutes required by the cell.

c) *Describe what would happen in terms of osmosis if a freshwater plant were immersed in salt water, which is a hypertonic solution.*

The plant cells would experience plasmolysis. Water travels to the area that is less concentrated; in this case, the salt water. The plant cell will lose water and, therefore, lose turgor pressure. The plasma membrane will pull away from the rigid cell wall, and the vacuole and cytoplasm will shrink. Compare the given diagram with the diagram in the solution to question **2a**.

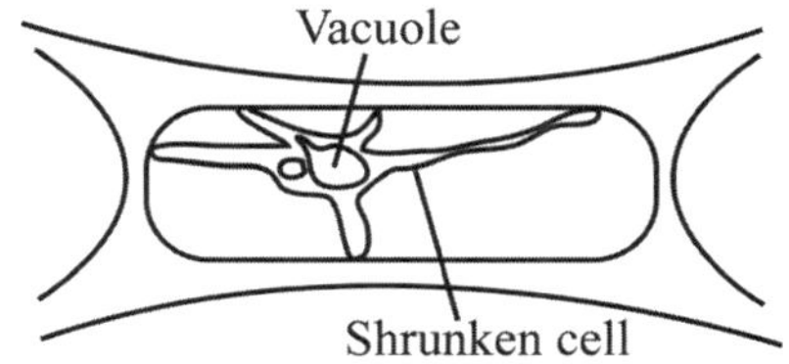

UNIT TEST—CYCLING OF MATTER IN LIVING SYSTEMS

1. What scientist first observed what he called "cells" in a section of cork?

A. Robert Hooke

B. Louis Pasteur

C. Matthias Schleiden

D. Anton van Leeuwenhoek

2. As the cells of cork are dead, the only part of a cell that can be observed in cork is the rigid outer covering known as the

A. vacuole

B. nucleus

C. cell wall

D. ribosome

3. A difference between the simple microscopes that Robert Hooke and Anton van Leeuwenhoek used and today's compound light microscopes is that compound light microscopes

A. can observe aquatic microbes

B. direct light through two lenses

C. use electric light rather than sunlight

D. can be used to observe living organisms

Use the following diagram to answer the next question.

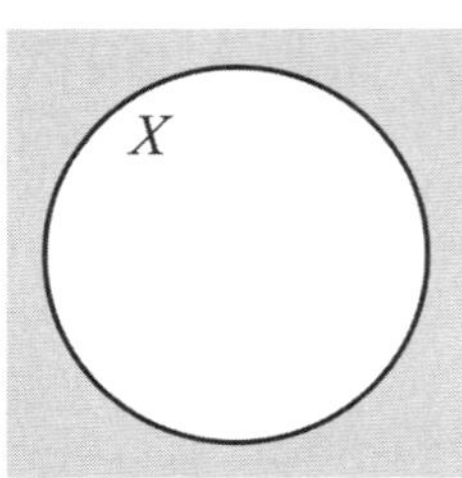

4. A student is observing the given letter *X* on a microscope slide under low power with a school microscope. Before switching to medium power, the student has to move the *X* to the centre of the field of view by moving the slide

A. up and to the left

B. up and to the right

C. down and to the left

D. down and to the right

5. Two changes caused by switching a light microscope from low power to medium power are that the light intensity is

A. lower and the resolution is increased

B. lower and the resolution is decreased

C. greater and the resolution is increased

D. greater and the resolution is decreased

Use the following information to answer the next five questions.

> The cells lining the small intestine make digestive enzymes. These enzymes are proteins that move into the intestine to digest food.

6. Since these enzymes are protein molecules, they would be assembled by

A. ribosomes

B. the nucleus

C. mitochondria

D. the endoplasmic reticulum

7. The synthesis of molecules inside cells requires chemical energy in the form of ATP. Most of the ATP needed is produced by the

   A. nucleus

   B. chloroplasts

   C. mitochondria

   D. cell membrane

8. Once the enzymes are produced, they have to be transported through the cell. The part of the cell that serves as a transportation system is the

   A. nucleus

   B. cell wall

   C. cell membrane

   D. endoplasmic reticulum

9. Which of the following organelles gathers the required enzymes to be packaged into a vacuole?

   A. Ribosome

   B. Chloroplast

   C. Mitochondrion

   D. Golgi apparatus

10. Once the enzymes are collected into vacuoles, the vacuoles are moved to the cell membrane. The membranes of the vacuoles fuse with the cell membrane, releasing the enzymes into the intestine. This removal of material from a cell is called

   A. exocytosis

   B. phagocytosis

   C. active transport

   D. cytoplasmic streaming

Use the following information to answer the next five questions.

For an experiment, Grace places dialysis tubing containing a starch solution into a glucose solution.

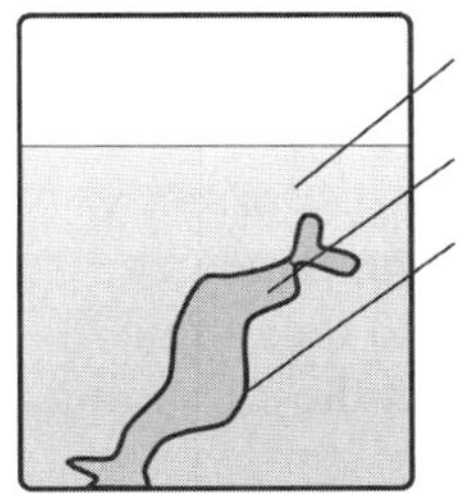

11. During the experiment shown in the diagram, water would

   A. neither enter nor leave the bag

   B. both enter and leave the bag

   C. leave the bag only

   D. enter the bag only

12. The results of this experiment would indicate that the size of the pores in the dialysis tubing is

   A. smaller than water, glucose, and starch molecules

   B. larger than water, glucose, and starch molecules

   C. larger than water and glucose molecules but smaller than starch molecules

   D. larger than starch molecules but smaller than water and glucose molecules

13. Measuring the mass of the bag and its contents before and after the experiment would show that, during the experiment, the bag

   A. lost mass because of the loss of water

   B. lost mass because of the loss of starch

   C. gained mass because of the increase of starch

   D. gained mass because of the increase of water and sugar

Use the following additional information to answer the next two questions.

Benedict's solution is blue, but it turns orange when it comes in contact with glucose.
Iodine solution is brown, but it turns dark blue when it comes in contact with starch.

14. Which of the following rows correctly describes the colours of the Benedict's solution inside the bag and the iodine solution outside the bag at the beginning of the experiment?

Row	Benedict's Solution Inside Bag	Iodine Solution Outside Bag
A.	Blue	Brown
B.	Orange	Brown
C.	Blue	Blue
D.	Orange	Blue

15. Which of the following rows correctly describes the colours of the iodine solution inside the bag and the Benedict's solution outside the bag after 10 hours?

Row	Iodine Solution Inside Bag	Benedict's Solution Outside Bag
A.	Blue	Brown
B.	Orange	Brown
C.	Blue	Orange
D.	Orange	Blue

Use the following information to answer the next three questions.

An experiment to measure the rate of transpiration was set up as shown. The level of the water in the graduated cylinder was recorded every hour. The mass of the plant was recorded before and after the experiment.

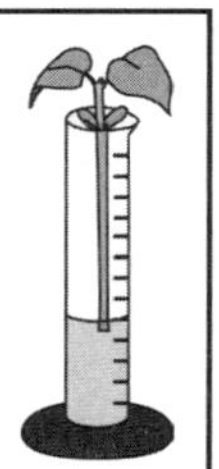

16. In this experiment, positive evidence for the occurrence of transpiration would be through

A. a decrease in the plant's mass

B. an increase in the plant's mass

C. a decrease in the level of the water

D. an increase in the level of the water

17. An increase in which of the following conditions would **not** cause an increase in the rate of transpiration in this experiment?

A. Humidity

B. Wind speed

C. Temperature

D. Light intensity

18. If you removed the leaves from this plant, the rate of transpiration would

A. increase

B. decrease

C. remain the same

D. fluctuate up and down

19. As a seedling grows, it responds to its environment through movements referred to as tropisms. Which of the following rows correctly describes a seedling's responses to Earth's gravity?

Row	Shoot of Seedling	Root of Seedling
A.	Positive gravitropism	Positive gravitropism
B.	Positive gravitropism	Negative gravitropism
C.	Negative gravitropism	Positive gravitropism
D.	Negative gravitropism	Negative gravitropism

20. A vascular bundle in the stem of a plant contains
   A. xylem and phloem
   B. guard cells and xylem
   C. phloem and root hairs
   D. root hairs and stomata

Written Response

Use the following information to answer the next two questions.

Oxalis is a common forest plant in southeastern Canada and the eastern United States. It has the unusual ability to alter its leaves from horizontal to vertical in response to the intensity of the sunlight. Usually, the leaves are in the horizontal position during the day and the vertical position at night. An experiment was set up to measure the effect of the light intensity on the transpiration rate.

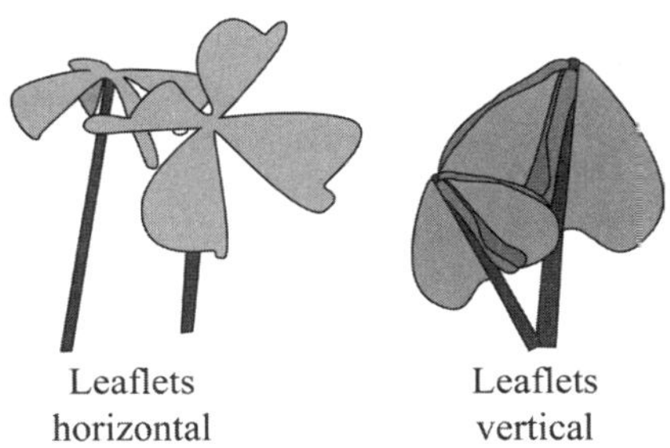

Transpiration rates were measured as weight loss from the leaves. During trial 1, some negative transpiration rates were measured. A negative transpiration rate meant that the leaves actually gained weight during the trial.

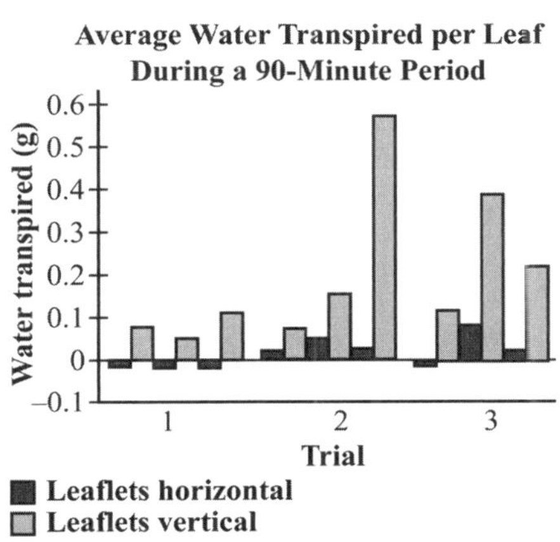

1. **a)** The term *negative transpiration* suggests that the water that was brought to the leaves through the __________ exceeded the water that was lost from the leaves through the ____________.

Fill in the blanks in the given sentence.

b) Describe how conditions may have varied between trials 1, 2, and 3.

c) Imagine that a chemical substance was sprayed onto the leaves, clogging the stomata so that nothing could pass through them. List the effects that spraying this substance would have on the functioning of the plant.

Use the following information to answer the next question.

During the spring, a sugary sap rises in the xylem of sugar maple trees. The sap contains about 2% to 3% sugar, along with other nutrients that the tree needs for growth.

2. Describe the forces inside roots, xylem, and leaves that help to move this sap up a sugar maple tree.

ANSWERS AND SOLUTIONS—UNIT TEST

1. A	**5. D**	**9. D**	**13. D**	**17. A**	**WR1. See Solution**
2. C	**6. A**	**10. A**	**14. A**	**18. B**	**WR2. See Solution**
3. B	**7. C**	**11. B**	**15. C**	**19. C**	
4. A	**8. D**	**12. C**	**16. C**	**20. A**	

1. A

Robert Hooke was the scientist who observed "cells" in a slice of cork. Cork is dead plant matter from the bark of trees. The structures that Hooke observed were actually cell walls—the rest of the cellular material was gone.

Where there normally would be cytoplasm in a living cell, Hooke saw nothing. It is not surprising that these empty boxes looked like cells. Louis Pasteur did experiments to show that microorganisms grow on food matter. Matthias Schleiden studied plant cells. Anton van Leeuwenhoek was the first scientist to observe living bacteria and other microorganisms.

2. C

Cork comes from plant bark. A cell wall is the non-living covering surrounding all plant cells. It will still exist after the living matter of the cells is gone. The nucleus, vacuole, and ribosomes are all living parts of the cell.

3. B

Anton van Leeuwenhoek observed aquatic microbes through his simple microscope. The microbes that he observed were living. A compound microscope is described as compound because the light travels through two lenses between the specimen and the observer. One lens is the eyepiece and the other is the objective lens. It is true that many microscopes now are fitted with an electric light, but many compound microscopes direct sunlight to the microscope with a mirror.

4. A

Anything you observe through a microscope is upside down and backward. If you want to move a specimen down and to the right, you have to adjust the microscope slide by moving it up and to the left.

5. D

By increasing the magnification, you are spreading the light out more, so your specimen will look darker. Therefore, you will have to increase the light intensity. Resolution refers to the clarity with which you can observe a specimen. The greater the magnification, the less clear the specimen; therefore, the resolution has been decreased.

6. A

The function of a ribosome is to assemble proteins. Most of the organic matter of a human body is protein, so humans are largely assembled by ribosomes. The nucleus houses the DNA, the mitochondria make ATP, and the endoplasmic reticulum is a transport network within a cell.

7. C

Mitochondria break down food molecules and use the energy in the food to assemble ATP. ATP is needed for all metabolic activities that consume energy. The nucleus houses DNA. Chloroplasts in green plants are the site of photosynthesis. The cell membrane is a selective barrier that controls the flow of matter into and out of the cell.

8. D

The endoplasmic reticulum is a system of interconnected tubules. The RER has ribosomes attached to it and the SER does not.

9. D

Materials that move through the endoplasmic reticulum are gathered into the Golgi apparatus, where they are then packaged into a vacuole. A vacuole is made of membrane, as is the Golgi apparatus. The vacuole is formed by simply pinching off a portion of the Golgi apparatus.

10. A

Exocytosis involves fusing a vacuole to the plasma membrane to move the vacuole out of the cell. The opposite, endocytosis, involves bringing a substance into a cell by forming a vacuole around it. Phagocytosis is endocytosis of larger solid materials. Active transport refers to pumping a large molecule through the membrane with the help of transport proteins. Cytoplasmic streaming is the stirring of cytoplasm in some cells.

11. B

If the material of the membrane is permeable to water, the water will cross the membrane in either direction.

12. C

If the membrane is permeable to water and glucose, then water and glucose molecules can pass through the pores in the membrane. Therefore, the pores are larger than water and glucose molecules. If the membrane is not permeable to starch, the pores must be too small for starch molecules to pass through.

13. D

Eventually, the glucose will be in equilibrium, which means there will be an equal concentration of glucose inside and outside of the bag. Water would also move into the bag by osmosis. The net flow of water will be into the bag, increasing the mass of the bag and its contents.

14. B

At the beginning of the experiment, glucose has not yet moved into the bag so the Benedict's solution will be blue. As starch cannot leave the bag, the solution outside will show a negative result for starch and the iodine solution will be brown.

15. C

As starch cannot leave the bag, the solution inside the bag will show a positive result for starch and the iodine solution will be blue. As glucose moves into and out of the bag, the solution outside the bag will show a positive test result for glucose and the Benedict's solution will be orange.

16. C

Transpiration is the evaporation of water from the leaves of a plant. Transpiration creates a pulling force, drawing water up the xylem. In the given experiment, water moving up the xylem (evidence of transpiration) will draw water into the plant from the graduated cylinder. As a result, there will be a decrease in the water level in the graduated cylinder.

17. A

Transpiration is the evaporation of water from the leaves of a plant. Anything that increases the evaporation rate, such as temperature, wind speed, and light intensity, will increase the transpiration rate. An increase in humidity will decrease the evaporation rate and the transpiration rate.

18. B

Since transpiration is the evaporation of water from the leaves of a plant, there can be no transpiration without leaves. Therefore, the transpiration rate decreases.

19. C

Gravitropism refers to growth in response to gravity. When a seed germinates, the root must grow down, which is positive gravitropism. The first shoot grows up, away from the pull of gravity, which is negative gravitropism.

20. A

Vascular tissue is tissue that transports materials. This material is composed of the xylem and phloem. Xylem and phloem both exist as tubes. Tiny tubes have a greater surface area relative to their diameter than large tubes do. A vascular bundle is a bundle of tiny xylem and phloem tubes. In a leaf, vascular bundles appear as veins.

1. **a)** *The term* negative transpiration *suggests that the water that was brought to the leaves through the _________ exceeded the water that was lost from the leaves through the ___________. Fill in the blanks in the given sentence.*

The words that fill in the blanks in the given sentence are *xylem* and *stomata*, respectively.

b) *Describe how conditions may have varied between trials 1, 2, and 3.*

Since the experiment is about the effect of the light intensity (the manipulated variable) on the transpiration rates (the responding variable), the light intensity must have varied between trials 1, 2, and 3. Trial 1 would have had the lowest light intensity because it showed the lowest transpiration rate. Trial 3 had the highest transpiration rate, so it would have been exposed to the highest light intensity.

c) *Imagine that a chemical substance was sprayed onto the leaves, clogging the stomata so that nothing could pass through them. List the effects that spraying this substance would have on the functioning of the plant.*

Blocking the stomata would mean that oxygen would not be able to leave the leaf and carbon dioxide would not be able to enter the leaf, so at some point, photosynthesis would stop. Since water would not be able to leave the stomata, the flow of water up the xylem would stop, preventing mineral nutrients from the roots getting to the leaves. Because the evaporation of water from the leaves has a cooling effect, the leaves could overheat.

2. *Describe the forces inside roots, xylem, and leaves that help to move sap up a sugar maple tree.*

Water moves into the roots by osmosis because there is a higher concentration of water outside the roots than there is inside. The force of the water entering the roots in this way is called root pressure. Water moves inside the xylem up through the roots, stems, and leaves. The xylem consists of tiny tubes, and there is an attraction between water molecules and the side of the xylem tubes. This is called adhesion, and it pulls water up the xylem. Water molecules themselves are attracted to each other through their hydrogen bonds, so each water molecule is pulled up by the water molecule ahead of it. The force of attraction between water molecules is called cohesion. The evaporation of water out of the stomata has a pulling effect, like sucking on a drinking straw, drawing water up the xylem. All of these forces together move water from the roots to the leaves.

Energy Flow in Global Systems

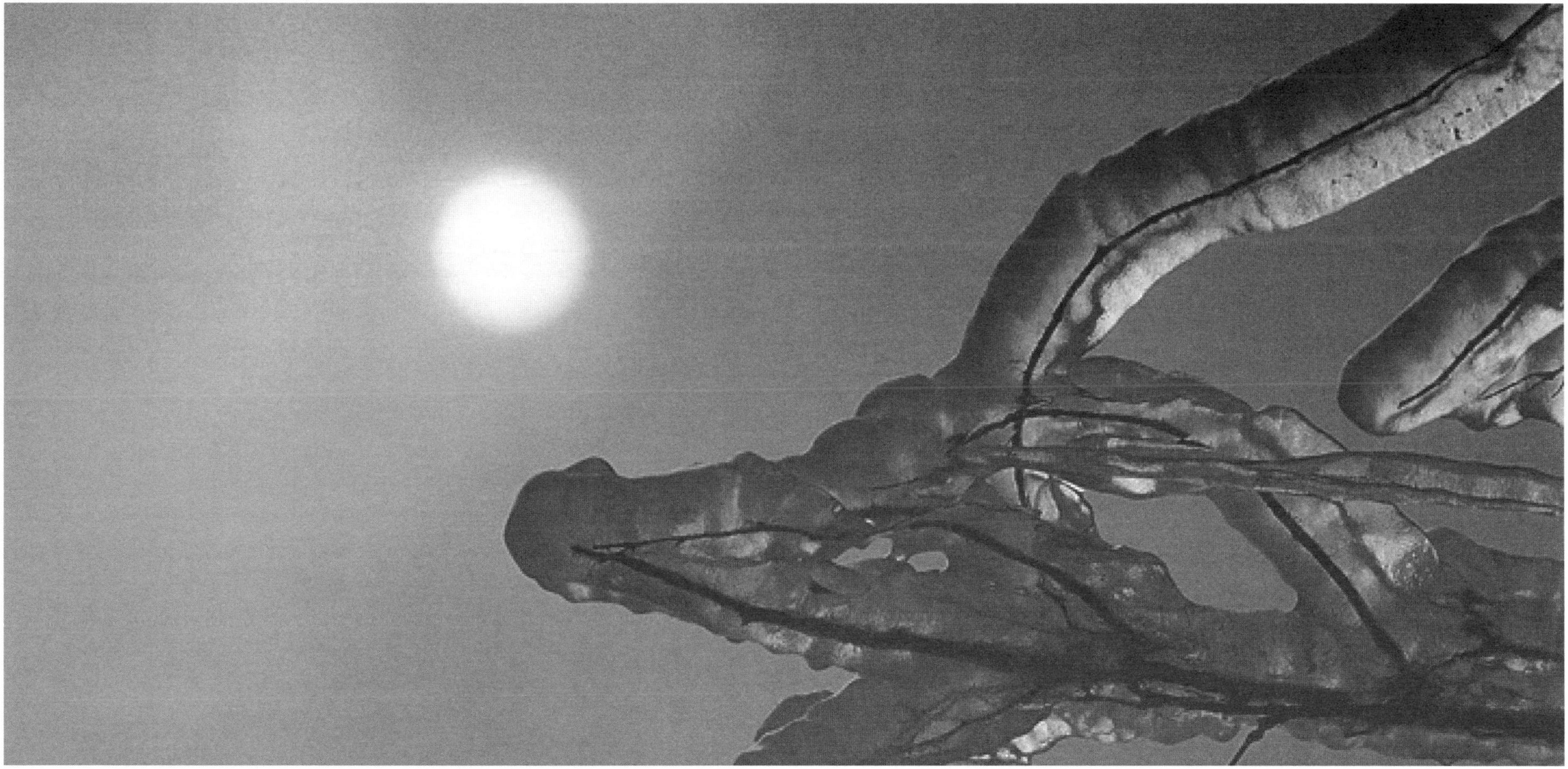

ENERGY FLOW IN GLOBAL SYSTEMS

Table of Correlations				
Specific Expectation	**Practice Questions**	**Unit Test Questions**	**Practice Test 1**	**Practice Test 2**
By the end of this course, students will:				
D1 Describe how the relationships among input solar energy, output terrestrial energy and energy flow within the biosphere affect the lives of humans and other species.				
D1.1 explain how climate affects the lives of people and other species, and explain the need to investigate climate change	28, WR2			
D1.2 identify the Sun as the source of all energy on Earth	2, 3, 4, 19, 21, WR1d			35
D1.3 analyze, in general terms, the net radiation budget, using per cent; i.e., solar energy input, terrestrial energy output, net radiant energy				
D1.4 describe the major characteristics of the atmosphere, the hydrosphere and the lithosphere, and explain their relationship to Earth's biosphere	7, 8	1		34
D1.5 describe and explain the greenhouse effect, and the role of various gases—including methane, carbon dioxide and water vapour—in determining the scope of the greenhouse effect	31	NR2		37
D2 Analyze the relationships among net solar energy, global energy transfer processes- primarily radiation, convection and hydrologic cycle- and climate.				
D2.1 describe, in general terms, how thermal energy is transferred through the atmosphere (i.e., global wind patterns, jet stream, Coriolis effect, weather systems) and through the hydrosphere (i.e., ocean currents, large bodies of water) from latitudes of net radiation surplus to latitudes of net radiation deficit, resulting in a variety of climatic zones	NR1, NR2, 5, 9, 10, 11, 17, 18, 22, 30, WR1c	NR1, 8, 9	32, 34	39, 40, 41
D2.2 investigate and describe, in general terms, the relationships among solar energy reaching Earth's surface and time of year, angle of inclination, length of daylight, cloud cover, albedo effect and aerosol or particulate distribution	23, 24, 25, 26, 31	2, 10	30, 37, 38	
D2.3 explain how thermal energy transfer through the atmosphere and hydrosphere affects climate	6	5	31, NR10	
D2.4 investigate and interpret how variations in thermal properties of materials can lead to uneven heating and cooling	16			36
D2.5 investigate and explain how evaporation, condensation, freezing and melting transfer thermal energy; i.e., use simple calculations of heat of fusion $H_{fus} = Q/n$ and vaporization $H_{vap} = mc\Delta t$ to convey amounts of thermal energy involved, and link these processes to the hydrologic cycle	NR3, NR4, NR5, 12, 13, 14, 15	4, 7	NR9, 33	NR4, NR5, 38

D3 Relate climate to characteristics of the world's major biomes, and compare biomes in different regions of the world.				
D3.1 describe a biome as an open system in terms of input and output of energy and matter and exchanges at its boundaries	20, 21, 31, WR1a, WR1b, WR1e	NR2, NR3, 6, 11, 12, 13, 14	35	
D3.3 analyze the climatographs of two major biomes (i.e., grasslands, desert, tundra, taiga, deciduous and rain forest) and explain why biomes with similar characteristics can exist in different geographical locations, latitudes and altitudes				
D4 Investigate and interpret the role of environmental factors on global energy transfer and climate change.				
D4.1 investigate and identify human actions affecting biomes that have a potential to change climate and critically examine the evidence that these factors play a role in climate change	27, 29, 31	3		
D4.2 identify evidence to investigate past changes in Earth's climate		15, 16, 17		
D4.3 describe and evaluate the role of science in furthering the understanding of climate and climate change through international programs				
D4.6 assess, from a variety of perspectives, the risks and benefits of human activity, and its impact on the biosphere and the climate	1, WR2, WR3			

ENERGY FLOW IN GLOBAL SYSTEMS

D1.2 *identify the Sun as the source of all energy on Earth*

D1.3 *analyze, in general terms, the net radiation budget, using per cent; i.e., solar energy input, terrestrial energy output, net radiant energy*

D1.4 *describe the major characteristics of the atmosphere, the hydrosphere and the lithosphere, and explain their relationship to Earth's biosphere*

ENERGY FLOW IN GLOBAL SYSTEMS

The sun provides a constant supply of energy to Earth in the form of sunlight. Sunlight is the source of almost all of the energy needed for all forms of life on Earth. Green plants (also called **producers** or **autotrophs**) store this energy in compounds through the process of **photosynthesis**.

The sun's radiation cascade as it hits Earth

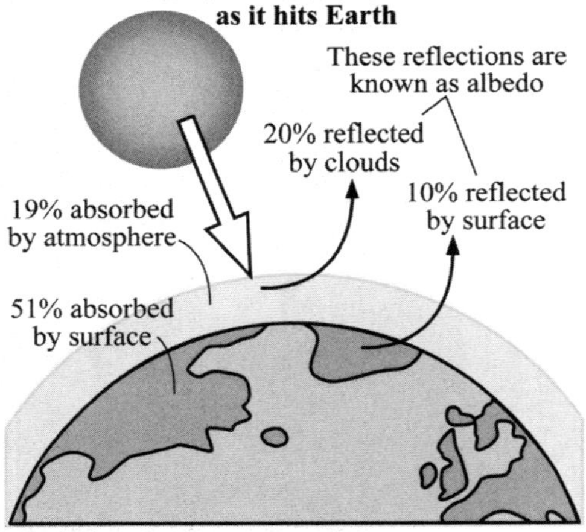

The **biosphere** can be defined as the parts of Earth that can support life. Generally speaking, the biosphere encompasses a thick layer that begins approximately 9000 m below sea level and extends to over 11300 m above sea level.

The **atmosphere** is composed of a mixture of gases that form a layer of air around Earth. It contains the gases needed for both protection against the sun's radiant energy and the survival of organisms on Earth. It also absorbs heat to form weather patterns.

The **lithosphere** is Earth's cool, rigid outer layer. It includes the crust and the cooled part of the uppermost mantle. The lithosphere is 100 to 200 km thick, depending on the location.

The **hydrosphere** is the area of Earth and its atmosphere in which water is present. This area extends from 100 km below the surface of Earth to 500 km above Earth's surface. Since every known kind of organism requires some form of water, life thrives in or close to the hydrosphere.

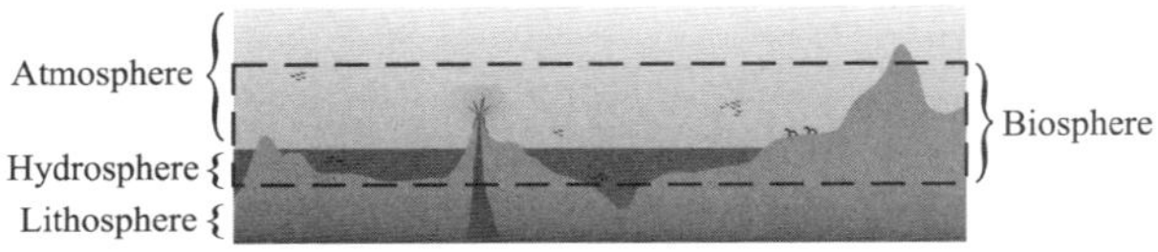

Practice Questions: 2, 3, 4, 7, 8, 19, 21, WR1d

D2.4 investigate and interpret how variations in thermal properties of materials can lead to uneven heating and cooling

D2.5 investigate and explain how evaporation, condensation, freezing and melting transfer thermal energy; i.e., use simple calculations of heat of fusion $H_{fus} = Q/n$ and vaporization $H_{vap} = mc\Delta t$ to convey amounts of thermal energy involved, and link these processes to the hydrologic cycle

PROPERTIES OF HEAT ENERGY

Materials are made up of many different combinations of molecules and exist as solids, liquids, or gases. Each material has its own set of physical properties, including boiling point, freezing point, and heat capacity. Due to the differences in the physical properties, some materials warm and cool quickly while others warm and cool slowly. These differences are characterized by the properties of heat energy.

Heat of fusion—the amount of heat energy required to change a substance from a solid to a liquid. Water has a high heat of fusion. It takes a lot of heat energy to pull the water molecules out of the ice crystals and into a liquid state. Water's heat of fusion can be quantified as 333 J/g. That means it takes 333 J of heat energy to change 1 g of solid water at 0°C to liquid water at 0°C.

If it takes 333 J to melt 1 g of ice, it will require the following amount of energy to melt 500 g of ice.
333 J/g × 500 g = 166 500 J (1.665×10^5 J)

The following equation can be used to calculate the heat of fusion:

$H_{\text{fus}} = \dfrac{Q}{n}$, to determine the heat of fusion in KJ/mol where
Q = quantity of thermal energy in kJ
n = number of moles of a substance

Example

If a student melts 7.2 mol of ice, how much energy is absorbed? The heat of fusion for water is 6.01 kJ/mol.

$$H_{\text{fus}} = \frac{Q}{n}$$
$$Q = H_{\text{fus}} \times n$$
$$Q = 6.01 \text{ kJ/mol} \times 7.2 \text{ mol}$$
$$Q = 43.3 \text{ kJ}$$

Heat of vaporization—the amount of heat energy needed to convert a liquid to a gas. Water has a high heat of vaporization for the same reason it has a high heat of fusion. The heat of vaporization of water is 2 260 J/g. It takes a lot of solar energy to evaporate liquid water on the ground. Later, when water vapour condenses to form clouds, that energy is released into the atmosphere.

Specific heat capacity—represents the amount of heat energy required to change the temperature of a substance. Water has a high specific heat capacity. In other words, it takes a lot of heat energy to change the temperature of water.
The specific heat capacity, which is indicated by the symbol *c*, can be quantified. Water has a specific heat capacity of 4.19 J/g°C. That means it takes 4.19 J of energy to increase the temperature of 1 g of water by 1°C. You can use the equation $Q = mc\Delta T$ to determine how much energy is taken into or released from water.

$$Q = \% \text{ efficiency}$$
$$= \frac{\text{useful energy output}}{\text{total energy input}} \times 100\%$$
$$\% \text{ efficiency} = \frac{1\ 149 \text{ kJ}}{2\ 874 \text{ kJ}} \times 100\%$$
$$= 40\% \text{ energy in joules}$$

m = mass in grams
ΔT = change in temperature in degrees Celcius

Example

A man put a pot containing 100 g of water at 20°C on a stove. After 5 min, the water was boiling (100°C). How many joules of heat energy did the heat of the stove add to the water?

$$\begin{aligned} Q &= mc\Delta T \\ &= 100\ \text{g} \times 4.19\ \text{J/g°C} \times 80°\text{C} \\ &= 33\ 520\ \text{J}\left(3.352 \times 10^4\ \text{J}\right) \end{aligned}$$

This equation can be manipulated in order to determine mass, specific heat capacity, or a change in temperature.

Use $m = \frac{Q}{c\Delta t}$ to determine the mass of a substance.

Use $c = \frac{Q}{m\Delta t}$ to determine the specific heat capacity of a substance.

Use $\Delta T = \frac{Q}{mc}$ to determine the temperature change.

Practice Questions: NR3, NR4, NR5, 12, 13, 14, 15, 16

D2.1 *describe, in general terms, how thermal energy is transferred through the atmosphere (i.e., global wind patterns, jet stream, Coriolis effect, weather systems) and through the hydrosphere (i.e., ocean currents, large bodies of water) from latitudes of net radiation surplus to latitudes of net radiation deficit, resulting in a variety of climatic zones*

D2.2 *investigate and describe, in general terms, the relationships among solar energy reaching Earth's surface and time of year, angle of inclination, length of daylight, cloud cover, albedo effect and aerosol or particulate distribution*

D2.3 *explain how thermal energy transfer through the atmosphere and hydrosphere affects climate*

Climate and Weather Systems

Solar energy entering the atmosphere, hydrosphere, and lithosphere drives weather systems. The effects of solar heating are not the same everywhere. The **albedo effect** determines the extent to which light reflects off a surface. Ice has a very high albedo; that is, most of the light hitting ice is reflected. In contrast, dark rocks have a low albedo; that is, most of the light hitting dark rocks is not reflected. Instead, it is absorbed and turned to heat.

At the border between the cold, arctic air and the warm, southern air high up in the atmosphere, there is a constant west-to-east wind called the **jet stream**. Normally, the jet stream flows above the southern border of Canada. Sometimes, the jet stream shifts more to the north, covering Canada with warm, southern air. Other times, the jet stream shifts to the south, leaving Canada completely covered in cold, northern air.

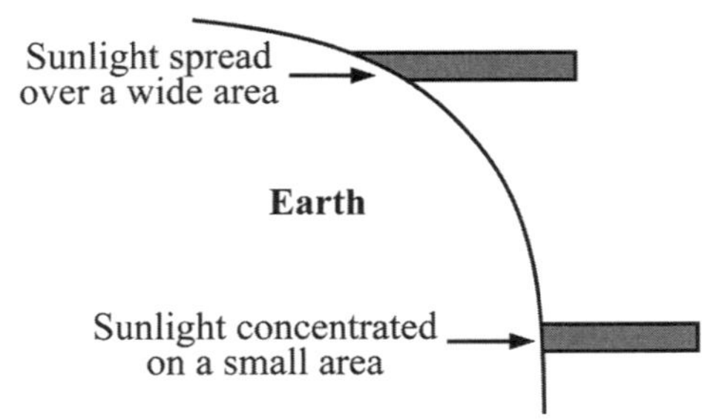

Another factor that affects solar heating is latitude. Close to the poles, sunlight must travel through a lot of atmosphere and is then spread thinly over a wide area. Close to the equator, sunlight travels through less atmosphere and is concentrated in a small area. Therefore, heating as a result of solar energy is much more intense near the equator. Air masses moving over the surface of Earth are also affected by the spinning of Earth. Air moving either toward or away from the equator curves, creating what is known as prevailing winds. This is called the **Coriolis effect**.

The given diagram illustrates how different surfaces affect air currents and temperatures.

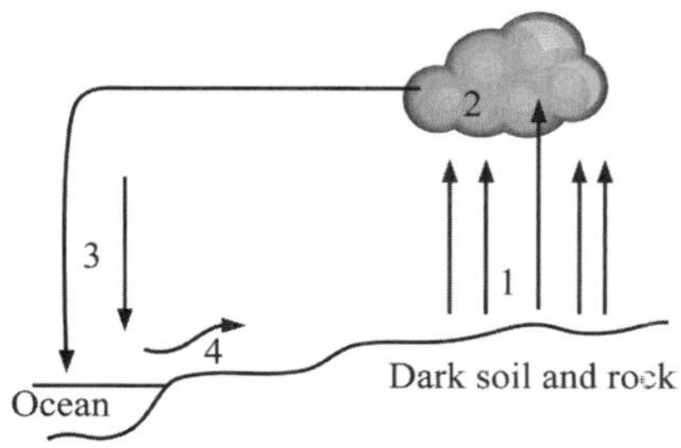

Dark soil and rock absorb sunlight, rapidly warming and evaporating soil moisture.
To change the liquid water on the ground to vapour, the heat of vaporization must be drawn from the environment (point 1). This keeps the surface from heating too quickly. The warm, moist air rises. As the rising air reaches a certain altitude (point 2), it has cooled enough for the moisture to condense and form clouds.
The process of condensation releases heat energy, which warms the air. When there is enough water in the atmosphere, it falls to the surface as precipitation (point 3).

Over the ocean, the falling air creates a region of high air pressure while over the land, the rising air results in a region of low air pressure. Therefore, there is a flow of air (point 4) that is known as a sea breeze—a wind from water to land.

The oceans also have flowing currents, which are created by temperature variance and the Coriolis effect. Areas of water with a warmer temperatures, such as those seen during El Niño events, can also dramatically change weather patterns by heating the air and changing the way low pressure systems are created and behave in different areas.

Because water has a high specific heat capacity, a large body of water can moderate an area's temperatures, thereby influencing the climate.
A warm current in the Pacific Ocean brings warm water north, making British Columbia's coastline warmer than it would otherwise be. In contrast, the cold Labrador Current carries cold water from the arctic southward, causing Labrador and Newfoundland to remain cool. A lot of moisture in the air, such as is found on the coast of British Columbia, further moderates temperatures.
In contrast, the temperature of the dry air of southern Alberta can fluctuate radically.

Earth experiences different seasons throughout the year. The tilt of Earth as it orbits the sun causes these seasons.

The tilt of something simply refers to how much it leans or slants to one side. Earth is tilted at 23.5°. Since its axis is tilted, different parts of Earth are turned toward the sun at different times of the year, affecting the angle at which sunlight hits Earth.

Thermal energy from the sun is transferred by radiation. When the sun's rays reach Earth, some are reflected back to space by the atmosphere, the clouds, and Earth's surface. Since clouds are made up of masses of water droplets, and water has a high specific heat capacity, the amount of solar energy reaching Earth is reduced.

Practice Questions: NR1, NR2, 5, 6, 9, 10, 11, 17, 18, 22, 23, 24, 25, 26, 31, WR1c

D3.3 analyze the climatographs of two major biomes (i.e., grasslands, desert, tundra, taiga, deciduous and rain forest) and explain why biomes with similar characteristics can exist in different geographical locations, latitudes and altitudes

CLIMATOGRAPHS

Climatographs, such as the one shown, can be used to analyze the temperature and precipitation of an area.

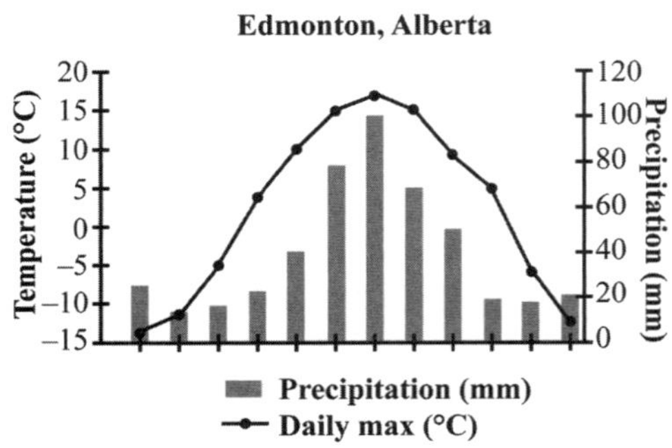

Solar energy determines climate, and climate has a major influence on the types of organisms that can exist in an area. A large area with a particular type of living community is called a **biome**. The table on the next page shows some characteristics of major biomes.

D3.1 describe a biome as an open system in terms of input and output of energy and matter and exchanges at its boundaries

D3.2 relate the characteristics of two major biomes (i.e., grassland, desert, tundra, taiga, deciduous and rain forest) to net radiant energy, climatic factors (temperature, moisture, sunlight and wind) and topography (mountain ranges, large bodies of water)

SYSTEMS

A **system** can be described as a group of separate things that work together. With regard to matter and energy, there are three types of systems. An **open system** exchanges matter and energy with its surroundings. A **closed system** allows energy in and out but does not allow matter to enter or leave. An **isolated system** does not allow either matter or energy to be exchanged with its surroundings. Any living cell is an open system. **Biomes**, such as a forest or a desert, are open systems.

The types of biomes found in an area are determined by two abiotic factors: climate and geography. A similar climate and geography in two different areas can produce the same type of biome. For example, high precipitation, cool temperatures, and coastal geography have promoted the development of a temperate rainforest biome on the west coast of British Columbia. Because of similar abiotic factors, the southwest coast of Chile also has a temperate rainforest biome. The types of plants and animals in both regions are very similar.

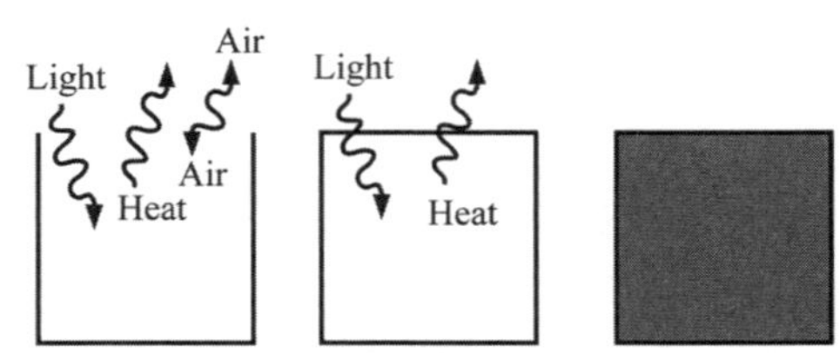

An open system. Matter and energy are exchanged.

A closed system prevents matter from entering or leaving but allows heat and energy to pass through.

An isolated system is a covering so solid that neither energy nor matter can enter it.

Characteristics of Biomes						
Characteristic	**Deciduous Forest**	**Tundra**	**Taiga**	**Grassland**	**Desert**	**Tropical Rainforest**
Temperature	Cold winters/hot summers	Extreme winters/short, cool summers	Long, cold winters/short, mild summers	Cold winters/hot summers with cool nights	Hot days/cold nights	Consistently moderate
Rainfall	Low; most falls in summer	Very low	Low; most falls in summer	Low	Very low	High; falls evenly throughout the year
Biodiversity	High	Low	High	Moderate	Low	Very high
Productivity (rate of photosynthesis)	Moderate	Very low	Moderate	Moderate	Low	Very high
Organic matter in soil	High	Low	Very low	Moderate	Very low	Very high

Practice Questions: 21, 31, WR1a, WR1b, WR1c

D1.1 *explain how climate affects the lives of people and other species, and explain the need to investigate climate change*

D1.5 *describe and explain the greenhouse effect, and the role of various gases—including methane, carbon dioxide and water vapour—in determining the scope of the greenhouse effect*

D3.4 *identify the potential effects of climate change on environmentally sensitive biomes*

D4.1 *investigate and identify human actions affecting biomes that have a potential to change climate and critically examine the evidence that these factors play a role in climate change*

D4.2 *identify evidence to investigate past changes in Earth's climate*

CLIMATE CHANGE

There are natural cycles of warming and cooling on Earth. Humans can study these cycles by examining the growth rings of trees or the ice cores from glaciers. However, in the past few decades, temperatures have been rising faster than they have in the past.

This accelerated warming has been associated with an increase in greenhouse gases. Many common chemical substances play an important role in temperature change. For example, carbon dioxide, methane, and nitrous oxide are important greenhouse gases.

Earth absorbs solar radiation and heats up. This heat radiates back up from Earth into the atmosphere. The gases in the atmosphere, including oxygen, water vapour, and carbon dioxide, prevent this heat from radiating into space, acting like the glass ceiling of a greenhouse. This radiates even more heat back to Earth's surface. As a result, Earth is gradually warmed up. This is called global warming.

A changing climate impacts biomes and the organisms living within them. For example, for most of the winter, the polar bears of Hudson Bay are on the sea ice, where they catch seals. During the summer, the ice melts, and the bears have to stay on land. While on land, they eat almost nothing. Because of global warming, the summers (when the bears do not eat) are getting longer, and soon the bears simply will not be able to survive.

Practice Questions: 27, 28, 29, 31, WR2

D4.3 *describe and evaluate the role of science in furthering the understanding of climate and climate change through international programs*

D4.4 *describe the role of technology in measuring, modeling and interpreting climate and climate change*

D4.5 *describe the limitations of scientific knowledge and technology in making predictions related to climate and weather*

D4.6 *assess, from a variety of perspectives, the risks and benefits of human activity, and its impact on the biosphere and the climate*

International Response to Climate Change

Scientists from around the world have come together to use general circulation models (GCMs) to look at the global effect of climate warming. Information from international scientists can be used to create computer simulations and models that predict the effects of human activity on climate change. This sharing of information has led to international cooperation to reduce the human contribution to global warming.

The **Intergovernmental Plan on Climate Change (IPCC)** is the biggest international initiative on climate change. Composed of governmental representatives and scientists from all over the world, the IPCC endeavours to bring together objective, high-quality science and information on climate change. It assembles a huge amount of information and produces comprehensive reports that can be used by policy-makers. More information on the IPCC can be found on their website, www.ipcc.ch.

Although Earth may be warming, it is far from certain what the long-term effects will be.
The **Gaia hypothesis** states that all living things on Earth are interconnected in the same way that all the cells in your body are. In the same way that the cells regulate the physical environment of your body, the Gaia hypothesis states that all living things on Earth maintain the climate of Earth. Therefore, life itself may regulate climate change in a way humans cannot predict.

Practice Questions: 1, WR2

PRACTICE QUESTIONS—ENERGY FLOW IN GLOBAL SYSTEMS

1. Prior to the turn of the twentieth century, the greenhouse effect was **most likely**
   - **A.** non-existent
   - **B.** as significant as it is now
   - **C.** less significant than it is now
   - **D.** more significant than it is now

Use the following information to answer the next three questions.

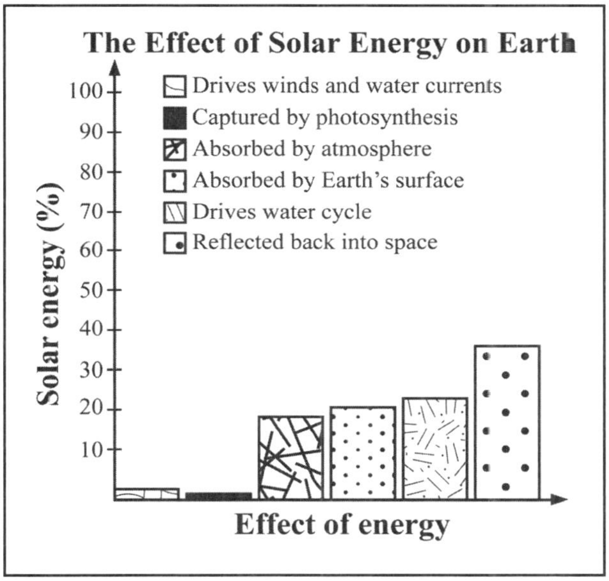

2. What percentage of solar radiation is captured by photosynthetic plants?
   - **A.** Less than 1%
   - **B.** 20%
   - **C.** 22%
   - **D.** 23%

3. Which of the given bars on the graph would have to be increased **most** in order to represent the effect of solar energy on Earth if the entire surface of Earth was covered by snow and ice?
   - **A.** Drives winds and water currents
   - **B.** Captured by photosynthesis
   - **C.** Reflected back into space
   - **D.** Drives water cycle

4. Which of the given bars on the graph does **not** represent a conversion of solar energy to thermal energy?
   - **A.** Drives winds and water currents
   - **B.** Captured by photosynthesis
   - **C.** Reflected back into space
   - **D.** Drives water cycle

Use the following information to answer the next question.

Four Events in the Creation of Convection Currents

1. Air is held aloft by rising warm air.
2. Dense air cools and descends.
3. Warm air expands and cools in areas of lower density.
4. Warm air rises.

Numerical Response

1. When listed in the order in which they occur during the creation of a convection current, the given events are ____, ____, ____, ____.

Use the following diagram to answer the next two questions.

The Biosphere

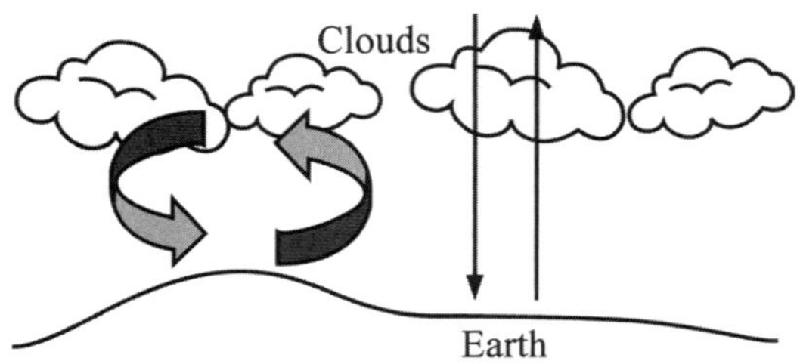

5. In the given diagram, the curving arrows represent
   A. radiation
   B. decomposition
   C. the water cycle
   D. the solar current

6. In the given diagram, the vertical arrows represent
   A. matter
   B. energy
   C. rainfall
   D. radiation

7. All known life on Earth exists in the biosphere. Which of the following characteristics of the biosphere is **not** necessary for life?
   A. assortment of gases
   B. water content
   C. temperature
   D. soil

Use the following information to answer the next question.

Venus has been dubbed Earth's twin because of its similar size and atmosphere. The Pioneer probe *Venera* and Earth-based radar studies have provided humanity with data that suggests the presence of highlands, lowlands, volcanoes, mountain belts, rifts, and ring structures on Venus. Scientists are puzzled by the apparent lack of water-related surface characteristics and water vapour in the atmosphere (less than 0.01%).

8. The **best** inference that can be drawn from the given information is that
   A. Earth and Venus are truly twin planets in that they have identical atmospheres, lithospheres, and hydrospheres
   B. Venus, like Earth, has an appreciable atmosphere, hydrosphere, and lithosphere
   C. Venus has an atmosphere and lithosphere but no hydrosphere
   D. Earth is unique because it has a lithosphere

Use the following information to answer the next question.

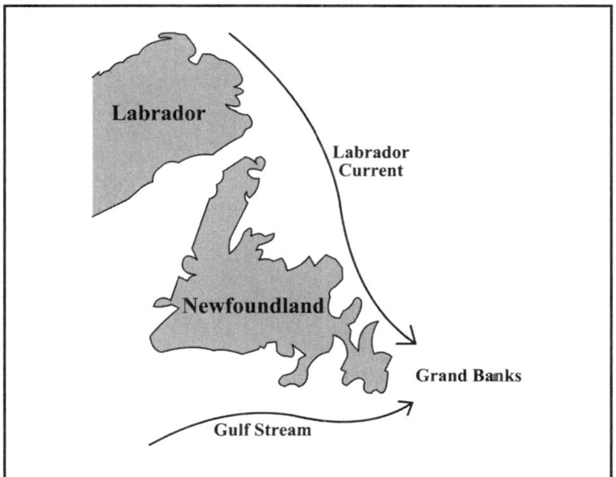

9. Newfoundland is surrounded by water, so there is always ample moisture, both on the ground and in fogs. In the summer, the temperature never gets very high because heat energy is removed from the air by the

A. water's specific heat capacity and its heat of fusion

B. water's specific heat capacity and its heat of vaporization

C. albedo effect and the heat of fusion from Newfoundland's surface

D. albedo effect and the heat of vaporization from Newfoundland's surface

10. The Grand Banks are famous fishing grounds off the coast of Newfoundland. The cold Labrador Current and the warm Gulf Stream converge at the Grand Banks. The meeting of these two currents would **most likely** cause which of the following events to occur?

A. The warm water of the Gulf Stream would rapidly cool, forming icebergs.

B. Very unstable conditions would result in some warm, sunny days and some cool, rainy days.

C. The air of the Labrador Current would be warmed by the Gulf Stream air, resulting in warm temperatures and clear skies.

D. Warm, moist air from the Gulf Stream would slide up over the top of the cold air of the Labrador Current, forming clouds.

Use the following information to answer the next question.

1. Alberta is located from 49° north to 60° north.
2. High-speed winds aloft affect precipitation patterns.
3. Almost all sunlight that hits snow is reflected back into space.
4. Convection currents twist as a result of Earth's rotation.

Numerical Response

2. Match each of the given statements with the term below that it corresponds with.

Answer: ____ Albedo
____ Jet stream
____ Latitude
____ Coriolis

11. Because Vancouver is near the ocean, it is very humid. Winter temperatures in Vancouver are moderate because

A. water molecules move quickly before they increase in temperature

B. water molecules, like all small molecules, are naturally resistant to a drop in temperature

C. the intermolecular bonds between water molecules ensure that as temperatures drops, heat energy is released

D. the intermolecular bonds between water molecules ensure that water will change its state rather than lower its temperature

Use the following information to answer the next question.

A chemistry experiment produces a clear, colourless solution comprised of a mixture of ethanol and hexane. Since ethanol and hexane do not mix at standard temperature and pressure, two distinct layers are formed.
To determine which of the layers is ethanol, a scientist separates them into two beakers and applies 5 000 J of heat to each. (c = 2.46 J/g°C for ethanol, c = 2.26 J/g°C for hexane, and the mass of each liquid is 57 g.)

12. Which of the following statements about this experiment is **true**?

A. Both compounds will reach the same temperature.

B. The hexane will reach a higher temperature than the ethanol.

C. The ethanol will reach a higher temperature than the hexane.

D. The specific heat capacity of ethanol is lower than the specific heat capacity of hexane.

Use the following information to answer the next three questions.

A metal cylinder was immersed in boiling water (100°C) and then quickly transferred to a calorimeter containing cold water.
The given information was recorded.

- Mass of cylinder = 125.00 g
- Mass of water in calorimeter = 152.00 g
- Initial temperature of water in calorimeter = 20.00°C
- Final temperature of water in calorimeter = 32.50°C
- For water, c = 4.19 J/g°C

Numerical Response

3. Correct to the nearest hundredth, how many kilojoules of energy were lost by the metal cylinder?
Answer: ________ kJ

4. To the nearest hundredth, what is the specific heat capacity of the metal of the cylinder in J/g°C ?
Answer: ________ J/g°C

13. What is the **minimum** amount of energy required to heat 1.3 L of water from 20°C to 45°C?

A. 1.3×10^{5} J

B. 1.4×10^{5} J

C. 2.4×10^{5} J

D. 2.6×10^{5} J

Use the following information to answer the next question.

With the aid of a fire, a stranded skier heats 75 g of snow with an initial temperature of –20°C in a cup. The specific heat capacity of snow is 2.01 J/g°C, the specific heat capacity of water is 4.19 J/g°C, the heat of fusion for water is 333 J/g, and the heat of vaporization for water is 2 260 J/g.

Numerical Response

5. If the water in the cup received 43.7 kJ of heat energy, what was the final temperature of the water in the cup, in °C. (Record your answer to **two** significant digits.)
Answer: ______°C

Use the following information to answer the next two questions.

It is believed that the surface of Mars was once covered by 50 m to 200 m of water. Now, however, the Martian hydrologic system is limited primarily to polar ice caps, ground ice, and daily frost cycles. Occasionally, a meteorite impacts the surface and melts the ground ice.

14. Given that the heat of fusion for water is 333 J/g, if 1 kg of ice is melted from the impact of a meteorite, how much heat energy is generated?

A. 133 J

B. 333 J

C. 3.33×10^5 J

D. 3.33×10^5 kJ

Use this additional information to answer the next question.

Water released from melted ground ice is believed to have been responsible for shaping much of the Martian surface by undercutting cliffs and creating outflow channels.

15. How much heat energy is required to heat 1 000 g of melted ice from 0°C to 87.4°C?

A. 87.4 J

B. 8.74×10^4 J

C. 3.66×10^5 J

D. 3.66×10^7 J

Use the following information to answer the next question.

The average human body temperature is 37°C. When a person dies, the body remains "warm" for a long period of time. In forensic investigations, the temperature of a corpse can help investigators approximate the time of death.

16. Soon after death, the temperature of a corpse remains higher than the ambient temperature because

A. air has a lower specific heat capacity than water; therefore, heat will be transferred from the air to the body

B. heat flowing into the body keeps the body temperature higher than the ambient temperature

C. the high specific heat capacity of water in the body helps to maintain a constant body temperature

D. metabolic activities continue even after death

Use the following information to answer the next two questions.

London, England is located at latitude 52°N, and its elevation is sea level. London is situated in close proximity to water.

Magnitogorsk, Russia is located at latitude 53°N, and its elevation is 1 000 m. Magnitogorsk is situated far from water.

17. The **best** inference that can be made about London and Magnitogorsk is that they

A. have similar climates

B. have similar temperatures throughout the year

C. receive about the same amount of rainfall throughout the year

D. receive sunlight at about the same angle throughout the year

18. Relative to the temperature of London, the temperature of Magnitogorsk is **most likely** to

A. be always cooler

B. have more stability

C. have greater variation

D. be warmer on average

19. If sunlight was cut off from a biome, life would

A. go on as usual, thereby demonstrating that energy is recycled

B. eventually stop, thereby demonstrating that energy is not recycled

C. go on as usual, thereby demonstrating that matter, such as carbon, is recycled

D. eventually stop, thereby demonstrating that matter, such as carbon, is not recycled

Use the following information to answer the next question.

In the given diagram, the system is defined as all the material inside the flask and the balloon. The hotplate underneath the flask is turned on.

20. The given information describes which of the following types of system?

A. Open system

B. Static system

C. Closed system

D. Isolated system

Use the following information to answer the next question.

A typical thundercloud contains over six trillion water droplets that eventually fall to Earth as precipitation. As rain and ground water evaporate, more thunderclouds form.

21. What type of energy drives this cycling of water?

A. Geothermal

B. Mechanical

C. Chemical

D. Solar

Use the following information to answer the next question.

A group of students tried to identify why Earth's surface is heated unevenly. They speculated that the following factors contributed to the climatic variations between tropical and arctic regions.

I. Latitude

II. Longitude

III. Tilt of Earth's axis

IV. Amount of solar radiation received

22. Which of the given factors is the **least responsible** for the given climatic differences?

A. I

B. II

C. III

D. IV

Use the following information to answer the next question.

The lowest temperature ever recorded on Earth was –89.2°C. It was recorded in Antarctica, near the South Pole. The highest temperature ever recorded on Earth was 57.8°C. It was recorded in North Africa, near the equator.

23. These regional temperature differences indicate that

A. solar energy does not reach the South Pole

B. convection currents draw the warm air toward the equator

C. more solar energy is absorbed at the equator than at the South Pole

D. surface characteristics at the South Pole aid in the absorption of solar radiation, thereby lowering the air temperature

Use the following information to answer the next four questions.

According to scientists, surface ice melt on the ice sheet covering Greenland was the highest in recorded history in 2003, and the amount of Arctic Sea ice also reached a record low. While some of the accelerated melting appears to be linked to natural atmospheric fluctuations, human influence could not be ruled out.

Measurements of the Greenland ice sheet taken from passive microwave satellite sensors show 685 000 km^2 of melt, an area that is more than double that of 1992. Such melting encourages further ice loss. The excess water weight pushes down on the glacier at the same time that water seeps through cracks to the underside. This combination accelerates the glacier's flow to the sea.

It has been calculated that warming has produced a roughly 20% loss in Arctic Sea ice since 1978. Likely not all warming is a result of natural factors.

Polar sea ice has an important function in moderating the global energy balance. Sea ice has an albedo of 0.8; that is, it reflects 80% of the solar radiation it receives. Sea water has an albedo of 0.2.

24. Which of the following statements about the given information is **true**?

A. The melting of Greenland ice will result in cooler climate.

B. The rate of the melting of Greenland ice has been increasing.

C. The ice sheet on Greenland has been melting for a long time.

D. The sea ice around Greenland has been melting, but the land ice has not.

25. Which of the following statements about the absorption of solar radiation and albedo is **true**?

A. Sea ice, which absorbs 20% of solar radiation, has a lower albedo than water.

B. Sea ice, which absorbs 80% of solar radiation, has a lower albedo than water.

C. Sea water, which absorbs 80% of solar radiation, has a lower albedo than ice.

D. Sea water, which absorbs 20% of solar radiation, has a lower albedo than ice.

26. According to the information, not only is the Greenland ice sheet melting, it is also

A. becoming warmer

B. acquiring a lower albedo

C. absorbing more solar radiation

D. sliding into the sea at a faster rate

27. According to the information, natural factors do not account for all the warming on Greenland. Human factors that may be linked to warming on Greenland would **most likely** include

A. a change in ocean currents

B. a change in Greenland's latitude

C. an increase in atmospheric carbon gases

D. an increase in the population of in Greenland

28. Maintaining a steady state in a living organism is called homeostasis. When this idea is applied to the biosphere, this concept is called the

A. heat budget

B. Gaia hypothesis

C. first law of thermodynamics

D. second law of thermodynamics

29. All of the following terms relate to an explanation of the greenhouse effect **except**

A. atmospheric temperature

B. ozone in the stratosphere

C. increased combustion

D. carbon compounds

30. Why is a cell often described as an open system?

A. The cell membrane contains pores.

B. Matter can enter a cell, but energy cannot.

C. Any molecule can pass in and out of a cell.

D. Molecules that contain chemical energy can enter a cell.

31. A farmer cuts trees and shrubs around a small pond with a white sand bottom. Topsoil then flows into the pond, which darkens the bottom and changes the pond bottom's

A. albedo

B. biosphere

C. Coriolis effect

D. hydrologic cycle

Written Response

Use the following information to answer the next question.

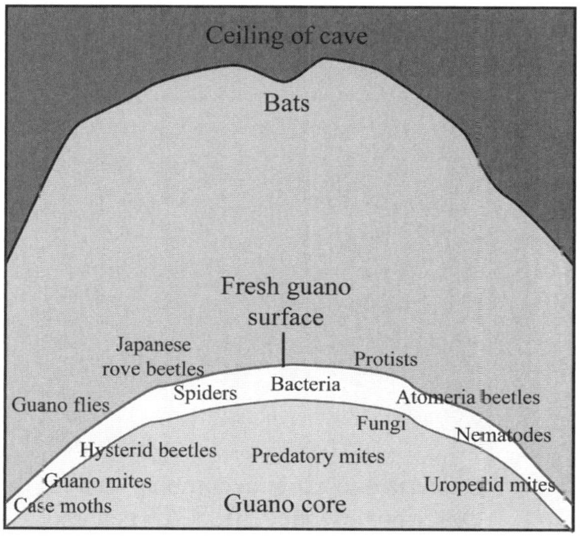

The given diagram outlines the communities that live in a cave in Australia. There is no light in the cave. The largest animals in the cave are insect-eating bats. The bats leave the cave to hunt each night, but they return to the cave to roost during the day. The bats have produced a large pile of guano. Guano is composed of the urine and feces (droppings) of the bats

Organism	Observations
Bent-winged bats	During the winter, they roost during the day. At night, they leave the cave to feed on the moths in the nearby forest. During the summer, they rarely enter the cave.
Fungi	Found on the freshest part of the guano pile. They decompose the guano and absorb the nutrients.
Bacteria	Similar to fungi
Protists	Feed on bacteria
Nematodes	Feed on protists and bacteria
Predatory mites	Feed on guano mites and uropedid mites
Guano mites	Feed on fungi
Uropedid mites	Feed on guano flies
Case moths	Larvae feed on fungi
Spiders	Feed on guano flies, case moths, and hysterid beetles
Hysterid beetles	Feed on fungi
Japanese rove beetles	Feed on guano fly pupae
Atomeria beetles	Feed on guano fly larvae
Guano flies	Feed on guano

1. **a)** Could this cave community be considered a biome? Explain why or why not.

b) Is this cave community a closed system, an open system, or an isolated system? Explain your answer.

c) The activities of all of the organisms in the cave create a lot of water vapour. As a result, the air of the cave is always saturated with water even though the climate of the region outside the cave is very dry. How would the high humidity affect the temperature of the cave air compared with the air outside the cave? Explain by describing the characteristics of water molecules and their effect on temperature.

d) Most communities are based on energy gained through photosynthesis. This cave community has no plants. Would it be correct to conclude that this community is **not** dependent on photosynthesis? Explain why or why not.

e) Bacteria and fungi decompose guano. Describe how they affect oxygen and carbon dioxide concentrations in the air of the cave.

Use the following information to answer the next question.

The burning of fossil fuels (coal, oil, and natural gas) contributes to the buildup of greenhouse gases. The greatest release of harmful gases occurs during the combustion of waste gases (flaring). The Kyoto Climate Convention, held in Japan in 1997, focused on reducing the global production of greenhouse gases. Because of Canada's reliance on the oil and gas industries, many Canadian companies are at the forefront of the development of alternative energy sources.

Between 1955 and early 1970, the edge of the ice meeting the sea at Antarctica receded roughly 28° in latitude (a 25% reduction). Information about the sea ice at Antarctica is collected as part of the records of whale capture because whales are most often captured at the ice edge. Environmental scientists predict that continued global warming will cause further melting of Antarctic ice.

Every spring in the Gulf of Mexico, oxygen concentrations near the ocean floor decrease to dangerously low levels. Fish and bottom-dwelling organisms, such as shrimp, snails, crab, and starfish, are either killed or driven away from the oxygen-poor waters, which are called hypoxic zones. The major cause of the low levels of oxygen is the polluted water dumped into the Gulf from the Mississippi River. This polluted water has caused an increase in the nitrogen and phosphorous levels, and ultimately, an increase in the population of oxygen-consuming bacteria living on the Gulf floor.

2. Consider the following statement: Water is essential to life on Earth. In a unified and organized essay, describe:

- three of the chemical properties of water, and explain why these properties are significant in terms of the survival of organism
- the hydrologic cycle, and indicate how and at which points the cycle can be affected by human influence. Use one or more of the given examples or examples of your own.

3. Responding from two different perspectives, such as environmental, economic, or social, analyze the risks of the province of Alberta signing the Kyoto Agreement.

ANSWERS AND SOLUTIONS—PRACTICE QUESTIONS

1. C	8. C	13. B	20. C	28. B
2. A	9. B	NR5. 50	21. D	29. B
3. C	10. D	14. C	22. B	30. D
4. C	NR2. 3 2 1 4	15. C	23. A	31. A
NR1. 4 3 1 2	11. C	16. C	24. C	WR1. See Solution
5. C	12. B	17. D	25. C	WR2. See Solution
6. B	NR3. 7.96	18. C	26. C	WR3. See Solution
7. D	NR4. 0.94	19. C	27. C	

1. C

Humans tend to think of the greenhouse effect as negative, but it is not all bad. Some greenhouse effect must exist. If it did not, Earth would be too cold for life of any kind. There has always been some greenhouse effect. The concern among many scientists now is the *rate* at which the greenhouse effect is increasing, probably because of pollution from burning fossil fuels. In previous centuries, fewer fossil fuels were burned than are being burned now, so the greenhouse effect probably had less of an impact than it currently does.

2. A

Sunlight is used to make glucose in the process of photosynthesis. Glucose is organic matter that contains stored energy, and the stored energy of glucose and other food was once sunlight. The fact that less than 1% of the sun's energy that reaches Earth is captured by plants demonstrates just how much solar energy is produced.

3. C

If the entire surface of Earth was covered by snow and ice, it would have a much higher albedo. The albedo is the tendency of a surface to reflect light. Therefore, more light would be reflected back into space. From space, Earth would look much brighter than it now does.

4. C

During photosynthesis, light energy is converted to chemical energy; however, some energy is converted to heat because no energy transfer is 100% efficient. The water cycle involves light energy heating Earth's surface and causing water to evaporate. Wind and water currents require more light to be converted to heat in some areas than in others. However, if light is reflected back to space, there is no conversion to heat.

NR 1 4 3 1 2

When the sun heats Earth, the air over Earth is warmed. It becomes less dense and rises. When this air is high above Earth, where the air is less dense, it expands. As the air expands, it cools because the air molecules are more spread out. For a time, this air is held aloft by rising air pushing on it from below. However, eventually this cooler, denser air falls back to Earth.

5. C

Water evaporates and rises up from Earth. At some point, the water will condense to form clouds and fall back to Earth, as rain. The curving arrows in the diagram represent the water cycle.

6. B

Energy can come to Earth as light and leave as heat. There is no cycling of energy. Once it leaves as heat, it does not return.

7. D

For life to exist on Earth, there must be an assortment of gases, a suitable temperature, and water. Soil is not necessary for life. For most of Earth's history, life existed only in water, which today covers over 70% of Earth's surface.

8. C

From the given information, the reader is told that Venus has surface features that suggest it has a lithosphere. The reader is also told that there is a lack of water-related surface characteristics and water vapour in the atmosphere, which indicates that Venus lacks a hydrosphere.

9. B

The high specific heat capacity of water means that a lot of heat energy is required to increase the temperature of air laden with moisture. The heat of vaporization is the amount of heat energy required to change liquid water to water vapour. Adding this energy changes the state of water without increasing the temperature. The heat of fusion is the energy required to melt snow or ice It also keeps temperatures low, but not in the summer. A high albedo would keep temperatures from getting too high, but during the summer, the albedo of Newfoundland would not be high. A covering of snow and ice would have a high albedo, but Newfoundland would not have that during the summer.

10. D

Warm air is less dense than cool air. Therefore, the cool air slides under the warm air when warm and cool air meet,. The warm air is then pushed up. As the warm air rises, it cools, and the moisture it holds condenses, forming clouds.

NR 2 3 2 1 4

Albedo refers to how much sunlight is reflected off a surface. Snow has a high albedo, so when the land is covered by snow, sunlight has little effect on temperature as most light is simply reflected back into space (3). The jet stream is a high-speed, high-altitude wind where warm, southern air and cold, northern air meet (2). Latitude is the distance from the equator a place is. Latitude affects the angle of sunlight that hits Earth. The higher the latitude, the lower the angle of sunlight. Thus, the cooler the temperatures (1). The point at which a convection current of warm, southern air and a convection current of cold, northern air meet, a twisting or bending effect occurs. As a result, winds do not flow north-south or south-north. They bend and come from the east or west. This effect is the known as the Coriolis effect (4).

11. C

The intermolecular bonds between water molecules are called hydrogen bonds. When water molecules absorb energy, they move faster, but any increase in the movement of molecules is resisted by the hydrogen bonds. Therefore, it takes a lot of heat energy to increase the temperature of water. The same is true for when the water temperature drops. Because the movement of molecules is resisted by the hydrogen bonds, a lot of heat energy must be lost to decrease the temperature of the water. With so much water in the air in Vancouver, the air temperature does not drop quickly.

12. B

The compound with the lower heat capacity will require less energy to increase its temperature, (i.e., for 1 g of each compound to increase 1°C, different amounts of heat are required). Ethanol requires 2.46 J, but hexane requires only 2.26 J. Therefore, hexane will reach a higher temperature than ethanol if 5 000 J of heat are applied to each.

NR 3 7.96

The energy lost by the cylinder was gained by the water, resulting in the change in temperature of the water. This concept underlies the function of a calorimeter.

$Q = mc\Delta T$
$Q = (152.00\ g)(4.19\ J/g°C)(32.50°C - 20.00°C)$
$Q = 7.96\ kJ$

NR 4 0.94

Given that $Q = mc\Delta T$, solve for c.

$$c = \frac{Q}{m\Delta T}$$
$$c = \frac{7\ 960\ J}{125.00\ g \times (100°C - 32.50°C)}$$
$$c = 0.94\ J/g°C$$

Therefore, the specific heat capacity of the metal cylinder is $0.94\ J/g°C$.

13. B

First, determine the mass of 1.3 L of water. Since 1 mL of water has a mass of 1 g, 1.3 L (1 300 mL) of water has a mass of 1.3 kg (1 300 g).

Next, use the formula $Q = mc\Delta T$.

$Q = (1\ 300\ g)(4.19\ J/g°C)(45°C - 20°C)$
$= 1.4 \times 10^5\ J$

NR 5 50

The snow undergoes a phase change once it is heated from its initial temperature to the melting/freezing temperature of 0°C. At this point, as more heat is added, the snow at 0°C will become water at 0°C. Once all the snow has been melted into water, the remaining heat will raise the water temperature.

Initially, energy applied to the cup will be used to heat the snow to the melting/freezing temperature of (0°C).

$Q = mc\Delta T$
$Q = (75\ g)(2.01\ J/g°C)(0°C - (-20°C))$
$Q = (75\ g)(2.01\ J/g°C)(20°C)$
$Q = 3\ 015\ J$

After the snow has reached the melting temperature (0°C), the heat energy will be used to melt the snow.

$Q = m\Delta H_{fus}$
$Q = (75\ g)(333\ J/g)$
$Q = 24\ 975\ J$

The remaining heat energy will be used to heat the water to its final temperature. The remaining heat energy can be calculated by subtracting the energy already used from the total energy applied.

Remaining heat energy
$= 43\ 700\ J - (3\ 015\ J + 24\ 975\ J)$
$= 15\ 710\ J$

Therefore, the final temperature of the water can be calculated.

$$Q = mc(T_{final} - T_{initial})$$
$$15\ 710\ J = (75\ g)(4.19\ J/g°C)(T_{final} - 0°C)$$
$$T_{final} = \frac{15\ 710\ J}{(75\ g)(4.19\ J/g°C)}$$
$$T_{final} = 50°C$$

14. C

Since ice undergoes a phase change to water, use the formula $Q = m\Delta H_{fusion}$, where ΔH_{fusion} is the heat of fusion of water, which is 333 J/g, to calculate the amount of heat energy generated.

$Q = (1\ 000\ g)(333\ J/g)$
$Q = 333\ 000\ J$
$Q = 3.33 \times 10^5\ J$

15. C

To calculate the heat energy required to heat the melted ice, use the formula $Q = mc\Delta T$.

$Q = (1\ 000\ g)(4.19\ J/g°C)(87.4°C - 0°C)$
$Q = 366\ 206\ J$
$Q = 3.66 \times 10^5\ kJ$

16. C

While it is true that air has a lower specific heat capacity than water, the transfer of heat energy always travels from matter at higher temperatures to matter at lower temperatures (second law of thermodynamics). Since the question states that the ambient temperature is lower than the initial temperature of the corpse, heat cannot flow into the body.

Metabolic activity is the chemical activity of a living cell.

The high specific heat capacity of water (4.19 J/g°C) means that 4.19 J of heat energy are required to increase the temperature of 1 g of water by 1°C. The reverse is also true. Before the temperature of 1 g of water drops by 1°C, 4.19 J of heat must be lost. Therefore, given that the human body is composed mainly of water, a large amount of heat must leave the body before the temperature drops significantly. As a result, a corpse can maintain a temperature higher than that of its surroundings for quite some time.

17. D

Because their latitudes are about the same, the angle at which both cities receive sunlight will be the same throughout the year. However, as a result of the differences in elevation and distance from water, they will have different climates with differing temperatures and rainfall.

18. C

Water has a moderating effect on temperature. The high specific heat capacity of water means that it takes a lot of heat energy to increase the temperature of water; the opposite is also true. Water must lose a lot of heat energy for its temperature to drop. If air contains a lot of moisture, like it does in London, temperature variation will be minimal. In contrast, the air of Magnitogorsk, being very dry, is able to have great temperature fluctuations.

19. C

Life would stop in the biome because life relies on energy from the sun. Through photosynthesis, plants take in energy, which is then passed to animals when they eat plants. This energy, stored as chemical energy, is not recycled. Eventually, the energy captured during photosynthesis is converted to heat during metabolic activities and is released. This heat passes out of the atmosphere and into space, never to be used by life on Earth again.

20. C

The given system is a closed system because no matter is leaving or entering the system. It is not an isolated system because heat is flowing through the system boundary from the hotplate to the material inside the flask.

21. D

The water cycle is driven by the energy of the sun (solar radiation). This energy heats the ground water, which evaporates and rises into the atmosphere. Eventually, it condenses into clouds as cooler air temperatures are encountered. This water eventually returns to Earth as precipitation. Chemical energy is the energy stored in carbohydrates and other molecules; it can be released when the molecule is involved in an exothermic, chemical reaction.

Geothermal energy is energy derived from the heated core of Earth. It can be observed in several forms, including volcanoes, geysers, and earthquakes. Mechanical energy is responsible for the physical movement of bodies of mass.

22. B

Variations in longitude cannot explain the uneven heating of Earth because noticeable changes in heating occur as one moves from north to south, not east to west. Lines of longitude extend north to south, dividing Earth into wedges.

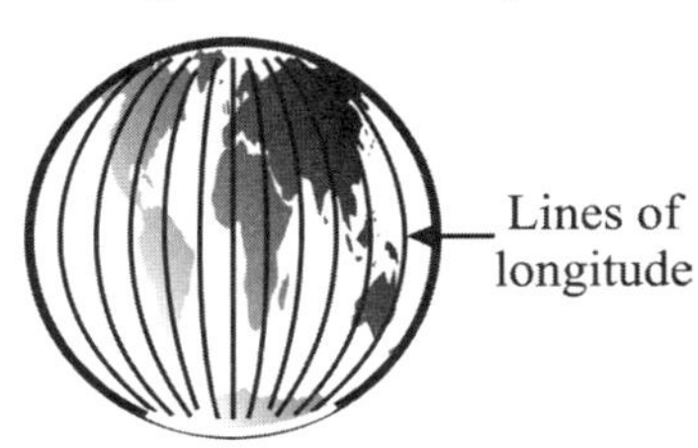

Lines of latitude run from east to west.

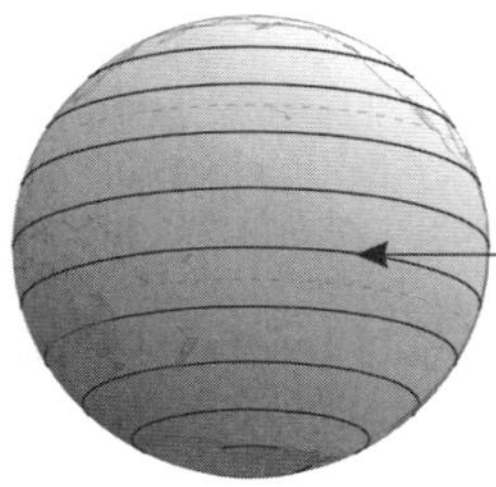

Latitude determines the amount and intensity of solar energy received at different points on Earth. The tilt of Earth's axis also causes uneven heating as the sun's rays strike different areas of Earth at different angles. At an area such as the equator, the sun's rays strike Earth more directly. Moving toward the poles, the sun's rays strike less directly. The more direct the sun's rays, the greater the amount of solar energy absorbed, and the lower the amount of radiation deflected back into the atmosphere.

23. A

At the equator, the sun's rays strike Earth more directly. As one moves toward the poles, the sun's rays strike Earth's surface less directly (as shown in the given diagram). More solar radiation is absorbed by Earth's surface through the direct impact of the sun's rays. Convection currents generally carry warm air away from the equator. The surface characteristics of the South Pole, such as polar ice caps, reflect radiation instead of absorbing it.

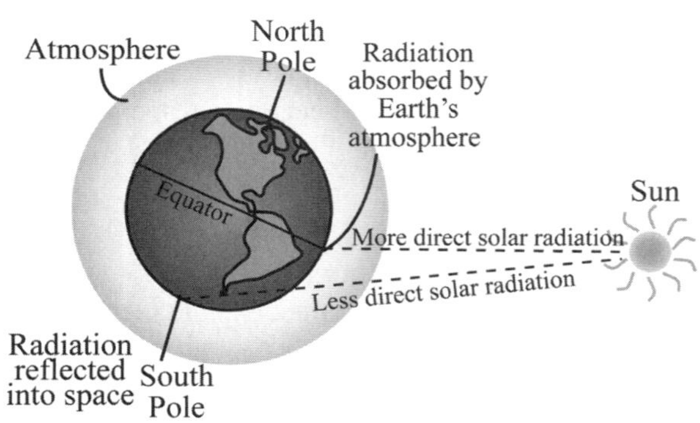

24. C

It is possible that the Greenland ice has been melting for a long time, and it may be that the melting ice is cooling the climate, but that is not stated. According to the information, both land ice and sea ice are melting. It is true that the article indicates that the rate of melting of the Greenland ice has been increasing.

25. C

If sea ice has an albedo of 0.8, it reflects 80% of the solar radiation it absorbs. Water has an albedo of 0.2; this indicates that water reflects 20% of the solar radiation it absorbs. If water reflects 20%, it must absorb and hold on to 80%. Since albedo is the ability to reflect solar radiation, water has a lower albedo than ice.

26. C

The information states that melt water slips down through cracks in the ice and causes the ice sheet to slide into the sea faster. The reader does not know if the ice is becoming warmer, changing its albedo, or absorbing more solar radiation.

27. C

Humans have caused an increase in atmospheric carbon gases through the burning of fossil fuels. Cars, furnaces, and industries all burn fossil fuels that send many tonnes of carbon dioxide into the atmosphere, causing Earth's temperatures to rise.

28. B

The Gaia hypothesis conceives of Earth as being like an organism in that it monitors and regulates its internal environment. The Gaia hypothesis also states that Earth can adapt to changes.

29. B

Ozone is a form of oxygen that exists high in the atmosphere. It is significant to life in that it blocks much of the ultraviolet (UV) radiation coming from the sun. UV radiation damages DNA, so it is a potential cause of cancer in humans and other organisms. The greenhouse effect affects global temperatures. As far as scientists know, the ozone layer does not have an effect on global temperatures.

30. D

An open system is one that can exchange both matter and energy with its environment. When a molecule enters a cell, the cell is taking in matter. The molecule contains chemical energy, so the cell is also taking in energy from its environment.

31. A

Albedo is the ability of a surface to reflect sunlight. A light-coloured surface reflects a lot of sunlight; it has a high albedo. A darker surface absorbs more sunlight; it has a lower albedo.

1. **a)** *Could this cave community be considered a biome? Explain why or why not?*

No, this cave community is not a biome. It shares certain characteristics with a biome, but a biome is a large geographical area dominated by a certain climate type and living organisms. Any biome contains various unique ecosystems. For example, the biome known as taiga (boreal or northern forest) may contain a lake ecosystem. a marsh ecosystem, or a section of grassland. Nonetheless, it is known as taiga because evergreen trees, a climate that provides cool temperatures, and adequate moisture characterize the area. The cave in Australia is part of the surrounding biome.

b) *Is this cave community a closed system, an open system, or an isolated system? Explain your answer.*

It is an open system. An open system exchanges matter and energy with its surroundings. Bats, air, and probably a lot of other materials move in and out of the cave. Bats move chemical energy into and out of the cave, and the bat droppings in guano provide other organisms energy. Eventually, the energy seeps out of the cave as heat.

c) *The activities of all the organisms in the cave create a lot of water vapour. As a result, the air of the cave is always saturated with water even though the climate of the region outside the cave is very dry. How would the high humidity affect the temperature of the cave air compared with the air outside the cave? Explain by describing the characteristics of water molecules and their effect on temperature.*

Temperatures inside the cave will fluctuate less than those outside the cave. Water molecules are attracted to each other by hydrogen bonds. When molecules gain energy, they speed up, and this increase in speed is noted as an increase in temperature. However, the hydrogen bonds make it difficult for water molecules to move faster. Therefore, water in the air of the cave will prevent the air from increasing or dropping in temperature. The more water there is in the air, the more stable the temperature will be.

d) *Most communities are based on energy gained through photosynthesis. This cave community has no plants. Would it be correct to conclude that this community is* ***not*** *dependent on photosynthesis? Explain why or why not*

Even though there are no plants, the cave is dependant on photosynthesis. Through photosynthesis, plants outside the cave capture the sun's energy. Insects feed on the plants and gain chemical energy. When the bats eat the insects, they acquire this energy. The bats enter the cave, and their droppings, which contain the energy from photosynthesis, are deposited on the cave floor for the other organisms to share.

e) *Bacteria and fungi decompose guano. Describe how they affect the oxygen and carbon dioxide concentrations in the air of the cave.*

When bacteria and fungi decompose guano, they use the food energy in the guano to generate ATP through a process called cellular respiration. Along with the food, oxygen is consumed. The waste products of cellular respiration are water and carbon dioxide. Therefore, the oxygen level of the cave drops and the carbon dioxide level rises in this process.

2. *Consider the following statement: Water is essential to life on Earth. In a unified and organized essay, describe:*

- *three chemical properties of water, and explain why these properties are significant in terms of the survival of organisms*
- *the hydrologic cycle, and indicate how and at which points the cycle can be affected by human influence. Use one or more of the given example, or examples of your own.*

Your unified, organized essay should contain three or more of the following points.

- Water has a high surface tension because of the relatively large force of cohesion (force of attraction) between water molecules. The surface tension of water is present because the molecules on the surface of the water are pulled toward the inner body of the water. As a result, some insects and aquatic plants (e.g., the water strider and the water lily) can maintain life on its surface.
- Many nutrients and minerals dissolve in water. Because of this, plants and animals obtain essential substances that allow them to carry on metabolic activities.
- Oceans moderate the world's climate. The ocean acts like a heat sink and retains heat much longer than land. Without the ocean, Earth would not be livable as the days would be extremely hot, and the nights would be freezing cold. Heat from the equator is also transferred to the poles while colder water is returned from the poles to be heated.
- Water has a high heat of vaporization, which is important for processes such as perspiration in animals. The purpose of perspiration is to get rid of excess body heat. A large amount of heat energy is required to vaporize water. The temperature of the environment is also affected. Expending large amounts of energy to evaporate water results in a narrower range in temperature, i.e., more heat energy is used for the phase change than to heat the air. For this reason, deserts (where there is very little water present) experience large variations in temperature.
- The density of ice is less than the density of liquid water. Water has a maximum density at 4°C, so water at 4°C will always be located at the lowest point in a body of water. Ice will always float, causing a lake to freeze from the surface down. Ice also insulates the water below, so complete freezing of lake water is rare. This property of water is significant for the winter survival of aquatic organisms living at the lake bottom when the lakes freeze over. If lakes were to freeze from the bottom up, thermal energy transferred continuously to the air may cause the lake to freeze completely, causing aquatic organisms to perish.

A description of the hydrologic cycle should include some of the following information.

- The hydrologic cycle is the cycle of water evaporation and condensation on Earth. It is driven by the energy of the sun. Ground water absorbs solar and heat energies, causing it to evaporate. Water vapour rises into the atmosphere and cools as it rises (mainly as a result of the decrease in pressure at higher altitudes). As the water vapour cools, it condenses, forms clouds, and eventually falls back to Earth as precipitation in the form of rain, snow, or hail. Organisms also comprise a portion of the hydrologic cycle because they take in and expel both atmospheric and ground water.

- The hydrologic cycle can be affected by human influence at virtually every point in the cycle. Waste gases from industries can react with moisture in the air. This produces acid rain, which destroys plants and waterways, thereby affecting all organisms. The relative amounts of water in different states may be affected by global warming as a result of the release of greenhouse gases into the atmosphere. For example, global warming may cause melting of polar ice, which has already occurred in Antarctica.

3. *Responding from two different perspectives, such as environmental, economic, or social, analyze the risks of the province of Alberta signing the Kyoto Agreement.*

Your response could contain some of the following arguments.

- Every perspective should include the risks and benefits that characterize that particular aspect of the issue.
- Economically, making changes to comply with the Kyoto Agreement will cost money and may cause job losses, but the potential benefits include the development of new technologies designed to reduce greenhouse gases. This may increase commercial profits in the long term.
- Environmentally, the risks of complying with the Kyoto Agreement include the possibility that the reduction of greenhouse gases may not be effective because the measures are implemented too slowly to have a significant impact. On the other hand, the benefits of reducing greenhouse gases include the reduction of global warming and the protection of ecosystems worldwide.
- Societal impacts, such as negative opinions, may cause a destructive backlash. People may feel threatened because of the economic impacts already mentioned. However, the benefits include a better standard of living and healthier natural living conditions.

UNIT TEST—ENERGY FLOW IN GLOBAL SYSTEMS

1. Which of the following parts of the biosphere experiences the **most direct** effects of solar radiation?

A. Cryosphere

B. Lithosphere

C. Atmosphere

D. Hydrosphere

2. A result of the tilt in Earth's axis is that

A. it is summer in Canada when it is winter in Australia

B. it is daytime in Canada when it is nighttime in Australia

C. in July, the sun's rays are most directed at Canada and Australia

D. in January, the sun's rays are most directed at Canada and Australia

3. Unrestricted logging may contribute to a greater greenhouse effect because it will result in

A. increased levels of oxygen in the atmosphere

B. decreased levels of oxygen in the atmosphere

C. decreased levels of carbon dioxide in the atmosphere

D. increased levels of carbon dioxide in the atmosphere

4. Which of the following values could represent a specific heat capacity?

A. 75°C

B. 500 g/L

C. 1.85 J · g

D. 2.25 J/g °C

Use the following information to answer the next three questions.

The Grand Banks are famous fishing grounds off the coast of Newfoundland. The cold Labrador Current and the warm Gulf Stream converge at the Grand Banks.

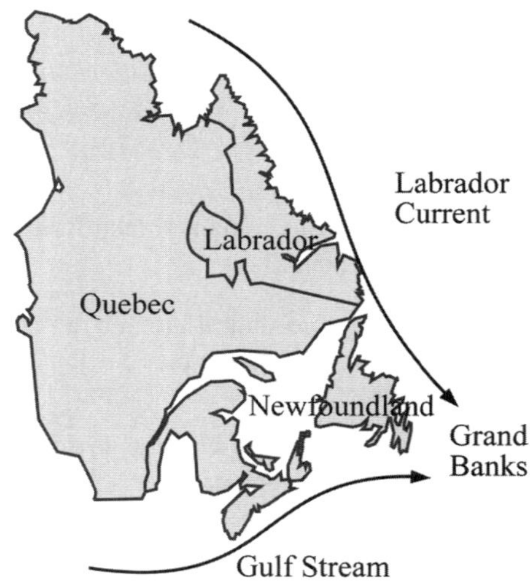

5. As a result of the convergence of these currents, which of the following weather conditions would be common on the Grand Banks?

A. Warm temperatures

B. Sunny skies

C. Heavy fogs

D. Hurricanes

6. The island of Newfoundland could be thought of as an open system because

A. it is surrounded by an ocean

B. it exchanges matter and energy with its surroundings

C. ocean currents bring energy to and remove energy from the island

D. moisture leaves the island through evaporation and returns through precipitation

7. The air above Newfoundland contains abundant clouds. The air in the clouds is warmer than air where there are no clouds. This is because when clouds form, heat energy is released as

   A. the heat of fusion

   B. a convection current

   C. a specific heat capacity

   D. the heat of vaporization

8. Because Vancouver is beside the ocean, it experiences high humidity. Summer temperatures in Vancouver are moderate as a result of the fact that water has a high

   A. albedo

   B. boiling point

   C. heat of fusion

   D. specific heat capacity

9. Winds move air from the Pacific Ocean, up the western side of the coastal mountains, and then down the eastern side of the mountains. Which of the following rows correctly describes the changes that occur to the water in the air as it moves over the mountains?

Row	Up the western side	Down the eastern side
A.	Condensation	Condensation
B.	Condensation	Evaporation
C.	Evaporation	Condensation
D.	Evaporation	Evaporation

Use the following information to answer the next question.

1. Fast-moving air
2. High altitude
3. Travels from west to east
4. Travels from east to west
5. Causes cloud formation
6. Forms where warm and cold air meet
7. Is greater in summer than in winter
8. Affects airplanes

Numerical Response

1. Listed in numerical order, the given descriptions that define a jet stream are ____, ____, ____, and ____.

10. The **highest** albedo would be found at which of the following places?

    A. Forest

    B. Ocean

    C. Desert

    D. Ice sheet

Use the following information to answer the next two questions.

Processes that Occur in a Grassland Biome

1. A ground squirrel breathes.
2. A prairie fire burns the grass.
3. Dead grass is decomposed by bacteria.
4. Water evaporates from the leaves of plants.
5. Algae in a slough undergo photosynthesis.
6. Life processes occur in green plants.

Numerical Response

2. Listed in numerical order, the given processes that add carbon dioxide to the atmosphere are ____, ____, ____, and ____.

3. Listed in numerical order, the given processes that recycle matter by returning nutrients to the soil are ____ and ____.

Use the following information to answer the next four questions.

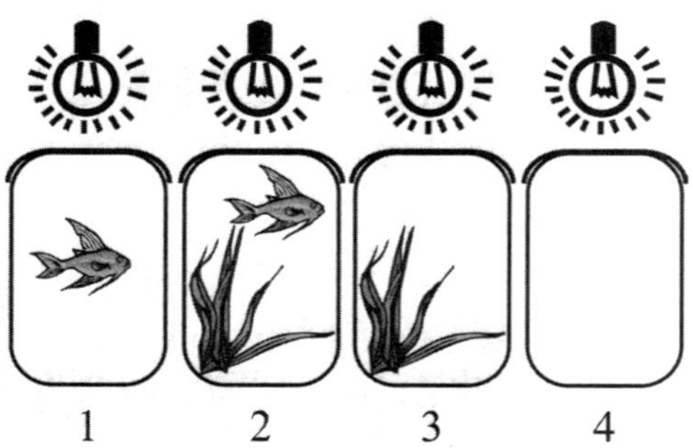

An experiment was set up as shown in the diagram. There was an indicator in the water of each sealed glass container that would colour the water if high levels of CO_2 were present. The four containers were left in the light for three days. By the end of the experiment, only the water in container 1 was coloured.

11. Which of the following statements does **not** explain a way in which container 2 is like a biome?

A. It contains energy, matter, and organisms.

B. Matter is cycled between the living organisms within it.

C. Energy is exchanged with its surroundings, but matter is not.

D. The solar energy that enters the system is equal to all the forms of energy that leave the system.

12. Each of the containers is representative of what type of system?

A. Open

B. Closed

C. Isolated

D. Steady state

13. The water in container 2 did **not** become coloured because

A. CO_2 is produced by burning and pollution only

B. the CO_2 produced was equal to the CO_2 consumed

C. in the presence of light, plants do not produce CO_2

D. the plants absorbed the indicator from the environment

14. Container 4 was included in the experiment in order to
    A. provide a control for comparison
    B. show what colour the water should be
    C. provide a greater number of containers
    D. show that CO_2 can be produced without organisms

Use the following information to answer the next three questions.

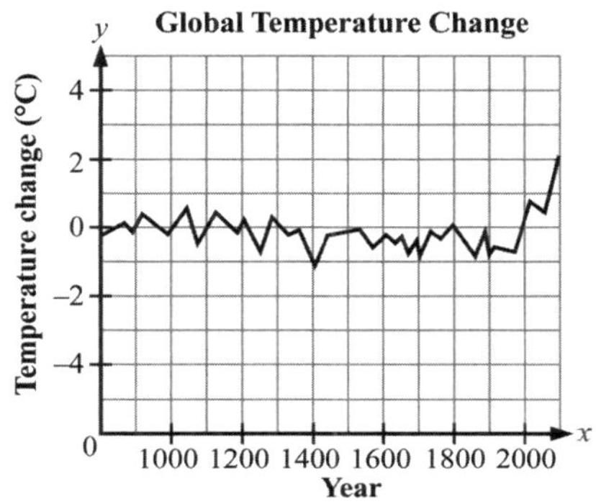

15. The graph indicates that prior to the year 1900, global temperatures
    A. rose sharply
    B. were constant
    C. varied by about 2°C
    D. varied by large amounts

16. Which of the following conditions does **not** provide a reasonable explanation for the temperature changes that occurred prior to 1900?
    A. Pollution from factories
    B. Changing ocean currents
    C. Changes in global CO_2 amounts
    D. Changes in global wind patterns

17. The **best** conclusion that can be drawn from the graph is that
    A. temperatures are currently the highest on record
    B. there has been a steady increase in temperature over the past 1 000 years
    C. temperature changes over the past 100 years have been as a result of human factors
    D. temperature changes have not been significant enough to affect biomes until recently

ANSWERS AND SOLUTIONS—UNIT TEST

1. B	**5. C**	**9. B**	**NR3. 2 3**	**14. A**
2. A	**6. B**	**NR1. 1 2 3 6**	**11. C**	**15. C**
3. D	**7. D**	**10. D**	**12. B**	**16. A**
4. D	**8. D**	**NR2. 1 2 3 6**	**13. B**	**17. A**

1. B

The lithosphere is the land. The temperature of the land fluctuates more in response to sunlight than other parts of the biosphere.
The lithosphere has the lowest albedo so most of the sunlight that hits it is converted to heat.
The land has a lower specific heat capacity than the hydrosphere, so the absorption of light energy causes a more rapid rise in temperature in the lithosphere than on other parts of the biosphere.

2. A

A result of the tilt of Earth's axis is that during the Canadian summer, Canada and the rest of the Northern Hemisphere are pointed toward the sun. Therefore, the sun's rays are more direct, and there is warm, sunny weather. At the same time, the Southern Hemisphere is pointed away from the sun, so the sun's rays are not very direct, and countries like Australia experience their coolest weather of the year (winter).

3. D

Plants, such as trees, carry out photosynthesis. During photosynthesis, plants produce oxygen and consume carbon dioxide. If trees are removed, there will be less carbon dioxide taken into plants. Therefore, there will be more carbon dioxide in the atmosphere, which will contribute to the greenhouse effect.

4. D

Specific heat capacity is defined as the amount of heat energy (J) required to raise a gram (g) of matter by 1 degree (^{o}C), that is J/g ^{o}C. It takes a lot of heat energy to raise the temperature of water, so water has a high specific heat capacity.
The temperature of aluminum, in contrast, rises with little energy input. Aluminum has a low specific heat capacity.

5. C

Fogs will form when the warm moist air of the Gulf Stream hits the cold air of the Labrador Current. When the warm moist air of the Gulf Stream cools quickly, the water condenses and forms fog.

6. B

An open system is one that exchanges matter and energy with its surroundings. Water evaporates from Newfoundland, and it returns as rain.
This is an exchange of matter. Energy reaches Newfoundland as light and leaves as heat, which is an exchange of energy. Therefore, the island of Newfoundland is an open system.

7. D

The heat of vaporization is the heat energy absorbed by water when it changes from a liquid to a gas. This same energy is released when gaseous water condenses to a liquid, which it does when clouds form. Therefore, during cloud formation, there is a release of heat. Rapid cloud formation during the late afternoon of the summer months can release enough heat energy to generate thunderstorms.

8. D

Specific heat capacity is the amount of energy needed to increase the temperature of a substance. Water has a high specific heat capacity. It takes a lot of heat energy to increase the temperature of water. With all the water in the air in Vancouver, the temperature does not increase quickly.

9. B

As the air moves up the mountains, it gains altitude. The air pressure drops, and the air cools. The moisture condenses to form clouds, and this results in rain or snow. When the air descends the western side of the mountain, the air pressure rises, and the air warms. The warmer air can hold more moisture, so the ground moisture evaporates into the air. This is why the western side of this mountain range is rainy and the eastern side is dry.

NR 1 1236

A jet stream is a very fast, high-altitude wind that forms at the border of warmer, southern air and cooler, northern air. Jet streams flow from west to east. If the jet stream that crosses Canada moves south, Canadians will be exposed to the cold northern winds from the east. If the jet stream moves north, Canadians will experience the warmer air from the southwest. Jet streams are greater in winter because the temperature difference between the southern, warm air and the northern, cool air is greatest during that time.

10. D

Albedo refers to how much light is reflected off a surface and back into space. Ice has the highest albedo of the given alternatives by far. About 90% of sunlight reflects off of ice and goes back into space. A desert also has quite a high albedo. An ocean's albedo is less, and a forest has a very low albedo. The darker colour of the forest causes it to absorb most of the sun's light.

NR 2 1236

When the ground squirrel breathes, it releases the carbon dioxide that it produced during the process of cellular respiration (1). During a fire, fuel and oxygen are consumed and carbon dioxide and water vapour are released (2). Bacteria carry out a process similar to cellular respiration when they decompose organic matter (3). Plants carry out photosynthesis, but they also carry out cellular respiration. Cellular respiration is like combustion. Food molecules are combined with oxygen, and carbon dioxide and water are produced as waste (6).

NR 3 23

During burning, energy is released from the fuel as heat and light, and molecules of carbon dioxide and water are released into the atmosphere. However, nitrogen compounds, phosphorous compounds, and other forms of matter, which are part of the ash, are added to soil. These compounds are mineral nutrients for plants, which absorb them with water. Decomposition is similar to burning. Bacteria use what they can of the plant matter, but quite a lot of compounds are added to the soil.

11. C

In container 2 energy, in the form of light and heat, goes in and out, but matter cannot. However, this is not true of a biome. Energy in the form of light and heat constantly moves in and out of a biome, but matter is also exchanged with neighbouring biomes. The matter can consist of air, water, and migrating animals. This makes a biome an open system while the containers in this experiment are all closed systems.

12. B

A closed system is one in which energy is exchanged but matter is not. As heat or light, energy can enter or leave these containers, but the containers are sealed to matter, whether it be gas, liquid, or solid.

13. B

The fish in container 2 produced CO_2; however, there was no CO_2 in the container because the plant consumed it during photosynthesis.

14. A

A control setup is used for comparison with the experimental setup. Presumably, the experimenter wanted to learn about CO_2 changes that occur as a result of living organisms. Therefore, no organisms were placed in container 4. If there is an increase in CO_2 in container 4, the experimenter will know that CO_2 production was related to something other than the plant or the fish.

15. C

Prior to the year 1900, there were fluctuations in global temperatures, but according to the temperature scale, the variations were not more than 2°C. Since the temperatures are only going up and down by that amount, it is impossible to conclude that temperatures were stable, but they certainly did not vary by large amounts. The sharp rise in temperature began after 1900.

16. A

There may have been changes in global CO_2 amounts, resulting in changes to the greenhouse effect, but prior to the year 1900, it is unlikely that those changes were a result of pollution from factories. Throughout the world, there was not enough industrial activity prior to 1900 to affect the climate in a measurable way. Ocean currents change with time, as do global wind patterns, and these may cause climate changes.

17. A

Current temperatures are the highest on this graph, which goes back 1 000 years. That is about as long as humans have been able to measure temperatures. Temperature changes may have been a result of human factors, but it is impossible to determine this from the graph. It is also impossible know from this graph what effects temperature changes have on biomes. There has not been a steady increase in temperatures until recent decades. Before that, temperatures fluctuated.

KEY Strategies for Success on Tests

Test Preparation and Test-Taking Skills

Things to Consider When Taking a Test

- It is normal to feel anxious before you write a test. You can manage this anxiety by:
  - –Thinking positive thoughts. Imagine yourself doing well on the test.
  - –Making a conscious effort to relax by taking several slow, deep, controlled breaths. Concentrate on the air going in and out of your body.
- Before you begin the test, ask questions if you are unsure of anything.
- Jot down key words or phrases from any instructions your teacher gives you.
- Look over the entire test to find out the number and kinds of questions on the test.
- Read each question closely and reread if necessary.
- Pay close attention to key vocabulary words. Sometimes these are **bolded** or *italicized*, and they are usually important words in the question.
- If you are putting your answers on an answer sheet, mark your answers carefully. Always print clearly. If you wish to change an answer, erase the mark completely and then ensure your final answer is darker than the one you have erased.
- Use highlighting to note directions, key words, and vocabulary that you find confusing or that are important to answering the question.
- Double-check to make sure you have answered everything before handing in your test.

When taking tests, students often overlook the easy words. Failure to pay close attention to these words can result in an incorrect answer. One way to avoid this is to be aware of these words and to underline, circle, or highlight them while you are taking the test.

Even though some words are easy to understand, they can change the meaning of the entire question, so it is important that you pay attention to them. Here are some examples:

all	**always**	**most likely**	**probably**	**best**	**not**
difference	**usually**	**except**	**most**	**unlikely**	**likely**

Example

1. Which of the following equations is **not** considered abiotic?

A. wind

B. bacteria

C. sunlight

D. precipitation

HELPFUL STRATEGIES FOR ANSWERING MULTIPLE-CHOICE QUESTIONS

A multiple-choice question gives you some information, and then asks you to select an answer from four choices. Each question has one correct answer. The other answers are distractors, which are incorrect. Below are some strategies to help you when answering multiple-choice questions.

- Quickly skim through the entire test. Find out how many questions there are and plan your time accordingly.
- Read and reread questions carefully. Underline key words and try to think of an answer before looking at the choices.
- If there is a graphic, look at the graphic, read the question, and go back to the graphic. Then, you may want to underline the important information from the question.
- Carefully read the choices. Read the question first and then each answer that goes with it.
- When choosing an answer, try to eliminate those choices that are clearly wrong or do not make sense.
- Some questions may ask you to select the best answer. These questions will always include words like *best*, *most appropriate*, or *most likely*. All of the answers will be correct to some degree, but one of the choices will be better than the others in some way. Carefully read all four choices before choosing the answer you think is the best.
- If you do not know the answer, or if the question does not make sense to you, it is better to guess than to leave it blank.
- Do not spend too much time on any one question. Make a mark (*) beside a difficult question and come back to it later. If you are leaving a question to come back to later, make sure you also leave the space on the answer sheet, if you are using one.
- Remember to go back to the difficult questions at the end of the test; sometimes clues are given throughout the test that will provide you with answers.
- Note any negative words like *no* or *not* and be sure your choice fits the question.
- Before changing an answer, be sure you have a very good reason to do so.
- Do not look for patterns on your answer sheet, if you are using one.

HELPFUL STRATEGIES FOR ANSWERING OPEN-RESPONSE QUESTIONS

A written response requires you to respond to a question or directive such as **explain**, **predict**, **list**, **describe**, **show your work**, **solve**, or **calculate.** In preparing for open-response tasks you may wish to:

- Read and reread the question carefully.
- Recognize and pay close attention to directing words such as *explain*, *show your work*, and *describe*.
- Underline key words and phrases that indicate what is required in your answer, such as *explain*, *estimate*, *answer*, *calculate*, or *show your work*.
- Write down rough, point-form notes regarding the information you want to include in your answer.
- Think about what you want to say and organize information and ideas in a coherent and concise manner within the time limit you have for the question.
- Be sure to answer every part of the question that is asked.
- Include as much information as you can when you are asked to explain your thinking.
- Include a picture or diagram if it will help to explain your thinking.
- Try to put your final answer to a problem in a complete sentence to be sure it is reasonable.
- Reread your response to ensure you have answered the question.
- Think: Does your answer make sense?
- Listen: Does it sound right?
- Use appropriate subject vocabulary and terms in your response.

About Science Tests

What You Need to Know about Science Tests

To do well on a science test, you need to understand and apply your knowledge of scientific concepts. Reading skills can also make a difference in how well you perform. Reading skills can help you follow instructions and find key words, as well as read graphs, diagrams, and tables.

Science tests usually have two types of questions: knowledge questions and skill questions. Knowledge questions test for your understanding of science ideas. Skill questions test how you would use your science knowledge.

How You Can Prepare for Science Tests

Below are some strategies that are particular to preparing for and writing science tests.

- Note-taking is a good way to review and study important information from your class notes and textbook.
- Sketch a picture of the process or idea being described in a question. Drawing is helpful for learning and remembering concepts.
- Check your answer to practice questions the require formulas by working backward to the beginning. You can find the beginning by going step-by-step in reverse order.
- When answering questions with graphics (pictures, diagrams, tables, or graphs), read the test question carefully.

  –Read the title of the graphic and any key words.
  –Read the test question carefully to figure out what information you need to find in the graphic.
  –Go back to the graphic to find the information you need.
- Always pay close attention when pressing the keys on your calculator. Repeat the procedure a second time to be sure you pressed the correct keys.

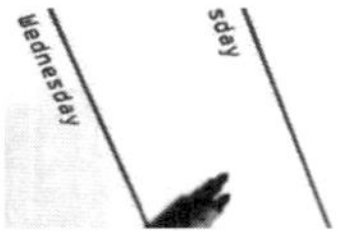

Test Preparation Countdown

If you develop a plan for studying and test preparation, you will perform well on tests.

Here is a general plan to follow seven days before you write a test.

Countdown: 7 Days before the Test

1. Review the following information:
   - Areas to be included on the test
   - Types of test items
   - General and specific test tips
2. Start preparing for the test at least 7 days before the test. Develop your test preparation plan and set time aside to prepare and study.

Countdown: 6, 5, 4, 3, 2 Days before the Test

1. Review old homework assignments, quizzes, and tests.
2. Rework problems on quizzes and tests to make sure you still know how to solve them.
3. Correct any errors made on quizzes and tests.
4. Review key concepts, processes, formulas, and vocabulary.
5. Create practice test questions for yourself and then answer them. Work out many sample problems.

Countdown: The Night before the Test

1. The night before the test is for final preparation, which includes reviewing and gathering material needed for the test before going to bed.
2. Most important is getting a good night's rest and knowing you have done everything possible to do well on the test.

Test Day

1. Eat a healthy and nutritious breakfast.
2. Ensure you have all the necessary materials.
3. Think positive thoughts: "I can do this." "I am ready." "I know I can do well."
4. Arrive at your school early so you are not rushing, which can cause you anxiety and stress.

Summary of How to Be Successful During a Test

You may find some of the following strategies useful for writing a test.

- Take two or three deep breaths to help you relax.
- Read the directions carefully and underline, circle, or highlight any important words.
- Look over the entire test to understand what you will need to do.
- Budget your time.
- Begin with an easy question, or a question you know you can answer correctly, rather than following the numerical question order of the test.
- If you cannot remember how to answer a question, try repeating the deep breathing and physical relaxation activities first. Then, move on to visualization and positive self-talk to get yourself going.
- When answering a question with graphics (pictures, diagrams, tables, or graphs), look at the question carefully.
  - Read the title of the graphic and any key words.
  - Read the test question carefully to figure out what information you need to find in the graphic.
  - Go back to the graphic to find the information you need.
- Write down anything you remember about the subject on the reverse side of your test paper. This activity sometimes helps to remind you that you do know something and you are capable of writing the test.
- Look over your test when you have finished and double-check your answers to be sure you did not forget anything.

NOTES

Practice Tests

PRACTICE TEST 1

Use the following information to answer the next question.

Albert Einstein proposed that light was made up of tiny bundles of energy called photons. Einstein believed that photons travelled at the speed of light, and contained energy. However, he believed that they could be classified as matter.

Some Properties of Matter

1. Matter must be visible.
2. Matter must have mass.
3. Matter must be composed of atoms.
4. Matter must occupy space.
5. Matter must be measurable.

Numerical Response

1. When listed numerically in ascending order, the properties given of matter that are correct are ____, and ____.

Use the following information to answer the next question.

By 1869, 63 different elements had been discovered. Dmitri Mendeleyev, a Russian scientist, grouped these elements according to their properties and atomic mass. In so doing, he found that these elements formed a regular pattern.

When moving across the periodic table from left to right, the elements change from ___*i*___ to ___*ii*___. In moving down the alkali metal group, the metals will ___*iii*___ in mass.

1. Which of the following rows contains words that complete the given statements?

Row	*i*	*ii*	*iii*
A.	metals	non-metals	decrease
B.	metals	non-metals	increase
C.	non-metals	metals	decrease
D.	non-metals	metals	increase

Use the following information to answer the next question.

Computer colleges are training students to work in a wide variety of fields, including the field of scientific research. Chan is using his knowledge of chemistry to categorize elements in a database according to the observed properties of the elements. He notes that a certain element has the following properties:

- Non-conductor
- Gas at room temperature
- Reacts vigorously with alkali metals

2. The given element is **most likely**

A. neon

B. sulfur

C. copper

D. chlorine

Use the following information to answer the next question.

Since the development of theories on the relationship between energy and matter (most notably Albert Einstein's theory of relativity), scientists and engineers have "released" vast amounts of energy by splitting atoms. Millions of dollars are poured into subatomic research in an effort to discover better ways of using nuclear energy for power. Nuclear power plants today use ^{235}U as a fuel. When ^{235}U is split, the heat energy generated turns water into steam, which in turn drives a steam turbine to produce electrical power.

3. The main difference between ^{235}U and ^{238}U is that ^{235}U is

A. a different element than ^{238}U

B. an ion and ^{238}U is an atom

C. a different isotope than ^{238}U

D. an atom and ^{238}U is an ion

Use the following information to answer the next question.

Protons, electrons, and neutrons are subatomic particles. The difference in charges between these subatomic particles is that protons are ***i***, electrons are ***ii***, and neutrons are ***iii***.

4. Which of the following rows contains the words that complete the given statement?

Row	*i*	*ii*	*iii*
A.	positively charged	negatively charged	neutral
B.	negatively charged	positively charged	neutral
C.	positively charged	negatively charged	positively charged
D.	positively charged	neutral	negatively charged

Use the following information to answer the next question.

Calcium is the most abundant mineral in the human body. Not only is calcium required for the functioning of nerve and muscle cells and blood clotting, it is also required for bone growth. Bone consists of dense, crystalline calcium phosphate. Minute amounts of magnesium and fluorine are also present to help strengthen bones.

5. The atomic radius or size of calcium is

A. larger than magnesium and fluorine

B. smaller than magnesium and fluorine

C. larger than magnesium, but smaller than fluorine

D. smaller than magnesium, but larger than fluorine

Use the following information to answer the next question.

Milk of magnesia (magnesium hydroxide) is used to neutralize excess stomach acid (hydrochloric acid) to prevent heartburn. The products of this reaction are magnesium chloride and water.

6. Which of the following chemical equations describes this reaction?

A. $Mg(OH)_2 + HCl \rightarrow MgCl_2 + H_2O$

B. $MgOH_2 + 2\,HCl \rightarrow MgCl_2 + H_2O$

C. $Mg(OH)_2 + HCl \rightarrow MgCl + H_2O$

D. $Mg(OH)_2 + 2\,HCl \rightarrow MgCl_2 + 2\,H_2O$

Use the following information to answer the next two questions.

Warning labels on most bottles of bleach state, "Do not use together with vinegar." Vinegar is an acid, and bleach, which contains the hypochlorite ion ClO^- in the form of sodium hypochlorite, is a base. A combination of these two substances would cause an exothermic neutralization reaction, producing toxic chlorine gas that is harmful, and sometimes deadly, when inhaled.

7. The formula for sodium hypochlorite is

A. $NaClO$

B. $NaCl$

C. Na_2ClO

D. $Na(ClO)_2$

Use the following information to answer the next question.

If vinegar was mixed with bleach in a fume hood, the temperature of the solution would _*i*_ and _*ii*_ would be produced.

8. Which if the following rows contains the words that complete the given statement?

Row	*i*	*ii*
A.	decrease	gas
B.	increase	gas
C.	decrease	precipitate
D.	increase	precipitate

Use the following information to answer the next question.

Scientists use various techniques to determine the chemical formula of an ionic compound. One method used to determine the type of positive ion present in a compound is to perform a flame test. With this test, a sample of the compound, dissolved in an appropriate solvent, is burned and the colour of the flame is observed. The following table contains cations and their distinctive flame colours.

Cation	Flame Colour
Cu^{2+}	Green
K^+	Purple
Na^+	Yellow
Sr^{2+}	Red

9. A scientist analyzes an unknown ionic compound known to contain one of the given cations. The compound is found to contain the OH^- ion, and has low solubility in water. If the compound is analyzed using the flame test, the colour of the flame would **most likely** be

A. green

B. purple

C. yellow

D. red

Use the following information to answer the next question.

Reactive metals usually react with oxygen to form metal oxides. However, some reactive metals, such as sodium (Na), are useful in their elemental form. In order to purify sodium, sodium compounds must be melted.
Pure sodium is then separated from the compound through the process of electrolysis.

Some Properties of a Compound

I. Its molten form conducts electricity.

II. It is a solid at standard temperature and pressure.

III. It has low solubility in water.

10. The compound sodium oxide can **best** be described by?

A. properties I and III

B. properties I and II

C. property II only

D. property III only

Use the following information to answer the next question.

Over the course of history, humans have used many substances only to later discover that the substance is toxic. Lead, for example, is poisonous to humans, but in Ancient Greece and Rome, lead was used in cosmetics. In the 15th and 16th century, mercury(I) chloride was used in eyedrops to make the user's eyes sparkle. However, because of the toxicity of mercury, this often caused the user to go blind.

11. The formula of mercury(I) chloride is

A. PbCl

B. AuCl

C. HgCl

D. MeCl

Use the following information to answer the next question.

In 1846, kerosene was discovered by a Canadian, Dr. Abraham Gesner. Compared with other lighting fuels used at the time, kerosene was safer, burned more brightly, and could be used in lighthouses. "Kerosene" is derived from the Greek words meaning "wax" and "oil."

12. The burning of kerosene can be described as what type of reaction

A. Formation

B. Combustion

C. Single replacement

D. Double replacement

13. Baking soda, sodium hydrogen carbonate, is used to protect car battery posts from corrosion that is caused by the acid inside the battery. Which of the following statements **best** describes the reaction between baking soda and car battery acid ($H_2SO_{4(aq)}$)?

A. Sodium hydrogen carbonate plus car battery acid yields sodium bisulfate plus carbon dioxide and water.

B. Sodium hydrogen carbonate plus hydrosulfuric acid yields sodium bisulfate, carbon dioxide, and water.

C. Sodium hydrogen carbonate plus sulfurous acid yields sodium bisulfate, carbon dioxide, and water.

D. Sodium hydrogen carbonate plus sulfuric acid yields sodium bisulfate, carbon dioxide, and water.

Use the following information to answer the next question.

The most durable batteries in the world are the zinc foil and sulfur dry pile batteries that were made in 1840. These batteries are still working today at the Clarendon Laboratory in England. Modern batteries are made from zinc and manganese oxide.

An unbalanced equation for a reaction in a battery is:

$$Zn + MnO_2 + H_2O \rightarrow 3Zn^{2+} + 2MnO_4 + 8H^+$$

Numerical Response

2. The correct coefficients for the reactants of the given equation, from left to right, are _____, _____, and _____.

Use the following information to answer the next question.

Portable hot packs that can be used to keep hands and feet warm often contain a mixture of powdered iron, activated carbon, sodium chloride, cellulose, zeolite, and water. Oxygen in the air permeates through the outer layer of the pack and oxidizes the iron inside. Iron, in powder form, has a large surface area and reacts quickly with oxygen to produce heat. The unbalanced reaction can be represented as:

$$Fe_{(s)} + O_{2(g)} \rightarrow Fe_2O_{3(s)}$$

Numerical Response

3. The correct coefficients for the given unbalanced reaction, from left to right, are _____, _____, and _____.

Use the following information to answer the next question.

An automobile uses the energy of gasoline for its motion. The energy used has gone through a series of conversions.

Forms of Energy

1.	Chemical	**2.**	Heat
3.	Kinetic	**4.**	Solar

Numerical Response

4. From its origin to its use in a car, the energy will take the given forms in the order of _____, _____, _____, and _____.

14. The energy for producing hydroelectric power can come from

A. gravity acting on the water behind a dam

B. the sun shining on the water behind a dam

C. the movement of air passing through a turbine

D. chemical energy turning a turbine

Use the following information to answer the next question.

The tallest living animal is the giraffe. Female giraffes reach average heights of 4.5 m, while male giraffes can reach average heights of 5.0 m. Blood from the heart must travel up, on average, 2.5 m to reach a giraffe's brain.

15. The increase in gravitational potential energy of 60 g of blood travelling from the heart to the brain in an average giraffe is

A. 1.5 J **B.** 2.7 J

C. 1.2 kJ **D.** 1.2 W

Numerical Response

5. What is the kinetic energy of a 60 kg skier traveling at 40 km/h, in kilojoules to **three** significant digits? _______

Use the following information to answer the next question.

Other than Earth, the most explored planetary surface is Mars. In 1976, the Viking spacecraft became the first man-made object to land on Mars. In 1997, the Pathfinder probe landed on the surface of Mars and relayed images of the planet back to Earth. The acceleration due to gravity on Mars is only 3.73 m/s^2.

Numerical Response

6. The work done to move a 60 kg space probe on Mars 10 m vertically upward at a constant velocity, can be expressed as $b \times 10^{w}$ J. What is the value of b, correct to **three** significant digits? _______

16. Which of the following statements **best** describes the process of photosynthesis?

A. It is an endothermic change in potential energy and an exothermic change in kinetic energy.

B. It is an exothermic change in potential energy and an endothermic change in kinetic energy.

C. Solar potential energy is released and chemical potential energy is stored in the glucose molecules.

D. Solar energy is converted to chemical energy in an endothermic process.

Use the following information to answer the next question.

Bamboo, which uses sunlight to produce glucose, can achieve growth rates of up to 91 cm per day. This plant converts ___*i*___ energy from the sun into stored ___*ii*___ energy in glucose.

17. Which of the following rows contains the words that complete the given statement?

Row	***i***	***ii***
A.	solar	chemical
B.	solar	mechanical
C.	electrical	chemical
D.	thermal	chemical

Use the following information to answer the next question.

In 1885, German inventor Karl Benz built the first car that ran on gasoline. With a top speed of 16 km/h, the "Motorwagen" had only three wheels, and a one-cylinder engine.

The car converted ___*i*___ energy in gasoline to ___*ii*___ energy for the motion of the car.

18. Which of the following rows contains the words that complete the given statement?

Row	***i***	***ii***
A.	chemical	potential
B.	chemical	kinetic
C.	physical	potential
D.	kinetic	Kinetic

Use the following information to answer the next question.

As an in-line skater begins her descent down one side of a 5 m half-pipe, she loses 10% of her potential energy to heat as a result of friction.

Numerical Response

7. What is the minimum initial velocity she needs to reach the opposite edge correct to **three** significant digits? _______

Use the following information to answer the next question.

Amtrak trains in the United States use diesel fuel and can move at speeds exceeding 346 km/h. Amtrak engineers must ensure that they have an efficient and safe means of stopping the high-speed trains. In other words, the kinetic energy built up by a high-speed train must, in some way, be lost if a train is to stop. Deceleration by braking is not the only way in which kinetic energy can be lost.

19. Kinetic energy may also be lost as

A. chemical energy and heat

B. potential energy and sound

C. heat and sound

D. potential energy and heat

Use the following information to answer the next question

Some Biological Structures

1. Virus	**2.** Prion
3. Blood cell	**4.** Bacterium

Numerical Response

8. If the given structures were ordered according to their size, from the smallest to the largest, the order would be ___, ___, ___, and ___.

20. The cell theory is the basis for biologists' understanding of organisms. Which of the following statements is **not** in accordance with the cell theory?

A. All cells come from other cells.

B. Cells are the smallest units of life.

C. All organisms are made up of cells.

D. Cells are specialized for different functions.

Use the following information to answer the next question.

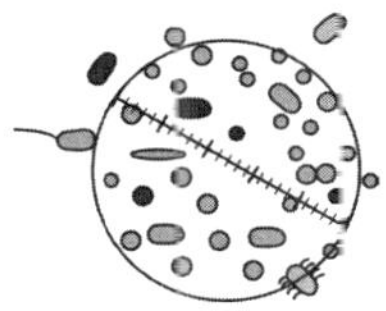

Penicillin is often used to prevent bacterial infection following minor surgical procedures such as the extraction of wisdom teeth. Penicillin prevents bacteria from multiplying by inhibiting the formation of new cell walls required for bacterial growth.

21. Human cells are **not** susceptible to the inhibiting effects of penicillin because

A. penicillin is quickly removed by lysosomes

B. human cells do not possess cell walls

C. human cells secrete a hormone that counteracts the effects of penicillin

D. penicillin is not active long enough to prevent the growth of human cells

Use the following information to answer the next question.

Patients awaiting kidney transplants must undergo regular dialysis. Dialysis is an artificial method of removing water, urea, and other toxic substances from the blood. The dialysis technique makes use of a special type of semi-permeable membrane known as Visking tubing, through which blood flows.

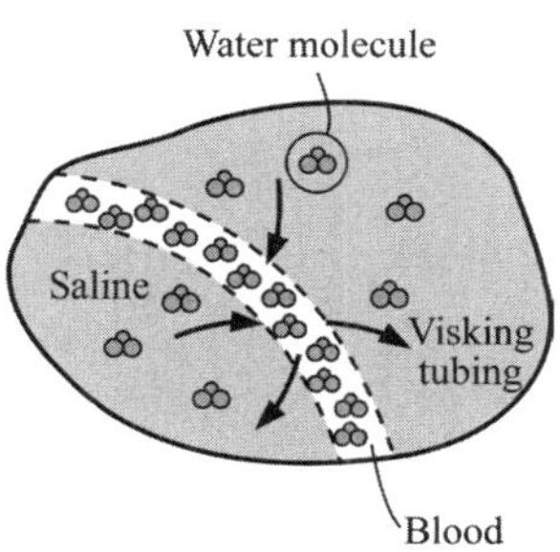

22. Water passes across the Visking tubing through the process of

A. diffusion

B. active transport

C. osmosis

D. osmoregulation

Use the following information to answer the next question.

Comparison of the Relative Surface Area and Volume of Two Organisms		
Organism	**Surface Area (cm^2)**	**Volume (cm^3)**
Mouse	14	12
Hummingbird	12	8

23. Which of the following rows correctly identifies the given animal with the higher metabolic rate and the explanation of why the metabolic rate is higher?

Row	Animal	Explanation
A.	Hummingbird	It has the higher surface area-to-volume ratio.
B.	Hummingbird	It has the lower surface area-to-volume ratio.
C.	Mouse	It has the higher surface area-to-volume ratio.
D.	Mouse	It has the lower surface area-to-volume ratio.

Use the following information to answer the next question.

Freshwater, single-celled organisms, such as *Euglena* possess organelles called contractile vacuoles. These vacuoles contract rhythmically and function to remove excess water from the cell.

24. Excess water accumulates in an organism such as the *Euglena* because

A. water movement follows a concentration gradient, from an area of high concentration to an area of low concentration

B. the interior of *Euglena* is hypotonic relative to the surrounding water

C. water is being transported actively into the cell

D. the membrane is selectively permeable, as water can enter, but cannot leave the cell

25. In plants, roots take up water from the ground, since the ground is hypotonic compared to the cytoplasm of root cells. Which of the following mechanisms would a root cell use to take in water from a hypotonic soil environment?

A. Transpiration

B. Osmosis

C. Facilitated diffusion

D. Active transport

Use the following information to answer the next question.

Glucose can be burned (combusted) to produce carbon dioxide, water, and energy. This energy is released as heat energy, and is not used to do any cellular work. In a cell, a complicated chemical process allows the cell to harvest the released energy as ATP during the breakdown of glucose.

26. The chemical reactions that release the energy in glucose occur **mainly** in the

A. mitochondria

B. chloroplasts

C. lysosomes

D. ribosomes

27. Water and dissolved nutrients reach the top of a tree through

A. transpiration and root pressure

B. respiration and photosynthesis

C. water surface tension

D. woody phloem

Use the following information to answer the next question.

I. Root hairs are valuable to a plant because of their large surface areas.

II. There is a lower concentration of minerals inside the roots than in the soil.

III. Water enters the roots down a concentration gradient.

IV. Along with water, minerals enter the roots through passive transport.

28. Which of the given statements are correct?

A. I, II, and III

B. I and III

C. I, II, and IV

D. I, III, and IV

29. Which of the following statements is **not** true for transpiration?

A. It cools the plant.

B. It involves a phase change of water.

C. It is necessary for photosynthesis to occur.

D. It draws water and nutrients from the roots.

30. The sun has less effect in Canada during the month of January for all of the following reasons **except** for the fact that

A. there is typically a higher albedo

B. there are more greenhouse gases

C. solar rays are spread over a larger surface area

D. solar radiation passes through more of the atmosphere

31. The primary function of the Intergovernmental Panel on Climate Change (IPCC) is to

A. monitor climate change

B. investigate past climate change

C. evaluate the risks of human-induced climate change

D. coordinate and carry out research related to climate change

Numerical Response

9. When 100 g of snow is melted in 1.0 L of water, the change in water's temperature, expressed in scientific notation, is $b \times 10^{w}$°C. The value of b, correct to **three** significant digits is __________.

Use the following information to answer the next question.

> Every two weeks, the Earth receives 4.92×10^{32} J of solar energy. This is equivalent to the energy stored in all the coal, oil, and gas reserves on Earth. Unlike these non-renewable resources, solar energy is a pollution-free way of generating electricity. Sunlight is used to heat water, eventually converting it to steam.

Numerical Response

10. By how many degrees would 1 000 J of sunlight raise the temperature of 10 g of water, correct to three significant digits?

____

32. As an air mass from the Rocky Mountains descends on Calgary, there would **most** *likely* be

A. an increase in temperature and pressure

B. an increase in pressure and relative humidity

C. a decrease in pressure and relative humidity

D. a decrease in temperature and relative humidity

Use the following information to answer the next question.

> The greatest temperature change ever recorded in one day occurred in Montana, USA, in 1916. The temperature fell from 7°C to –49°C, which is a decrease of 56°C.

33. If water underwent a similar temperature change, it would undergo a decrease in

A. kinetic energy, then a decrease in potential energy, and finally another decrease in kinetic energy

B. potential energy, then a decrease in kinetic energy, and finally another decrease in potential energy

C. kinetic energy, then an increase in potential energy, and finally another decrease in kinetic energy

D. kinetic energy, but not potential energy

34. During the winter, temperatures in Calgary can drop as low as –40°C. Vancouver, which is relatively at the same latitude but at a lower altitude, experiences much milder temperatures. What accounts for this difference in temperature?

A. The higher altitude of Calgary means that the air is more dense and has a lower specific heat capacity.

B. The large body of water near Vancouver moderates the temperature of the surrounding environment.

C. The specific heat capacity of water is lower at higher altitudes.

D. Brisk winds in Calgary bring about rapid changes in pressure.

Use the following information to answer the next question.

Humans must maintain a relatively constant body temperature to maximize the efficiency of the various biochemical reactions that take place inside the body. The body takes in food that it uses to produce heat (amongst other things), to replace the heat that is lost to the environment.

35. The human body is an example of what type of system?

A. Open

B. Closed

C. Isolated

D. Ecological

36. Which of the following terms is **not** like the others given?

A. Evaporation

B. Transpiration

C. Perspiration

D. Condensation

Use the following information to answer the next two questions

The following graph shows the preferred temperatures for three common freshwater algae.

Temperature Tolerances of Three Common Freshwater Algae

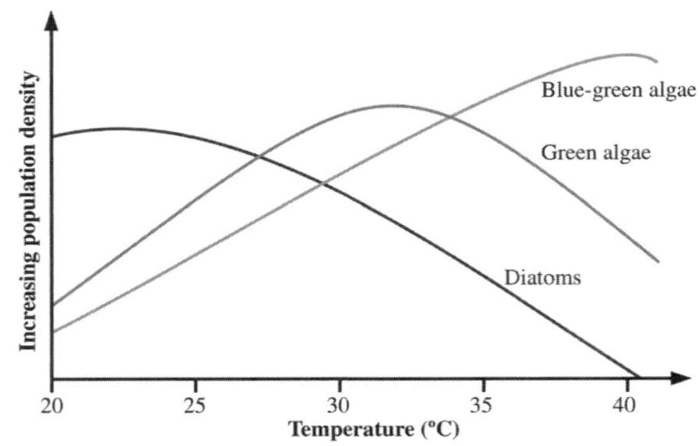

37. Imagine a small pond that has a white sand bottom. A farmer cuts trees and shrubs around the pond and topsoil flows into the pond, darkening the bottom. What effect will this have on the water?

A. It will raise the albedo, which will lower the water's temperature.

B. It will raise the albedo, which will raise the water's temperature.

C. It will lower the albedo, which will lower the water's temperature.

D. It will lower the albedo, which will raise the water's temperature.

38. Blue-green algae are quite toxic to many animals. How will the farmer's actions affect his cattle that drink from the pond?

A. They will benefit from the increased algae in the water.

B. They will be less healthy as a result of the toxins produced by the algae.

C. There will be no difference as long as the cattle have enough to drink.

D. There will be no difference since the concentration of blue-green algae is so low.

Written Response

Use the following information to answer the next question

Elodea is a common weed that flourishes in Canadian ponds, and is commonly used in aquariums. The plant produces tiny white flowers that are suspended on the water surface by long, thin, flexible stems. The roots are either anchored in the pond soil or are free-floating. Elodea grows best in cool, nutrient-rich water that is exposed to full sunlight. This weed is a food source for ducks and beavers, and a habitat for pond-dwelling insects. Additionally, Elodea appears to remove pollutants from water, yet does not overgrow to become a pest weed.

The following diagram shows the setup for a controlled experiment using Elodea.

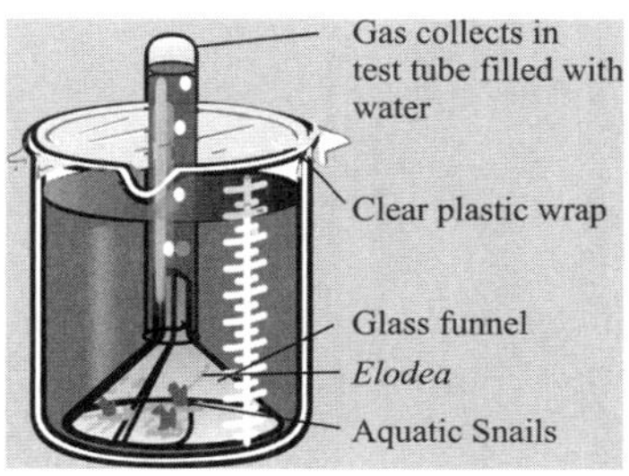

The investigator places two such setups in bright light for 24 hours. Two identical setups are placed in a dark closet for the same amount of time. At the end of the 24 hours, the investigator removes the test tubes from the setups, and performs the following two tests on the gas collected.

A glowing splint is inserted into the mouth of one test tube exposed to light and one from the closet.

The gas in two test tubes (one exposed to light and one from the closet) is bubbled through lime water.

The results of the experiment are shown in the following chart.

Amount of Gas Collected and Results of Gas Identification Tests Using the Setup

Test Tube	Test	Result	Amount of Gas Collected (cm)
1 (exposed to light)	1	Splint burst into flames	5
2 (exposed to light)	2	Limewater is clear	5.5
3 (closet)	1	?	?
4 (closet)	2	?	?

1. **a)** Predict the results for test tubes 3 and 4 by filling in the blanks on the chart.

b) Identify the gas collected in the test tubes from set-ups 1 and 2, which were the ones exposed to light. From what process is this gas derived?

c) Why are set-ups 3 and 4 included in this experiment?

Use the following information to answer the next three questions

> The experiment is identical to the setup of the first of the written response questions found on the previous page except that:
>
> - clear plastic wrap is used to seal the beaker, making it airtight
> - three aquatic snails are placed inside the funnel
>
> Each set-up is left for 5 days.

2. **a)** Will the snails and *Elodea* survive in the set-up exposed to light? What about the set-up in the dark closet? Explain your answer.

b) Is the set-up exposed to light an open, a closed, or an isolated system? Explain your answer.

c) What is the common manipulated variable in both sets of experiments?

Use the following information to answer the next question.

> To prevent injuries due to collisions, air bags are a standard feature in vehicles. The airbag is inflated through a process involving sodium trinitrogen, which is ignited by a spark upon impact. The sodium trinitrogen explodes and produces sodium metal and nitrogen gas as well as some heat. The nitrogen gas rushes into the deflated airbag, which inflates, and then cushions the driver of the car. All of this occurs in less than $\frac{1}{25}$ of a second. Recently, airbags have been criticized because of several child injuries and deaths in the United States and Canada as a result of the excessive force that airbags put on small bodies.

3. **a)** What are some of the advantages and disadvantages of using airbags?
In answering this question, be sure to discuss the following ideas:

- the process involved in airbag inflation
- the balanced reaction that occurs
- why this reaction inflates the airbag
- the advantages and disadvantages of relying on this reaction

b) What suggestions can be made to change current airbag technology to make them more safe and effective

ANSWERS AND SOLUTIONS—PRACTICE TEST 1

NR1. 2 4	**11. C**	**17. A**	**26. A**	**35. A**
1. B	**12. B**	**18. B**	**27. A**	**36. D**
2. D	**13. D**	**NR7. 3.13**	**28. D**	**37. D**
3. C	**NR2. 3 2 4**	**19. C**	**29. C**	**38. B**
4. A	**NR3. 4 3 2**	**NR8. 2 1 4 3**	**30. B**	**WR1. See Solution**
5. A	**NR4. 4 1 2 3**	**20. D**	**31. C**	**WR2. See Solution**
6. D	**14. A**	**21. B**	**NR9. 7.95**	**WR3. See Solution**
7. A	**15. A**	**22. C**	**NR10. 23.9**	
8. B	**NR5. 3.70**	**23. A**	**32. A**	
9. A	**NR6. 2.24**	**24. A**	**33. A**	
10. B	**16. D**	**25. B**	**34. B**	

NR 1 2 4

Matter is anything that has mass and occupies space.

1. Matter does not have to be visible. An example of this is oxygen. Therefore, property **1** is incorrect.

2. Matter must have mass, therefore, property **2** is correct.

3. Matter does not have to be composed of atoms. An example of this is an electron. Therefore, property **3** is incorrect.

4. Matter must occupy space, therefore, property **4** is correct.

5. Matter does not have to be measurable. For example, the universe has a mass, but it is not measurable. Therefore, property **5** is incorrect.

In ascending order, the correct statements are **2** and **4**.

1. B

Elements on the far left side of the periodic table are metals, and elements on the far right side are non-metals. The reactivity and mass of metals regardless of groups increases from the top of a group to the bottom. Only alternative **B** has the correct order of the words needed to complete the given statements.

2. D

Neon (group 18) is a noble gas and has very low reactivity. Therefore, neon will not react vigorously with alkali metals.

Sulfur (group 16) is a solid at room temperature, not a gas.

Copper (group 11) is a transition metal, therefore, it is a conductor.

Chlorine (group 17) is a halogen, which means that it reacts vigorously with alkali metals. It is also a non-metal, which means it is a non-conductor. It is a gas at room temperature.

Only chlorine, alternative **D**, matches the properties of the given element.

3. C

The number on the top left-hand side of the symbol of an element is called the mass number of that element. In this case, ^{235}U is a uranium atom with a mass number of 235 and ^{238}U is a uranium atom with a mass number of 238. Since both ^{235}U and ^{238}U are the same element (they are both uranium), they will both still have the same atomic number of 92. Isotopes are elements that have the same atomic number but different mass numbers. Therefore, ^{235}U and ^{238}U are different isotopes, and alternative **C** is the correct answer.

4. A

Protons have a charge of +1, electrons have a charge of –1, and neutrons have no charge (they are neutral). Thus alternative **A** is the correct answer.

5. A

The atomic radius or size of an element changes in relation to its location on the periodic table. Atomic size increases from the top of a group to the bottom. Therefore, since calcium (Ca) is lower in group 2 than magnesium (Mg) is, calcium will have a larger ionic size than magnesium. Atomic size decreases from the left to right on the periodic table. Since fluorine (F) is on the right side of the periodic table, and calcium (Ca) is on the left side, calcium will have a larger atomic size than fluorine. Therefore, calcium has a larger atomic size than both fluorine and magnesium.

6. D

In a balanced chemical equation, the total number of atoms of each element on the left-hand side of the equation must equal the total number of atoms of each element on the right-hand side of the equation. In addition, the correct chemical formula for each reactant and product must be given. The correctly balanced equation for this reaction is as follows.

$$Mg(OH)_2 + 2\,HCl \rightarrow MgCl_2 + 2\,H_2O$$

In the other alternatives $Mg(OH)_2$ is incorrectly written as $MgOH_2$ or the Cl or O atoms are not balanced in the equations.

7. A

Since the hypochlorite ion (ClO^-) has a net charge of –1, and the sodium ion (Na^+) has a net charge of +1, they must form a compound in a 1 to 1 ratio in order to maintain a net charge of zero. The only response that satisfies this condition is alternative **A**, with the formula NaClO.

8. B

Since the neutralization of bleach with vinegar is an exothermic reaction, it releases energy into its surroundings. The energy (in the form of heat) would be transferred to the solution, causing the temperature of the solution to increase. Chlorine gas is produced.

9. A

From the information given, the unknown compound was found to contain the OH^- ion.

A green flame would show the presence of the Cu^{2+} ion in the compound. Cu^{2+} has low solubility in water when matched with OH^-.

A purple flame would indicate the presence of a K^+ ion. On a solubility chart, the OH^- ion is listed as having high solubility with group 1 ions, which includes K^+. Therefore, this compound will dissolve in water. A yellow flame would indicate the presence of an Na^+ ion. The OH^- ion is listed as having high solubility with group 1 ions, which includes Na^+. Therefore, this compound will dissolve in water. A red flame would indicate the presence of a Sr^{2+} ion. The OH^- ion is listed as having high solubility with the Sr^{2+}. Therefore, this compound will dissolve in water.

10. B

Sodium oxide is an ionic compound, which means that it contains metallic and non-metallic ions. The molten, or liquid, form of an ionic compound will conduct electricity. Ionic compounds usually have very high solubilities and high melting points.

11. C

Mercury(I) chloride is an ionic compound, because it contains a metallic ion (mercury(I)) and a non-metallic ion (chloride). The mercury(I) ion is represented as Hg^+, and the chloride ion is Cl^-. Since the mercury(I) ion has a charge of +1, and the chloride ion has a charge of −1, they will form a compound in a one to one ratio, in order to maintain a net charge of zero. The formula for mercury(I) chloride is HgCl.

12. B

A formation reaction is one in which simple elements combine to form larger, more complex compounds. A combustion reaction is the reaction of a substance with oxygen that produces energy. A single replacement reaction is one that involves the exchange of one ion between reactants. A double replacement reaction is one that involves the simultaneous exchange of two ions between the reactants. When kerosene burns, it combines with oxygen to produce heat energy. It is an exothermic reaction and can best be described as a combustion reaction.

13. D

In order to answer this question, one must apply the rules for naming acids to the reaction between baking soda and car battery acid ($H_2SO_{4(aq)}$).

Rule	Ionic Name	Acid Name
1	Hydrogen____ide	Hydro____ic acid
2	Hydrogen____ate	____ic acid
3	Hydrogen____ite	____ous acid

For the acid ($H_2SO_{4(aq)}$), the negatively charged ion is $SO_{4(aq)}^{2-}$, which is the sulfate ion. Therefore, the ionic name for H_2SO_4 is hydrogen sulfate, and according to rule 2, the correct name for this acid is sulfuric acid. Using the term car battery acid is not specific enough.

NR 2 3 2 4

The balanced reaction is
$$\underline{3}Zn + \underline{2}MnO_2 + \underline{4}H_2O \rightarrow 3Zn^{2+} + 2MnO_4 + 8H^+$$

The coefficients of the reactants from left to right are 3, 2, and 4.

NR 3 4 3 2

This question tests the ability to correctly balance the oxidation reaction of iron:
$$4Fe_{(s)} + 3O_{2(g)} \rightarrow 2Fe_2O_{3(s)}$$

In the above given balanced equation, there are four iron atoms and six oxygen atoms on each side of the equation. The coefficients from left to right are 4, 3, and 2.

NR 4 4 1 2 3

The sun exerts solar or light energy. The sunlight may be captured by plants in the process of photosynthesis. During photosynthesis, light energy is converted to chemical energy. Hundreds of millions of years ago plants that underwent photosynthesis did not decay and their organic matter was eventually converted to petroleum. When we burn the petroleum, the chemical energy of the petroleum is converted to heat that causes the engine of the car to turn. This results in the car's kinetic, or movement, energy.

14. A

Hydroelectric power can be produced when a dam is placed in a river. The water will back up behind the dam, and a generating turbine can be placed in the dam. Water, under great pressure, rushes through the turbine and generates electricity. It is the potential energy of the water building up behind the dam that provides the force to move the water through the dam. The potential energy exists because gravity is pulling on the water behind the dam.

15. A

You need to calculate the net potential energy gain of 60 grams (6.0×10^{-2} kg) of blood from the change in the height of the blood as it travels from the giraffe's heart to its head. The total change in the height is 2.5 m. The increase in height creates an increase in potential energy.

$$E_p = mgh$$
$$= (6.0\times10^{-2}\text{ kg})(9.81\text{ m/s}^2)(2.5\text{ m})$$
$$= 1.5\text{ J}$$

Therefore, there is an increase in the potential energy of the blood of the giraffe by 1.5 Joules (alternative **A**).

NR 5 3.70

In the equation for kinetic energy, the mass must be in kilograms and the velocity in metres per second. Therefore, the *velocity given* must be converted to metres per second.

$$\frac{40\text{ km}}{\text{h}}\times\frac{1\ 000\text{ m}}{\text{km}}\times\frac{1\text{ h}}{3\ 600\text{ s}} = 11.11\text{ m/s}$$

The kinetic energy the skier will have at this velocity is:

$$KE = \frac{1}{2}mv^2 = \frac{1}{2}(60\text{ kg})(11.11\text{ m/s})^2$$
$$= 3\ 703\text{ J}$$
$$= 3.70\text{ kJ}$$

Therefore, the kinetic energy of a 60 kg skier travelling at 11.11 m/s is 3.70 kJ.

NR 6 2.24

This question tests understanding of the nature of work, and its relationship to potential energy. The work done on the probe will be equal to the amount of energy needed to lift the mass to a height of 10 m.

Remember that the acceleration due to gravity on Mars is only 3.73 m/s^2, not 9.81 m/s^2, as it is on Earth.

$$E_p = mgh$$
$$E_p = (60\text{ kg})(3.73\text{ m/s}^2)(10\text{ m})$$
$$E_p = 2\ 238\text{ J}$$
$$E_p = 2.24\times10^3\text{ J}$$

Therefore, the amount of work done on the probe will also be 2.24×10^3 J. The value of *b*, correct to three significant digits is 2.24.

16. D

The reaction for photosynthesis is:

$$6CO_{2(g)} + 6H_2O_{(g)} + \text{light} \rightarrow \underset{\text{glucose}}{C_6H_{12}O_{6(s)}} + \underset{\text{oxygen}}{6O_2}$$

This reaction stores light energy as chemical energy in the form of glucose, $C_6H_{12}O_{6(s)}$, which is a form of potential energy.
As endothermic reactions use energy, and exothermic reactions release energy, the photosynthetic reaction is endothermic since energy is one of the reactants (light).

17. A

This question requires the proper classification of energy into one of the following types.

- Solar energy is energy derived from the radiation and heat emitted from the sun.
- Chemical energy is energy that is stored in the chemical bonds of a molecule.
- Thermal energy is a form of kinetic energy that is due to the random motion of molecules, also referred to as heat.
- Mechanical energy is the sum of the potential and kinetic energies of a system.
- Electrical energy is derived from the force between charged particles. A force of attraction exists between two particles with unlike charges, and a force of repulsion exists between particles with like charges.

During photosynthesis, the bamboo converts the solar energy of the sun into chemical energy, which is stored in the chemical bonds of glucose. Therefore, alternative **A** is correct.

18. B

Chemical energy is stored in the chemical bonds of the gasoline. When the gasoline is ignited, it releases this energy, which is then used to move the pistons in the engine and provide the car with motion. This motion is kinetic energy. Therefore, in the car, energy is converted from chemical energy to kinetic energy.

NR 7 3.13

Using the law of conservation of energy, all of the skater's potential energy is converted to kinetic energy ($K_E = P_E$). However, because she loses 10% of her potential energy to friction, we must add 10% to the initial kinetic energy to ensure she makes it to the top on the other side.

$$\frac{E_k}{0.1} = E_p \quad \text{(0.1 represents 10\%)}$$

$$\frac{\frac{1}{2}mv^2}{0.1} = mgh$$

$$\frac{\frac{1}{2}v^2}{0.1} = gh$$

$$v = \sqrt{(2)(0.1)gh}$$

$$v = \sqrt{(2)(0.1)(9.81\ \text{m/s}^2)(5.0\ \text{m})}$$

$$v = 3.13\ \text{m/s}$$

Correct to three significant digits, the answer is 3.13.

19. C

Energy can also be lost as heat and sound produced by the brakes. There is no evidence that kinetic energy is converted into chemical energy or potential energy. Therefore, alternative **C** is correct.

NR 8 2 1 4 3

A prion, such as the one that causes mad cow disease, is incredibly tiny. It is composed of only one protein molecule. A virus is only slightly larger. A virus contains a section of DNA surrounded by a protein coat. A bacterium is a very small cell. But, being a cell, it contains cytoplasm, a cell wall and DNA. One bacterium is larger than hundreds of viruses. Finally, a red blood cell is small for a human cell, but it is much larger than a bacterium.

20. D

It is true that most cells are specialized for specific functions, although one-celled organisms are composed of single cells that are completely unspecialized. But, the cell theory does not include anything about cell specialization. The other three statements are in accordance with the cell theory.

21. B

Penicillin is an antibiotic that disrupts the formation of cell walls. Cell walls are absent in animal cells, but are present in bacteria and plant cells.

22. C

Diffusion is a type of transport that does not require energy. During diffusion, molecules move from areas of high concentration to areas of low concentrations. Osmoregulation is the regulation of the water balance in an organism. Active transport requires energy to transport molecules across a semipermeable membrane.

23. A

The surface area to volume ratio (SA:V) in a hummingbird is 1.5:1. The SA:V for a mouse is 1.17:1. With a higher SA:V ratio, the hummingbird loses more heat across its skin for equal amounts of energy generated. Thus, the hummingbird must have a higher metabolic rate, i.e., it must break down glucose for energy at a faster rate than the mouse.

24. A

Water diffuses through the process of osmosis. Water moves toward the solution with the lower concentration. In this case, the lower concentration of water (hypertonic environment) is inside *Euglena*, so water moves into it. Water is never transported actively. It always diffuses across a semi-permeable membrane.

25. B

The cells of roots take in water from a hypotonic environment through the process of osmosis. The diffusion of water proceeds from the hypotonic environment (low solute concentration, high water concentration) to the area where the water concentration is lower. Transpiration refers to the loss of water from plants as a result of evaporation. In facilitated diffusion, special structures within a membrane facilitate the movement of matter across the membrane. Active transport involves the movement of molecules across a concentration gradient, requiring the expenditure of energy.

26. A

You are given that ATP is released through glucose metabolization. Glucose is metabolized in the mitochondria. The ribosomes are responsible for protein synthesis. Lysomes break up cellular debris.

27. A

Openings in leaves at the top of a plant are coated with a thin layer of moisture that escapes from the plant since the concentration of water in the air is lower than in the leaf openings. This process of water loss is called transpiration. To replace the water lost as a result of transpiration, more water is pulled up through the plant, carrying nutrients to the top. Phloem transports carbohydrates, not water.

28. D

Three of the four given statements are correct.

I. Root hairs are thin appendages on roots. Root hairs serve to increase the surface area across which nutrient and water absorption can occur in a plant.

II. This statement is not correct because it is not always true; see the explanation below for statement **IV**. Sometimes, the concentration of minerals in the roots is higher than in the soil. However, it is true that the solute concentration in the root cells is always higher than the solute concentration in the soil water. If this were not the case, water could not move into the roots passively (osmosis).

Recall that water moves from a hypotonic (low solute concentration) to a hypertonic (high solute concentration) environment.

III. Plants absorb water through their roots. Water is taken up by osmosis from the surrounding soil. For osmosis to occur, the concentration of water in the soil must be greater than the concentration of water in the root cells, such that the water travels down its concentration gradient (from an area of high concentration to an area of low concentration).

IV. Along with water, the roots also absorb minerals from the soil. Minerals are taken up either by passive or active transport. During passive transport, minerals are carried by water into the roots. Active transport of minerals is used by root cells when the concentration of minerals in the soil is lower than the concentration of minerals in the cells cytoplasm.

29. C

Transpiration is the cooling process in which water evaporates out of the stomata. The movement of water out of the leaf creates a pulling force that draws water and nutrients up the xylem. Transpiration is not necessary for photosynthesis to occur. This is reinforced by the fact that photosynthesis occurs in underwater plants that cannot perform transpiration.

30. B

In January, the sun's rays hit Canada at a low angle. One reason that the sun has less effect in January is that the sun's rays have to travel through a lot more of the atmosphere, so some of the solar energy is absorbed or reflected back into space. The sun's rays are spread over a larger area because they hit the Earth at a low angle. This reduces their heating effect. There is typically a higher albedo in the winter because snow is much more reflective than land. Greenhouse gas amounts do not vary with the seasons enough to change the sun's effect.

31. C

The IPCC evaluates the risks of human-induced climate change by assessing peer reviewed and scientific literature related to current climate change. The IPCC also composes reports on topics relevant to the implementation of the United Nations Framework Convention on Climate Change. They are not directly responsible for any research or monitoring of climatic conditions, and they do not focus on past (non-human) climate change episodes.

NR 9 7.95

The energy gained by the ice is calculated as follows:
$Q = mH_{\text{fusion}} = (100\ \text{g})(333\ \text{J/g}) = 33.3\ \text{k J}$

The same amount of energy is lost by the water. The decrease in temperature is calculated as follows:
$(1.00\ \text{L} = 1.00 \times 10^3\ \text{g})$

$$\Delta t = \frac{Q}{mc}$$
$$= \frac{3.33 \times 10^4\ \text{J}}{(1.00 \times 10^3\ \text{g})(4.19\ \text{J/g°C})}$$
$$= 7.95\text{°C}$$

Thus, the value of $b = 7.95$.

NR 10 23.9

The change in temperature is calculated as follows:
$$Q = mc\Delta t$$
$$\Delta t = \frac{Q}{mc}$$
$$= \frac{1000\ \text{J}}{(10\ \text{g})(4.19\ \text{J/g°C})}$$
$$= 23.9\text{°C}$$

32. A

An air mass is a large portion of the atmosphere that possesses uniform temperature and humidity. Both the temperature and humidity of an air mass are affected by atmospheric pressure. Atmospheric/air pressure is the downward force exerted by the weight of the atmosphere per unit area (in units of N/m^2 or Pascals, Pa). Pressure increases as an air mass descends in altitude because at lower elevations, the volume of air and mass of the air) above is greater (see diagram).

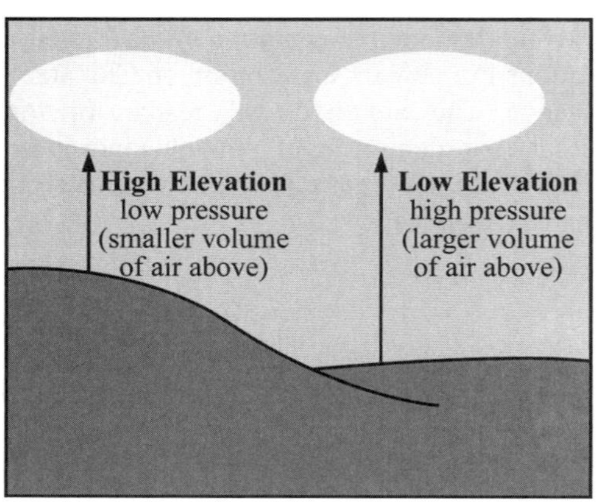

Increasing atmospheric pressure causes the air mass to compress, causing an increase in temperature. Warmer air can hold more water. Recall that relative humidity is a measure of the amount of water that one air mass can hold in comparison to another air mass. The descending air mass in the question will therefore experience an increase in pressure, causing compression of the air and a corresponding increase in temperature. The increase in temperature should cause a relative increase in the humidity as well.

33. A

As water cools from 7°C to 0°C, there is a decrease in temperature, which means there is a decrease in kinetic energy. This is because the faster the molecules in a substance move, the greater the kinetic energy and the temperature of the substance. Conversely, as molecules slow down, there is a drop in temperature and less kinetic energy. As the water undergoes a phase change from a liquid to a solid (ice), there is a decrease in potential energy. As the temperature of the ice goes from 0°C to –49°C, there is another decrease in the kinetic energy.

34. B

The large body of water located along Vancouver's coast (Pacific Ocean) serves to moderate the temperature because of the high heat capacity of water. The presence of water prevents the relatively large temperature changes that are experienced further inland. High heat capacity means that a large amount of energy is needed to change the temperature of the substance by even a small amount.

35. A

Matter and energy are exchanged between the body and its environment. Therefore, the body must be considered an open system. Isolated systems exchange neither matter nor energy with the surroundings, and closed systems exchange energy, but not matter with the surroundings.

36. D

Evaporation, transpiration, and perspiration all involve the phase change from a liquid to a gas. In condensation, there is a phase change from a gas to a liquid.

37. D

Albedo is the ability of a surface to reflect sunlight. Lighter colours reflect more light. Originally, the pond had a high albedo. When the bottom darkened, the albedo dropped. This would cause the bottom to absorb more sunlight, which would be converted to heat, which would raise the water's temperature.

38. B

The farmer's actions will cause the water temperature to rise, making it a better place for blue-green algae to grow. Therefore, the toxins produced by the blue-green algae would also increase. Animals, such as cattle, that drink from the pond will consume these toxins and may be harmed. Poisoning by blue-green algae is a significant problem where water is warm enough for blue-green algae to grow in abundance, such as in Australia.

1. **a)** *In the table, make a prediction by filling in the results for test tubes #3 and #4 (from the setups left in the dark).*

Test Tube	Test	Result	Amount of Gas Collected (cm^3)
3	1	Splint does not burst into flames	~ 0
4	2	Limewater is clear	~ 0

b) *Identify the gas collected in the test tubes from setups #1 and #2 exposed to light. From what process is this gas derived?*

Gas collected: oxygen
Process: photosynthesis
In the presence of light, *Elodea* (a green plant) undergoes photosynthesis.

Recall that the reaction for photosynthesis is as follows:

$$6CO_{2(g)} + 6H_2O_{(g)} + \text{light} \rightarrow \underset{\text{glucose}}{C_6H_{12}O_{6(s)}} + \underset{\text{oxygen}}{6O_2}$$

Because photosynthesis is dependent on solar energy (sunlight), the reaction should not occur in the set-ups that are in the dark closet.

c) *Why are setups #3 and #4 included in this experiment?*

Set-ups 3 and 4 are controls.

The manipulated variable (light) is absent in set-ups 3 and 4. Photosynthesis requires light and, therefore, should not occur in the dark. See the solution to part **a**.

2. **a)** *Will the snail and Elodea survive in the light setup? The dark setup? Explain.*

When exposed to light, *Elodea* should survive because it can perform photosynthesis. The snails should also survive because they can respire using the oxygen produced by *Elodea*. In turn, cellular respiration in the snail produces carbon dioxide that the plant can use for photosynthesis. Recall that cellular respiration and photosynthesis are essentially reverse reactions. In the dark, photosynthesis should not occur because photosynthesis is light-dependent. In the absence of photosynthesis, oxygen will not be produced by *Elodea*. Consequently, the snails would be expected to use up a majority of the oxygen dissolved in the pond water initially, until no oxygen remains.

Once all the oxygen is gone, the snails will suffocate. Therefore, the expected results, in terms of the survival of the snails and *Elodea*, is that both organisms will perish in the absence of light when the set-up is airtight.

b) *Is the setup exposed to light an open, closed or isolated system? Explain.*

Because energy (solar energy), but not matter, is able to enter the set-up when the plastic wrap seals the set-up, the system is considered a closed system.

c) *What is the common manipulated variable in all of the experiments above?*

In both sets of experiments, with or without the plastic wrap and snails, the factor of light exposure is the one that is manipulated or varied. Therefore, the manipulated variable is the presence or absence of light.

3. **a)** *What are some of the advantages and disadvantages of using airbags?*
In answering this question, be sure to discuss the following ideas:

- *the process involved in airbag inflation*
- *the balanced reaction that occurs*
- *why this reaction inflates the airbag*
- *the advantages and disadvantages of using this reaction*

The reaction that occurs in airbag inflation is a chemical process. The balanced reaction is:
$2\ NaN_3 + \text{energy} \rightarrow 2\ Na + 3\ N_2 + \text{energy}$

(2 moles of sodium trinitrogen + spark $\rightarrow$ 2 moles of sodium metal + 3 moles of nitrogen gas + heat) The reaction works because two moles of the reactant is chemically changed into three moles of nitrogen gas, which will inflate the airbag. It is a decomposition reaction that generates gas.

The advantages of using this reaction are that it is very quick (much quicker than a physical reaction), it takes very little energy to start, and the products are all harmless. One of the disadvantages of this reaction is that it is exothermic (produces heat), which could be dangerous in an accident.

b) *What suggestions can be made to change current airbag technology to make them more safe and effective?*

The current problems with this safety device could be avoided if the car had sensors for the size and position of the passenger of the vehicle, or if there was a way to control the size and force of the inflation of the airbag according to the passenger it is protecting. If these problems could be fixed, airbags would be a more efficient and excellent safety device in passenger vehicles.

PRACTICE TEST 2

Use the following information to answer the next question.

It is not uncommon for scientists to discover bottles containing unknown liquids in their labs. One such bottle is labelled with a Workplace Hazardous Material Information System (WHMIS) symbol.

1. From this given WHMIS label, it is **most likely** that this liquid is

A. corrosive

B. flammable

C. an oxidizing agent

D. dangerously reactive

Use the following information to answer the next question.

In the mid-nineteenth century, Dmitri Mendeleyev began constructing what is now known as the periodic table of the elements. Mendeleyev assigned each element an atomic number and an atomic molar mass and sorted them into groups according to their properties.

2. The atomic number of an element indicates the

A. number of protons in an atom

B. number of neutrons in an atom

C. number of electrons in an atom

D. mass of an atom

Use the following information to answer the next question.

Computer colleges are training students to work in a wide variety of fields, including scientific research. Chan is using his knowledge of chemistry to categorize elements in a database according to the observed properties of the element. Chan cross-references his database with information from the periodic table of elements.

3. Based on their chemical properties, copper (Cu), sodium (Na), argon (Ar), and iodine (I_2) would be classified, respectively, as a

A. transition metal, halogen, alkali metal, and noble gas

B. noble gas, transition metal, alkali metal, and halogen

C. transition metal, alkali metal, noble gas, and halogen

D. transition metal, alkali metal, halogen, and noble gas

Numerical Response

1. How many protons, electrons, and neutrons, respectively, are in one atom of carbon-14? _____, _____, and _____

Use the following information to answer the next question.

	Subatomic Particle Name	Charge	Mass unit
I	Electron	–1	0.0005
II	Neutron	0	1
III	Proton	+1	0.0005

4. The correct charge and mass unit are assigned to

A. subatomic particles I and III

B. subatomic particle I only

C. subatomic particle II only

D. subatomic particles I and II

5. Which of the following statements about an atom is **not** correct?

A. The nucleus makes up most of the volume and mass of an atom.

B. Electrons account for most of the volume of an atom, but very little of the mass.

C. The nucleus of an atom is much more dense than the rest of the atom.

D. Though the volume of the nucleus is smaller than the volume of the atom, the nucleus makes up most of the atom's mass.

Use the following information to answer the next question.

An unknown liquid was tested by:

- dipping red litmus paper into it
- applying an electric current to it

It was found that the red litmus paper remained red and that the solution conducted electricity.

6. The liquid is **most likely**

A. an ionic compound

B. a molecular compound

C. a base

D. an alcohol

7. The formula for ammonium carbonate is

A. NH_4CO_3

B. $NH_4(CO_3)_2$

C. $N_2H_8CO_3$

D. $(NH_4)_2CO_3$

8. The name for $CuHSO_4$ is

A. copper(I) hydrogen sulfate

B. copper(I) hydride sulfate

C. copper(II) hydrogen sulfate

D. copper(II) hydride sulfate

Use the following information to answer the next question.

A thermite reaction can be used to weld railroad rails, to produce bombs, and to ignite solid-fuel rocket engines. In a thermite reaction, iron(III) oxide reacts with aluminum to produce iron and aluminum oxide.

9. Which of the following thermite reactions is balanced?

A. $FeO_{(s)} + Al_{(s)} \rightarrow Fe_{(l)} + Al_2O_{3(s)}$

B. $3FeO_{(s)} + 2Al_{(s)} \rightarrow 3Fe_{(l)} + Al_2O_{3(s)}$

C. $Fe_2O_{3(s)} + Al_{(s)} \rightarrow Fe_{(l)} + Al_2O_{3(s)}$

D. $Fe_2O_{3(s)} + 2Al_{(s)} \rightarrow 2Fe_{(l)} + Al_2O_{3(s)}$

Use the following information to answer the next question.

Aconitum is a substance that is often used as a homeopathic remedy for colds. A chemist performed some tests on aconitum and made the following observations.

- The substance is highly soluble in water.
- A solution of the substance conducts electricity.
- A solution of the substance has a pH greater than 7.

10. The formula for aconitum is **most likely**

A. $Pb(OH)_2$

B. CH_3COOH

C. NaOH

D. $C_6H_{12}O_6$

Use the following information to answer the next question.

"Bomb calorimetry" is used to measure the amount of heat released or absorbed during chemical reactions. A bomb calorimeter is suspended in water and the heat released during a chemical reaction is measured by the temperature change in the water.

11. If an unknown metal reacts with oxygen in a bomb calorimeter and increases the water's temperature, then the reaction can be described as

A. exothermic

B. endothermic

C. a double replacement reaction

D. a physical change

Use the following information to answer the next three questions.

A chemist receives a sample of lake water that supposedly contains poisonous levels of lead ions. She uses potassium iodide to test for the presence of lead(II) ions. If lead(II) ions are present, a yellow precipitate, lead(II) iodide, will form. The reaction, expressed as an unbalanced chemical equation, is:
$PbSO_4 + KI \rightarrow PbI_2 + K_2SO_4$

12. The reaction may be **best** described as what type of reaction?

A. Formation

B. Double replacement

C. Decomposition

D. Combustion

Numerical Response

2. The coefficients of the given balanced equation, from left to right, are _____, _____, _____, and _____.

13. According to the solubility chart, which of the reactants or products has the **lowest** solubility?

A. $PbSO_4$

B. KI

C. PbI_2

D. K_2SO_4

14. Analysis of a compound found in epiphytic orchids reveals that the compound dissolves when placed in water. The unknown compound is **most likely**

A. $CaCO_3$

B. $AgCH_3COO$

C. CuBr

D. KOH

Use the following information to answer the next question.

It is believed that the first steam engine ever built was constructed by Hero of Alexandria. It consisted of a hollow metal ball filled with water. When the ball was heated, steam exited small holes and caused the ball to spin.

15. As the water in the ball underwent a phase change to steam, there was an increase in the

A. kinetic energy

B. temperature

C. potential energy

D. chemical energy

Use the following information to answer the next question.

Pendulums are used in grandfather clocks as timing devices. The period of a pendulum, which is the time required for it to complete one swing, is always the same. The time for one complete swing changes only when the length of the pendulum changes. A pendulum swing is an example of periodic motion.

16. If the end of a pendulum is held stationary at the top of one of its swings, what type of energy does it have?

A. Kinetic

B. Mechanical

C. Potential

D. Thermal

Use the following information to answer the next two questions.

The largest recorded hailstone to have fallen in Canada had a mass of approximately 290 g and fell in Cedoux, Saskatchewan in 1973.

Hailstones form in large rain clouds with very high updrafts. These high winds keep the hail from falling, allowing them to grow larger. Eventually the hailstone will acquire a large enough mass and fall to the ground.

Numerical Response

3. The potential energy of a 290 g hailstone at an altitude of 1 km can be expressed in scientific notation as $b \times 10^{w}$ J. What is the value of b, correct to three significant digits? ________.

17. If a 290 g hailstone starts at rest from an altitude of 1 km, at what velocity will it hit the ground, given that it loses 35% of its energy to friction?

A. 59 m/s **B.** 83 m/s

C. 113 m/s **D.** 166 m/s

Use the following information to answer the next question.

An average person requires approximately 2 500 calories of energy each day. The caloric content of food is dependent on its chemical composition. For example, fats contain more calories than proteins, which contain about the same amount of calories as carbohydrates.

18. What type of energy does food represent before it is eaten?

A. Mechanical

B. Kinetic

C. Potential

D. Thermal

Use the following information to answer the next question.

An important part of many automated factories is the industrial robot. Robots are machines that can perform a set of preprogrammed instructions without supervision. Some robots navigate by following the magnetic field around an electric cable buried beneath a floor. In this way, they are used in factories to carry materials from one place to another.

A robot converts ***i*** energy into ***ii*** energy.

19. Which of the following rows contains terms that complete the given statement?

Row	*i*	*ii*
A.	electrical	potential
B.	potential	electrical
C.	kinetic	electrical
D.	electrical	kinetic

Use the following information to answer the next two questions.

Albert Einstein's equation, $E = mc^2$, provides a relationship for the conversion of energy and mass. In a nuclear reactor, mass is converted into energy as a nuclear reaction splits the nucleus of an atom and releases the energy stored within. As more massive elements contain more energy, nuclear reactors often use the element uranium for fuel.

20. If a nuclear reactor produces 1 500 MW of useful energy with an efficiency of 30%, then the total energy input into the reactor is

A. 450 MW

B. 500 MW

C. 4 500 MW

D. 5 000 MW

21. Einstein's equation appears to contradict which of the following laws?

A. First law of thermodynamics

B. Second law of thermodynamics

C. First law of motion

D. Second law of motion

Use the following information to answer the next question.

Maglev trains use large electromagnets to lift them off a metal track, called a guideway, and propel them forward.

Using these principles, a 2 100 kg German maglev train can reach speeds of 110 m/s.

22. If another train is only 73% as efficient as the given train, it can only attain speeds of

A. 8.96 m/s

B. 17.92 m/s

C. 93.98 m/s

D. 187.96 m/s

Use the following information to answer the next question.

In incandescent light bulbs, an electric current passes through a tungsten filament. This influx of energy causes the temperature of the filament to rise. As a result, energy is radiated in the form of thermal (heat) energy as well as visible light. Modern incandescent bulbs convert electrical energy into light with an efficiency of approximately 5%.

23. How much energy is converted to heat in a 100 W incandescent light bulb?

A. 5 W

B. 25 W

C. 60 W

D. 95 W

24. The Human Genome Project has been a massive undertaking and was a major step forward in biological research. The purpose of the Human Genome Project was to

A. develop techniques for producing a human clone

B. identify and sequence all the genes that code for a human

C. develop an understanding of how a gene determines a human trait

D. produce guidelines for what types of genetic research is to be allowed

Use the following information to answer the next question.

> Artificial kidneys remove waste molecules from the blood, while allowing useful molecules to stay in the blood. This is done using an artificial membrane that works much like a cell membrane. Blood flows on one side of the membrane and a special solution flows on the other side. By adjusting the components of the solution, molecules can be added or removed from the blood by diffusion.

25. To increase the number of molecules crossing the membrane, the

A. volume of the solution should be decreased

B. size of the membrane pores should be decreased

C. size of the entire membrane should be increased

D. size of the molecules in the solution should be increased

26. A cell organelle where carbon dioxide is produced and an organelle where carbon dioxide is consumed, respectively, are

A. mitochondrion and a chloroplast

B. chloroplast and a mitochondrion

C. nucleus and a chloroplast

D. mitochondrion and a nucleus

Use the following information to answer the next three questions.

> Scientists have discovered that mitochondria are remarkably similar to bacteria. Like bacteria, mitochondria have their own DNA. Also, when cells divide, mitochondria divide in a process that is similar to bacterial reproduction. In light of this evidence, scientists have suggested that hundreds of millions of years ago, one primitive cell engulfed another cell. Instead of digesting it, the primitive cell offered the engulfed cell protection from other cells, and in exchange, the trapped cell serviced the host cell.

27. The process by which a cell engulfs a smaller cell is called

A. diffusion

B. endocytosis

C. osmosis

D. active transport

28. The engulfed cell evolved into the organelle that is responsible for the production of

A. digestive enzymes

B. transport vacuoles

C. proteins

D. adenosine triphosphate

Use this additional information to answer the next question.

29. The structure labelled is the site of ATP synthesis in mitochondria. The structure in bacteria that performs the same function is the

A. plasma membrane

B. DNA

C. ribosome

D. endoplasmic reticulum

Use the following information to answer the next two questions.

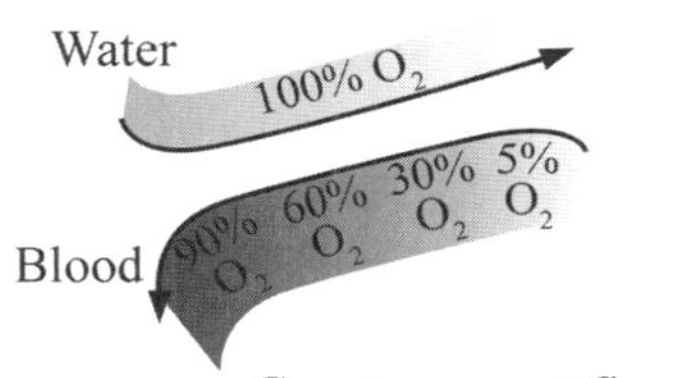

Fish use gills to extract oxygen from water. Water is pumped past the gill surface in the opposite direction (countercurrent) to blood flow. As a result, fish are able to extract roughly 85–90% of the dissolved oxygen entering the gills.

30. At point *A* in the diagram, oxygen enters the blood by diffusion. At point *B*, oxygen

A. neither enters nor leaves the blood

B. enters the blood by diffusion as well

C. enters the water by diffusion

D. enters the blood by active transport

Use the following information to answer the next question.

To follow the flow of carbon in a photosynthetic tobacco plant, scientists can expose the plant to radioactive carbon dioxide, $^{14}CO_2$, for a short period of time. Traces of radioactivity are then detected at various locations throughout the plant using a special device. Using this method, scientists discovered that CO_2 is first incorporated into organic molecules before it is transported to other parts of the plant.

31. The incorporation and transportation of CO_2 would occur, respectively, in

A. chloroplasts and phloem

B. mitochondria and root hairs

C. chloroplasts and xylem

D. mitochondria and endoplasmic reticulum

32. If the lenticels on a plant were destroyed by herbicides, the plant would die from something similar to

A. drowning

B. starvation

C. suffocation

D. dehydration

33. On a sunny day, the gas exchange between a leaf and the atmosphere would involve

A. oxygen and water leaving the leaf, and carbon dioxide coming in

B. carbon dioxide and water leaving the leaf, and oxygen coming in

C. oxygen leaving the leaf, and carbon dioxide and water coming in

D. carbon dioxide leaving the leaf, and oxygen and coming in

Use the following information to answer the next question.

The Kilauea Volcano in Hawaii is perhaps the most studied volcano in the world. Instruments monitor the chemistry of gases emitted and the movement of magma (molten rock) within the volcano. When the volcano erupts, lava and gases (comprised mainly of water vapour, carbon dioxide, and sulfur dioxide) are released.

34. Which of the following statements **best** describes the effects of a volcanic eruption?

A. Only the atmosphere is altered.

B. Only the hydrosphere is altered.

C. Only the lithosphere is altered.

D. The lithosphere, hydrosphere and atmosphere are all altered.

Use the following information to answer the next question.

The atmosphere contains over 13 million tonnes of water vapour. This amount of water equals the total amount that falls to the Earth as precipitation over 11 days. Precipitation represents a major portion of the water that moves through the hydrologic cycle.

35. The hydrologic cycle is driven by

A. all of the light energy that reaches Earth

B. 23–24% of the solar radiation that reaches the biosphere

C. all of the solar radiation that reaches the biosphere

D. the light energy absorbed by both the atmosphere and Earth's surface

Use the following information to answer the next question.

Earth's crust contains many mineral-rich "veins" that can extend for great distances underground. One of the most famous veins was discovered in California during the 1849 gold rush. It contained gold-laden quartz crystals and was named the "Mother Lode."

Numerical Response

4. A piece of gold is heated and placed in 250 mL of water, raising the water temperature by 8°C. If the specific heat capacity of water is 4.19 J/g°C and its density is 1.09 g/L, how much energy is transferred from the gold to the water correct to **four** significant digits? _______ J

Use the following information to answer the next question.

In 1912, the Titanic sunk after hitting an iceberg. The crew of the Titanic could have avoided this disaster if they had seen the iceberg sooner. Approximately 10% of an iceberg is visible above the surface of the water.

36. Ice floats because

A. ice weighs less than water

B. the density of ice is greater than the density of water

C. there are fewer water molecules in one millilitre of ice than in one millilitre of liquid water

D. the density of ice and water are equal

Numerical Response

5. The minimum amount of heat energy required to completely evaporate 100 g of water, expressed in scientific notation, is $b \times 10^{W}$ J. If the heat of fusion of water is 333 J/g and water's heat of vaporization is 2 260 J/g, what is the value of b correct to **three** significant digits? _______

37. The greater the greenhouse effect, the

- **A.** greater the heat produced on Earth
- **B.** less heat energy leaves Earth
- **C.** greater the heat energy leaving Earth
- **D.** lesser the albedo effect on Earth's surface

Use the following information to answer the next question

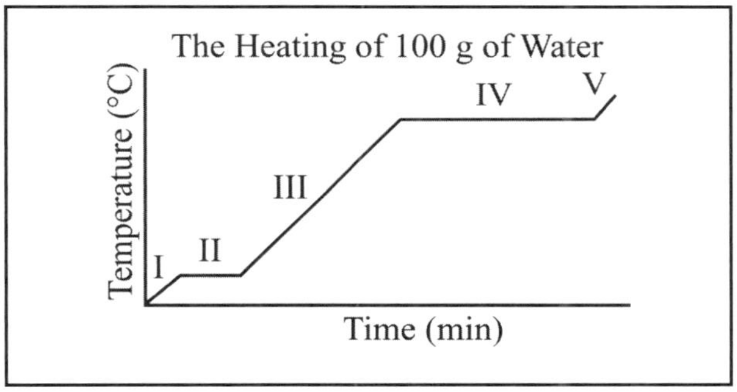

38. At what points on the graph were water molecules increasing their kinetic energy?

- **A.** II, IV
- **B.** I, III, V
- **C.** II, III, IV
- **D.** I, II, III, IV, V

Use the following map to answer the next three questions.

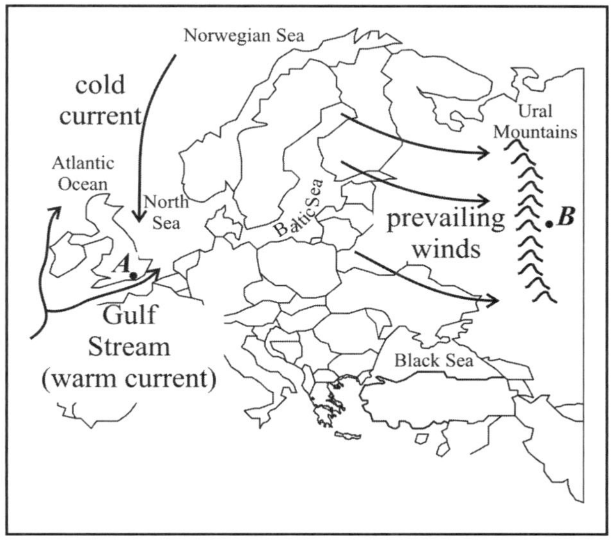

39. London (A) and Magnitogorsk (B) have different elevations. Differing elevations will **not** result in different

- **A.** vegetation
- **B.** relative humidities
- **C.** temperature variations
- **D.** angles of solar radiation

40. Notice that there is a cold current from the north meeting the warm Gulf Stream in the sea close to London. What will happen when the warm air mass and the cold air mass meet?

- **A.** The warmer air, with its higher thermal energy, will push the cold air back up north.
- **B.** The meeting of the warm and cold currents will result in unstable weather, with frequent tornadoes.
- **C.** There will be a rapid evaporation of sea water, causing the formation of high clouds or clear skies.
- **D.** A quick cooling of the air over the Gulf Stream water will cause condensation, resulting in frequent fog and rain.

41. Magnitogorsk is on the eastern slope of a mountain. As the air sweeps down the mountains onto Magnitogorsk, the air will become,

A. warmer, drier, and more dense

B. cooler, drier, and more dense

C. warmer, moister, and more dense

D. cooler, moister, and more dense

Written Response

Use the following information to answer the next question.

Roughly 20 million years ago, the movement of land masses created new ocean currents that chilled the once-temperate waters of Antarctica. Ancient perch-like fish living in the previously warmer waters of the South Pole either died or adapted to the new freezing environment. Their descendants, groups of fish known as the notothenioids, now thrive in the icy waters near Antarctica. They have special adaptations that keep them from freezing. For example, some notothenioids have little or no red blood cells or hemoglobin. Instead, these fish absorb oxygen directly through body tissues from the oxygen-rich Antarctic water. Lightweight cartilage skeletons and specialized fat distribution designed for neutral buoyancy enable these fish to conserve energy during movement. Most significantly, the blood of these remarkable fish contains molecules that act like anti-freeze. These molecules bind to minute ice crystals to prevent crystals from growing into obstructive and possibly lethal masses of frozen tissue.

1. Write a unified organized essay.

a) Compare gas exchange in the notothenioid with gas exchange in both humans and non-notothenioid fish. Describe the structure and function of the specific tissues involved.

b) Describe the dependence of gas exchange on semi-permeable membranes, including the type that involve membrane transport.

Use the following information to answer the next question.

The American tennis player Pete Sampras owes much of his success to his serve (one of the hardest serves in professional tennis). His serve has been measured at over 200 km/h.

2. **a)** If the tennis ball reaches maximum velocity at the net, a distance of 17 m, in a time of 0.6 s. What is the acceleration of the ball?

b) Draw a distance-time graph and a velocity-time graph of the ball's motion. Assume the ball undergoes uniform acceleration.

c) A tennis net has a height of 1.0 m. What is the total energy of a 50 g tennis ball as it passes just over the net at 200 km/h?

ANSWERS AND SOLUTIONS—PRACTICE TEST 2

1. C	10. C	18. C	28. D	NR5. 2.26
2. A	11. A	19. D	29. A	37. B
3. C	12. B	20. D	30. B	38. B
NR1. 6 6 8	NR2. 1 2 1 1	21. A	31. A	39. D
4. D	13. C	22. C	32. C	40. D
5. A	14. D	23. D	33. A	41. A
6. A	15. C	24. B	34. D	WR1. See Solution
7. D	16. C	25. C	35. B	WR2. See Solution
8. A	NR3. 2.85	26. A	NR4. 8 380	
9. D	17. C	27. B	36. C	

1. C

WHMIS symbols and their appropriate meanings are as follows.

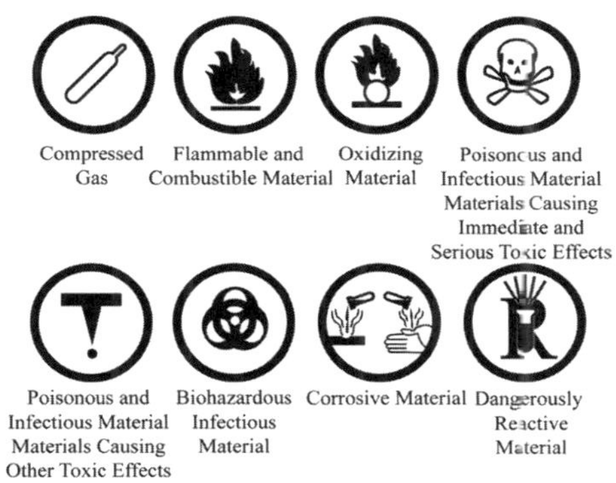

2. A

The atomic number is the number of protons contained in the nucleus of an atom. A common mistake is to assume that the atomic number also conveys the number of electrons in an atom. This is only true for the non-ionized form of the atom. Ions will have a different number of electrons than protons, resulting in a net positive or negative charge.

For example, chlorine (Cl), which has an atomic number of 17, has 17 electrons in its non-ionized form, but it has 18 electrons when it is an ion (Cl^-). Both the ionized form and the non-ionized form have 17 protons.

3. C

Elements in group 1 are called alkali metals. Sodium (Na) is in group 1 and, therefore, it is an alkali metal.

Elements in groups 3 to 12 are called transition metals. Copper (Cu) is in group 11 and, therefore, it is a transition metal.

Elements in group 17 are called halogens. Iodine (I) is in group 17 and, therefore, it is a halogen.

Elements in group 18 are called the noble gases. Argon (Ar) is in group 18 and, therefore, it is a noble gas.

NR 1 6 6 8

Carbon-14 is an isotope of carbon 12, which has 6 protons, 6 neutrons, and 6 electrons.

Isotopes of an element have the same atomic number (number of protons), but different mass number, which is the number of protons and neutrons. The relation between the mass number, the atomic number, and the number of subatomic particles in an atom is as follows.

Number of protons = atomic number

Number of neutrons = mass number – atomic number

Number of electrons = atomic number (non-ionized form only)

Therefore, the carbon 14 isotope atom contains 6 protons, 6 electrons, and 8 neutrons.

4. D

Electrons have a charge of –1 and a mass unit of 0.0005, which means that they have a mass of about $\frac{1}{2\ 000}$th of one mass unit.

Neutrons have a charge of 0 and a mass unit of 1.

Protons have a charge of +1 and a mass unit of 1.

Since particle III lists a proton as having a mass unit of 0.000 5, it is incorrect. However, particles I and II are both correct.

5. A

In an atom, the nucleus contains the relatively heavy protons and neutrons but only makes up a tiny volume of the atom. The electrons, which have much less mass than protons and neutrons, are contained in the "electron cloud," which makes up most of the volume of the atom.

6. A

Because the red litmus paper remained red, the solution cannot be a base. If it were a base, the paper would have turned blue.

Because the solution conducted electricity the solute must be an ionic compound. Molecular compounds do not conduct electricity when in solution.

7. D

Ammonium, NH_4^{1+}, has a charge of +1. Carbonate, CO_3^{2-}, has a charge of –2. Therefore, to have a balanced charge, we need two molecules of NH_4 for every one molecule of CO_3.
The correct formula is $(NH_4)_2CO_3$.

8. A

$CuHSO_4$ can be broken down into:
Cu^{1+} [copper (I)]
HSO_4^{1-} [hydrogen sulfate]

Therefore, $CuHSO_4$ is copper(I) hydrogen sulfate.

9. D

The correct reaction equation for the thermite reaction will include the correct chemical formula for each species and will include the correct coefficients to balance the equation. The correct equation is:
$Fe_2O_{3(s)} + 2\,Al_{(s)} \rightarrow 2\,Fe_{(l)} + Al_2O_{3(s)}$
Fe: 2 atoms on each side
O: 3 atoms on each side
Al: 2 atoms on each side

10. C

Using a solubility table, one can determine the solubility of all of the compounds listed.

Lead(II) hydroxide, $Pb(OH)_2$, is insoluble in water.

Only ionic compounds will conduct electricity when dissolved in water.

When acids are dissolved in water, the pH of the solution is less than 7. Since CH_3COOH is an acid, it will have a pH of less than 7 when dissolved in water.

Only NaOH (sodium hydroxide) fits all the criteria.

11. A

From the information in the question, the water in the bomb calorimeter surrounds the reaction involving the oxidation of the metal. The reaction released energy into the water, causing the temperature of the water to rise. A reaction that releases energy into its surroundings is called an exothermic reaction.

12. B

In a double replacement reaction, there are two simultaneous exchanges of similarly charged ions between two ionic compounds.
i.e., $AB + CD \rightarrow AD + BC$

Since there is no change in the coefficients of either of the products, indicating that ions *B* and *D* have the same charge and that ions *A* and *C* have the same charge, this reaction is a double replacement reaction.

NR 2 1 2 1 1

The balanced chemical reaction is:
$PbSO_4 + 2KI \rightarrow PbI_2 + K_2SO_4$

Therefore, the coefficients, from left to right, are 1, 2, 1, 1.

13. C

Anything containing group I elements (KI, K_2SO_4) will dissolve. According to the solubility chart, $PbSO_4$ has high solubility, but PbI_2 does not.

14. D

The SO_4^{-2} ion is listed as having low solubility with the Ag^+ ion. Therefore Ag_2SO_4 will not dissolve when placed in water.

The CH_3COO^- ion is listed as having low solubility with the silver ion (Ag^+). Therefore, $AgCH_3COO$ will not dissolve when placed in water.

The Br^- ion is listed as having low solubility with the Cu^+ ion. Therefore, CuBr will not dissolve in water.

The OH^- ion is listed as having high solubility with the K^+ ion. Therefore, KOH will dissolve in water.

The only compound that will dissolve in water is KOH, therefore, it is the possible identity of the unknown compound.

15. C

From the information in the question, we are given that the water in the ball underwent a phase change. During a phase change, there is a change in the potential energy. When liquid water changes to steam, the molecules experience an increase in potential energy. A change in kinetic energy would cause a change in temperature, which is an indication of how fast the molecules are moving.

16. C

In this question, the energy that the pendulum has at the top of its swing must be classified as either kinetic, mechanical, potential, or thermal.

Kinetic energy is energy due to motion. Since the pendulum is stationary, it has no motion, and therefore no kinetic energy.

Chemical energy is the energy stored in the bonds of molecules. The energy of the pendulum, is not due to chemical energy.

Potential energy is energy due to position or condition. The potential energy of a system increases as its height increases, and decreases as its height decreases. Because the pendulum at the top of its swing is at its greatest height, it has potential energy.

Thermal energy is energy due to the random motion of molecules (also known as heat).
The temperature of the pendulum is not due to its swing, therefore, the pendulum does not have thermal energy.

NR 3 2.85

To calculate the potential energy of a hailstone, use the formula $E_p = mgh$. Remember that the mass (m) must be in kilograms and the height (h) in metres.
$m = 290 \text{ g} = 0.290 \text{ kg}$
$h = 1 \text{ km} = 1\ 000 \text{ m}$

Substituting $m = 0.29$, $g = 9.81$, and $h = 1\ 000$, we get:
$E_p = mgh = (0.29 \text{ kg})(9.81 \text{ m/s}^2)(1\ 000 \text{ m})$
$E_p = 2\ 845 \text{ J}$
$E_p = 2.85 \times 10^3 \text{ J}$

Therefore, the potential energy of a hailstone at a height of 1 km is 2.85×10^{3} J.

The value of *b* correct to 3 significant digits is 2.85.

17. C

Recall that as an object falls, potential energy in the object as a result of its height is converted to kinetic energy, and as a result, the velocity increases. Therefore, the first step in solving this problem is to calculate the 0.29 kg hailstone's potential energy at a height of 1 km (1 000 m).

$$E_{\text{p}} = mgh$$
$$E_{\text{p}} = (0.29\text{ kg})(9.81\text{ m/s}^2)(1\ 000\text{ m})$$
$$E_{\text{p}} = 2\ 845\text{ J}$$

Because 35% of this potential energy is lost as a result of friction, the amount of energy that remains to be converted into kinetic energy is 65% of the total potential energy, or (0.65)(2 845 J) = 1 849 J. This is the amount of kinetic energy the hailstone has when it hits the ground. We can then calculate the velocity of the hailstone using the following formula.

$$E_{\text{k}} = \frac{1}{2}mv^2$$
$$v = \sqrt{\frac{2E_{\text{k}}}{\text{m}}}$$
$$v = \sqrt{\frac{(2)(1\ 849\text{ J})}{(0.29\text{ kg})}}$$
$$v = 113\text{ m/s}$$

Therefore, the speed of the hailstone just before it hits the ground would be 113 m/s.

18. C

This question requires the classification of the energy contained by food as one of the following forms.

Mechanical energy is the sum of the potential and kinetic energy of a system. Since the food has no potential or kinetic energy, it has no mechanical energy.

Kinetic energy is energy due to motion. Since the food is stationary, it has no motion, and therefore no kinetic energy.

Chemical energy is the energy stored in the bonds of molecules. Since the molecules in food are broken down when eaten, releasing energy, this energy is chemical

Thermal energy is energy due to the random motion of molecules (also known as heat). The energy stored in food is not due to its temperature, and therefore it does not represent thermal energy.

19. D

Electrical energy is energy due to the motion of charged particles, and includes electricity.

Potential energy is energy due to an object's position (height) or condition.

Kinetic energy is energy due to motion.

A robot converts the electrical energy running through its cable into motion, which is kinetic energy.

20. D

The efficiency of a system is a ratio of the energy output of the system to the energy input, and can be calculated using the following equation.

$$\text{efficiency} = \frac{\text{energy output}}{\text{energy input}}$$

In this question, we are given the energy output of the reactor (1 500 MW), and the efficiency of the reactor (30%). We can then calculate the energy input by rearranging the above equation:

$$\text{efficiency} = \frac{\text{energy output}}{\text{energy input}}$$
$$\text{energy input} = \frac{1\ 500\text{ MW}}{0.30} = 5\ 000\text{ MW}$$

It is important to note that we used the decimal equivalent of the efficiency 30% in the equation in order to obtain the correct answer of 5 000 MW.

21. A

The first law of thermodynamics states that energy cannot be created or destroyed. Einstein calculated that energy can be converted to mass, and mass to energy.

22. C

It is important to note that a train that is 73% efficient will not travel at 73% of the velocity of a maglev train, because the train's efficiency is describing the energy of the train, not its velocity.

Therefore, we must first calculate how much kinetic energy the maglev train has, based on its velocity.

$$\begin{aligned} E_k &= \frac{1}{2}mv^2 \\ &= \frac{1}{2}(2\ 100\ \text{kg})(110\ \text{m/s})^2 \\ &= 1.27 \times 10^7\ \text{J} \end{aligned}$$

To calculate how much kinetic energy the other train has:

$$\begin{aligned} E_{k\ \text{Regular}} &= (E_{k\ \text{Magley}})(\textit{efficiency}) \\ &= (1.27 \times 10^7\ \text{J})(0.73) \\ &= 9.27 \times 10^6\ \text{J} \end{aligned}$$

Next, calculate the velocity the train will require:

$$E_k = \frac{1}{2}mv^2$$

$$v = \sqrt{2\frac{E_k}{m}}$$

$$v = \sqrt{(2)\frac{9.27 \times 10^6\ \text{J}}{2\ 100\ \text{kg}}}$$

$$v = 93.98\ \text{m/s}$$

Therefore, a train that is 73% as efficient as a maglev train will be able to reach a speed of 93.98 m/s.

23. D

The first law of thermodynamics states that energy cannot be created or destroyed, only converted from one form to another. If 5% of the electrical energy is converted to light, we can assume that the other 95% of the electrical energy is converted to heat. 95% of 100 watts is $(0.95)(100\ \text{W}) = 95\ \text{W}$

Therefore, 95 W of power are converted to heat in a 100-W light bulb.

24. B

Cloning, determining how a gene works, and producing ethical guidelines are related to the Human Genome Project, but they are not the focus of the project. A genome is all of the genes that make up the instructions for one type of organism. The aim of the Human Genome Project was to analyze human DNA to identify all the genes and map the genes' positions.

25. C

By increasing the size of the membrane, the surface area of the filter is increasing. The greater the surface area, the more filtration will occur. Hence, more molecules will cross the membrane. The only other way to increase the number of molecules that will cross the membrane is to adjust the concentration gradients of the solutes. None of the other alternatives are related to concentration gradients.

26. A

Mitochondria break down food molecules in order to generate ATP. During this process, water and carbon dioxide are given off as waste. This occurs in all cells. The cells of green plants have chloroplasts. Inside chloroplasts, the energy of sunlight is used to assemble water and carbon dioxide into glucose. Therefore, in chloroplasts, carbon dioxide is consumed.

27. B

Diffusion involves the movement of very small molecules across a membrane. Osmosis is the diffusion of water across a membrane.
Active transport allows larger molecules to move across a membrane. Endocytosis is the process by which one-celled organisms "eat." One cell engulfs another in this process.

28. D

From the information given in the question, the engulfed cell evolved into a mitochondrion. Mitochondria carry out respiration by breaking down glucose in the presence of oxygen, releasing oxygen and water as waste. Adenosine triphosphate (ATP) is the product of respiration. ATP is the source of energy for all of a cell's metabolic activities.

29. A

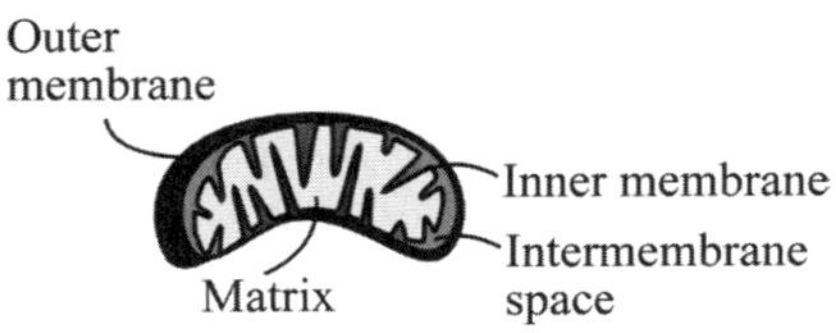

Mitochondria have a double membrane. If the theory about one cell engulfing another is correct, the outer membrane represents one vacuole. The inner membrane also represents the other vacuole, and the inner membrane corresponds to the plasma membrane of the engulfed cell. As bacteria do not have mitochondria, ATP is produced on the plasma membrane.

30. B

As the water moves from point *A* to point *B* through the gills, oxygen diffuses continuously from the water to the blood in the gill capillaries. At point *A*, for example, the higher concentration of $O_{2(g)}$ is in the water (100% in the water versus 90% in blood), so $O_{2(g)}$ moves down its concentration gradient. If fish are able to extract roughly 85% of the oxygen entering the gills, then 15% (100%–85%) of the $O_{2(g)}$ remains in the water at point *B*. As 15% is still higher than 5%, $O_{2(g)}$ still enters the blood by diffusion (down its concentration gradient).

31. A

From the information in the question, we are given that CO_2 is first incorporated into organic molecules before it is transported. The incorporation of CO_2 incorporated into organic molecules refers to photosynthesis, wherein CO_2 is used to assemble glucose. Photosynthesis occurs in the chloroplasts. The transportation of food within the plant occurs through the phloem.

32. C

Lenticels are pores in the epidermis of the stem, similar to the stomata of leaves. If the lenticels were destroyed, gas exchange between the atmosphere and the stem would stop. That would essentially suffocate the plant to death.

33. A

On a sunny day, photosynthesis would be occurring. Photosynthesis consumes carbon dioxide, which must enter the leaf, and produces oxygen, which leaves the leaf. As well, to keep from overheating, the leaf allows water to evaporate out of the stomata. This release of water is a cooling process called transpiration.

34. D

From the information given in the question, we know that lava, water vapour, and gases are released when a volcano erupts. The flow of lava would affect the lithosphere, which is the portion of the biosphere that includes all the land and its formations. Water vapour released into the air would have an impact on the hydrosphere, which is the water portion of the biosphere. Various other gases would alter the composition of the atmosphere, which is the thin layer of gases that make up the upper layer of the biosphere. Therefore, a volcanic eruption would alter the lithosphere, hydrosphere, and atmosphere.

35. B

The following diagram illustrates what happens to sunlight when it reaches Earth.

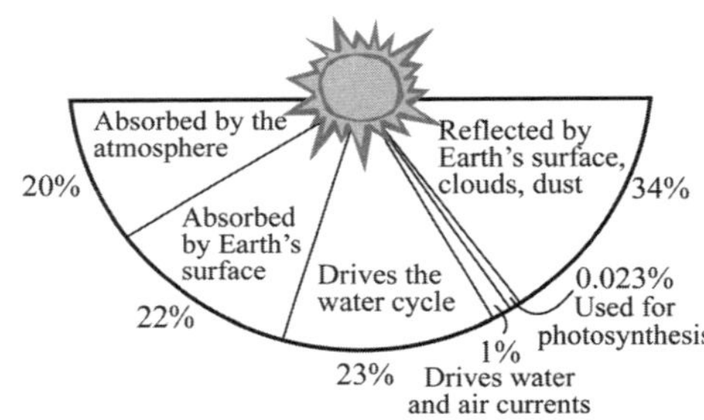

We can see that about 23 – 24% of the solar energy that reaches the biosphere drives the hydrologic cycle.

NR 4 8 380

1 mL of water has a mass of 1 g.
To find how much energy is transformed we can use the formula, $Q = mc\Delta t$.

$= (250\ \text{g})(4.19\ \text{J/g°C})(8\text{°C})$

$= 8.38 \times 10^3\ \text{J} = 8\ 380\ \text{J}$

Correct to four significant digits, the answer is 8 380 J.

36. C

Density is a measure of how many molecules of a substance occupy a particular volume. The higher the density, the more molecules occupy a particular volume. Relative to a defined liquid, a more dense substance will sink and a less dense substance will float (see diagram). Because ice is less dense than water (there are fewer water molecules in the same volume), it floats on top of water.

NR 5 2.26

Recall that as water evaporates from the human body, such as during perspiration, all the water present does not reach the boiling temperature of 100°C. Individual molecules of water absorb enough energy to evaporate, whereas other molecules will stay in a liquid state. Therefore only the energy of vaporization is involved in this question, not the energy required to change the temperature of the water.

$$Q = mH_{\text{vaporization}}$$
$$= (100\text{ g})(2\ 260\text{ J/G})$$
$$= 2.26 \times 10^5\text{ J}$$

Therefore, the value of b is 2.26.

37. B

The greenhouse effect refers to the atmosphere blocking heat from escaping from Earth. That is somewhat like the glass of a greenhouse blocking the escape of heat. As a result, a greenhouse can become very warm. The most important greenhouse gas is water vapour, however, carbon gases are also important.

38. B

Temperature is the average kinetic, or movement, energy of molecules. Whenever temperature is rising, the speed of molecules is also increasing. Heat energy is used to make molecules move faster. At points II and IV, the heat energy is used to change the state from a solid to a liquid or a liquid to a gas. There is no increase in temperature or molecular movement at these stages.

39. D

Because London and Magnitogorsk are at about the same latitude, the angle of the Sun's radiation will be about the same throughout the year. There will be a difference in vegetation as a result of the differences in elevation and there will be a difference in their humidities. With Magnitogorsk being at a higher altitude, the air will be less dense, so there will be greater temperature variations.

40. D

The famous fogs of London result from the meeting of the warm Gulf Stream air and the cool North Sea air. The moisture of the warm air condenses to form fog at ground level and clouds at higher elevations. When warm and cool air meet, the less dense warm air will slide up over top of the cold air. With so much moisture around, there will not be a rapid enough temperature increase for a tornado. There will be a rapid evaporation of sea water, but that results in heavy clouds and fog, not clear skies.

41. A

At the top of the mountains, the air is cool because it is not very dense. At cool temperatures, air may be saturated with moisture because cool air can hold more moisture. As the air descends the eastern slopes of the mountains, it becomes denser. This makes the air temperature rise. Warmer air can hold more water vapour. Therefore, the air is actively evaporating moisture and it feels dry.

1. *Write a unified organized essay*

Your essay should contain the following points.

- Animals—Specialized tissues in multicellular organisms are responsible for gas exchange. In animals, the tissues responsible for gas exchange are part of the respiratory system.
- Fish—Fish only live in aquatic environments and, therefore, have specialized structures for absorbing oxygen and expelling carbon dioxide, respectively, from and to the water. The special structures in fish are called gills. Gills provide a large surface area of tissue across which gas exchange occurs as water is pumped across the gills. Water flows across gill tissue in the opposite direction to blood flow through blood vessels in the gills which is called countercurrent flow. Countercurrent flow maximizes the amount of oxygen that can be extracted from the water.
- Oxygen binds to hemoglobin molecules in the blood. Blood that has passed through the gills and has exchanged gases then travels to the rest of the fish's body to distribute oxygen and collect the carbon dioxide present as a result of from cellular respiration. Blood circulates throughout the entire body (pumped by the muscular heart) within enclosed blood vessels until it returns to the gills.
- Humans—The specialized organs for gas exchange are the lungs. The lungs are specialized for gas exchange in a terrestrial environment where oxygen must be obtained from the surrounding air. They expand to inhale air. During inhalation, air is cleaned of particles, warmed, and then moisturized. Moist air and the moist surface area of the lung tissue is essential for gas exchange. Gases must first dissolve in water before they can travel across the lung tissue membranes. Gas exchange occurs in the lungs in alveoli—numerous small "sacs" that are lined by a single layer of cells.
- The purpose of the alveoli, as with fish gills, is to provide a large surface area across which gas exchange can occur. Also, as in fish, once blood in the lungs has absorbed oxygen through the binding of oxygen to hemoglobin molecules in red blood cells, the blood is circulated through the rest of the body, and pumped by a heart.
- Notothenioids—The information states that the nototheniods absorb oxygen directly through body tissues from the oxygen-rich Antarctic waters, and do not need to rely on pumping water across gills. Therefore, in comparison with non-notothenioid fish and humans, the notothenioids apparently do not rely on a specialized organ for gas exchange. Probably, the notothenioids conserve valuable energy by not having to pump water across gills. This is an activity that is a major energy expenditure for non-notothenioid fish.
- Dependence of gas exchange on semi-permeable membranes—gas exchange in all organisms occurs across a semi-permeable membrane. This is a membrane that is selective in the transport of substances.
  In most organisms, gas exchange occurs by diffusion (plants may absorb gases by some form of active transport). Diffusion occurs without the expenditure of energy; instead molecules travel passively down their concentration gradient. For gas exchange to be possible, membranes must be moist by way of a thin film of water wherein gases dissolve in order to travel across the membrane.

2. **a)** *If the tennis ball reaches maximum velocity at the net, a distance of 17 m, in a time of 0.6 s. What is the acceleration of the ball?*

First, we must convert the velocity of the ball into the required units (m/s).

$$200 \text{ km/h} = \frac{200 \times 1\ 000 \text{ m}}{3\ 600 \text{ s}} = 55.6 \text{ m/s}$$

Now, use this velocity in the equation for acceleration.

$$a = \frac{55.6 \text{ m/s}}{0.6 \text{ s}}$$
$$a = 92.7 \text{ m/s}^2$$

b) *Draw a distance-time graph and a velocity-time graph of the ball's motion. Assume the ball undergoes uniform acceleration.*

A distance-time graph will have distance on the vertical axis and time on the horizontal. The total distance travelled is 17 m and the total time taken is 0.6 s.

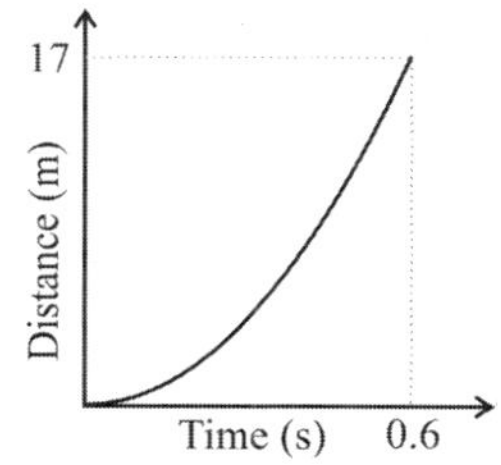

A velocity-time graph will have velocity on the vertical axis and time on the horizontal. The velocity calculated in part (a) is 55.6 m/s and the total time is 0.6 s.

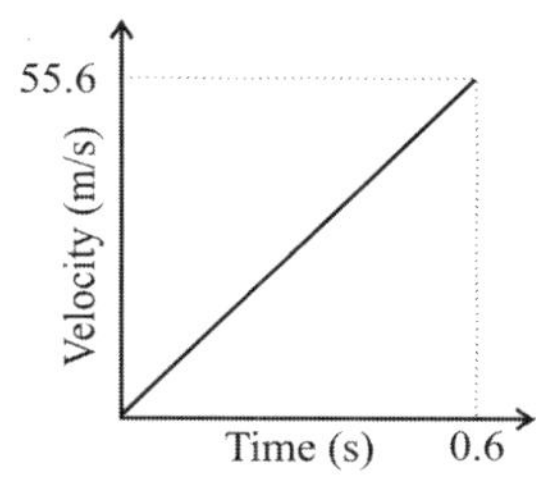

c) A tennis net has a height of 1.0 m. What is the total energy of a 50 g tennis ball as it passes just over the net at 200 km/h?

The total energy of the ball will be the sum of its kinetic and potential energies.
$E_{total} = E_k + E_p$

Kinetic energy is energy due to the ball's motion.
$E_k = \frac{1}{2}mv^2$

Potential energy is the stored energy due to its position above the net.
$E_p = mgh$

The total energy is, $E_{total} = mgh + \frac{1}{2}mv^2$

$$m = 50\text{ g} \times \frac{\text{kg}}{1000\text{ g}} = 0.05\text{ kg}$$
$$g = \frac{9.81\text{ kg}\times\text{m}}{\text{s}^2}$$
$$h = 1.0\text{ m}$$
$$v = 200\text{ km/h} = 55.6\text{ m/s}$$
$$\begin{aligned} E_{total} &= (0.05\text{ kg})(9.81\text{ m/s}^2)(1.0\text{ m}) \\ &\quad + \frac{1}{2}(0.05\text{ kg})(55.6\text{ m/s})^2 \\ &= 0.49\text{ J} + 77.28\text{ J} \\ &= 77.77\text{ J} \end{aligned}$$

NOTES

Appendices

Scientific Digits, Scientific Notation, and Useful Equations

Significant Digits

Digits that are the result of careful measurement are called significant digits. Significant digits indicate the accuracy of the measurement: the greater the number of significant digits, the greater the accuracy.

1. All non-zero digits are always significant.
2. Zeros between two non-zero numbers are always significant. For example, 1.01 has three significant digits.
3. Zeros at the end of a number and after the decimal point are significant. For example, 2.20 has three significant digits.
4. Trailing zeros may or may not be significant depending on the precision of the measurement. Scientific notation is preferred for expressing these large numbers because of this ambiguity. However, for simplicity all trailing zeros in a whole number will be considered significant. For example, 300 will be considered to have three significant digits.
5. Zeros at the beginning of a number are not significant. For example, 0.0045 has two significant digits.
6. When adding or subtracting measurements, the answer cannot be more precise than the least precise measurement. Therefore, the answer is expressed with the same number of decimal places as the least precise measurement.
   For example, $8.98 + 15.682 = 24.662 = 24.66$
7. When multiplying or dividing measurements, the answer cannot be more certain than the least certain value used. Therefore, the answer is expressed with the same number of significant digits as the least certain value.
   For example,
   $59.097 \div 3.45 = 17.12957 = 17.13$.

Scientific Notation

To work with extremely large or small numbers, scientists express numbers in a form called scientific notation. To convert a number to scientific notation, follow these steps:

1. Move the decimal point left or right so only one whole number is to the left of it.
2. Delete any non-significant zeros.
3. Multiply by 10^n, where n is the number of places the decimal point has been moved.
   If the decimal point was moved to the right, then n is negative. If the decimal point was moved to the left, then n is positive.
   For example the speed of light, 300 000 000 m/s, expressed in scientific notation is3×10^8 m/s

Useful Equations:

Physics:

$\vec{v} = \frac{\Delta d}{\Delta t}$	$\vec{a} = \frac{\Delta \vec{v}}{\Delta t}$	$F = ma$
$W = Fd$	$E_p = mgh$	
$E_k = \frac{1}{2}mv^2$		
$\% \text{ efficiency} = \frac{\text{useful energy output}}{\text{total energy input}} \times 100\%$		

Weather:

$Q = mc\Delta T$	$Q = H_{fus}n$
$Q = H_{vap}n$	

TABLE 1: SYSTEM OF PREFIXES

Prefix	Symbol	Multiplication factor
peta	P	$100\,000\,000\,000\,000 = 10^{15}$
tera	T	$100\,000\,000\,000 = 10^{12}$
giga	G	$100\,000\,000 = 10^{9}$
mega	M	$1\,000\,000 = 10^{6}$
kilo	k	$1\,000 = 10^{3}$
hecto	h	$100 = 10^{2}$
deca	da	$10 = 10^{1}$
deci	d	$0.1 = 10^{-1}$
centi	c	$0.01 = 10^{-2}$
milli	m	$0.001 = 10^{-3}$
micro	μ	$0.000\,001 = 10^{-6}$
nano	n	$0.000\,000\,001 = 10^{-9}$
pico	p	$0.000\,000\,000\,001 = 10^{-12}$
femto	f	$0.000\,000\,000\,000\,001 = 10^{-15}$

TABLE 2: SI UNITS

Quantity	Unit	Symbol
length/ distance	metre	m
mass	kilogram	kg
time	second	s
temperature	degree Celsius	°C
amount of substance	mole	mol

TABLE 3: COMMON POLYATOMIC IONS

Polyatomic ion	Formula
acetate	CH_3COO^-
ammonium	NH_4^+
benzoate	$C_6H_5COO^-$
carbide	C_2^{2-}
carbonate	CO_3^{2-}
hydrogen carbonate (bicarbonate)	HCO_3^-
chlorate	ClO_3^-
chlorite	ClO_2^-
chromate	CrO_4^{2-}
cyanide	CN^-
hydroxide	OH^-
nitrate	NO_3^-
perchlorate	ClO_4^-
permanganate	MnO_4^-
peroxide	O_2^{2-}
phosphate	PO_4^{3-}
silicate	SiO_3^{2-}
sulfate	SO_4^{2-}
hydrogen sulfate	HSO_4^-
sulfite	SO_3^{2-}
hydrogen sulfite	HSO_3^-

TABLE 4: DERIVED UNITS

Quantity	Unit	Symbol	Alternative units
Force	newton	N	kg·m/ s^2
Pressure	pascal	Pa	N/m^2
Air pressure	kilopascal	kPa	1 000 N/m^2
Energy/ work/ heat	joule	J	Nm, kg·m^2/s^2, cal
Power	Watt	W	J/s
Electrical energy	Kilowatt hour	kWh	
Area	square metre	m^2	
Velocity (linear)	Metre per second	m/s	
Acceleration (linear)	Metre per second squared	m/s^2	
Density	Kilogram per cubic metre	kg/m^3	
Specific heat capacity	Joule per kilogram by degree Celsius	$\frac{J}{kg°C}$	
Heat of fusion/ heat of vaporization/ heat of combustion	Joule per kilogram Joule per mole	J/kg J/mol	
Molar mass	Gram per mole	g/mol	
Volume	metre cubed	m^3	

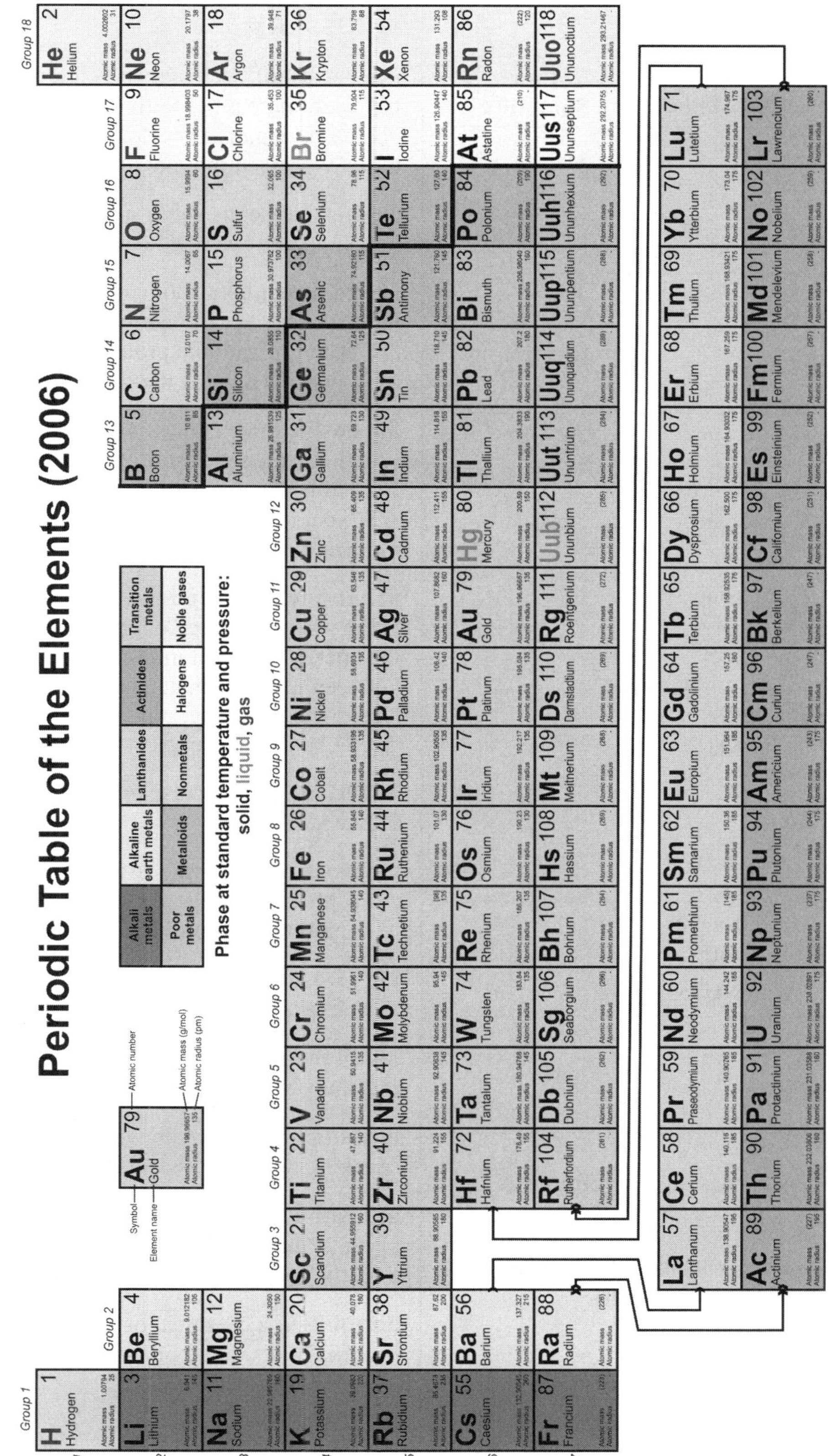
Periodic Table of the Elements (2006)
Symbol
Element name
Atomic number
Atomic mass (g/mol)
Atomic radius (pm)
Alkali metals
Alkaline earth metals
Lanthanides
Actinides
Transition metals
Poor metals
Metalloids
Nonmetals
Halogens
Noble gases
Phase at standard temperature and pressure:
solid, liquid, gas

SOLUBILITY CHART

Ion	High Solubility	Low Solubility
NO_3^- ClO_4^- ClO_3^-	All	None
Cl^- Br^- I^-	Most	Ag^+, Hg_2^{2+}, Hg^+, Pb^{2+}, Cu^+, Tl^+
SO_4^{2-}	Most	Ca^{2+}, Ba^{2+}, Sr^{2+}, Hg^{2+}, Pb^{2+}, Ag^+, Ra^{2+}
CO_3^{2-} SO_3^{2-} PO_4^{3-}	Group 1 NH_4^+	Most
OH^-	Group 1 NH_4^+ SR^{2+} Ba^{2+} Tl^+	Most
S^{2-}	Group 1 Group 2 NH_4^+	Most
Li^+, Na^+, K^+, NH_4^+, Cs^+, Rb^+	All	None

Some additional guidelines are also provided.

- Most silver salts are insoluble. $AgNO_3$ and $Ag(C_2H_3O_2)$ are common soluble salts of silver; virtually anything else is insoluble.

GLOSSARY

acceleration: a change in velocity (speed) over time; an increase (positive acceleration) or decrease (negative acceleration) in velocity over time; expressed in units of m/s^2

acid: an aqueous solution that contains hydrogen ions (H^+) and has a pH of less than 7

active transport: movement of molecules requiring the use of energy (usually in the form of ATP) and membrane proteins; used for movement of molecules against their concentration gradient

adenosine diphosphate (ADP): a molecule that functions in the transfer of energy in living cells; formed by the loss of one phosphate group from ATP; composed of one molecule of adenosine, one molecule of ribose, and two phosphate groups

adenosine triphosphate (ATP): a molecule that is the primary source of energy in all living cells; the energy is stored in high-energy chemical bonds between the phosphate groups; composed of one adenosine molecule, one ribose molecule, and three phosphate groups

adhesion: a molecular force of attraction between unlike substances

air mass: a relatively large volume of atmospheric gas that possesses fairly uniform temperature and humidity

air pressure: the force exerted by air per unit area, expressed in units of N/m^2

alkali metal: a metallic element that is a member of group 1 on the periodic table

altitude: the height above sea level when speaking about the weather

altocumulus cloud: **alto** is a prefix for high altitude, and a **cumulus** cloud is large and piled, e.g., the form of a thundercloud

antibiotic: a chemical or protein that causes bacterial cells to die or stop reproducing

atmosphere: the thin, gaseous layer that surrounds and protects Earth (or other heavenly body). Earth's atmosphere is comprised (in order of decreasing concentration) of: nitrogen, oxygen, carbon dioxide, water vapours and other rare gases; one portion of the biosphere

atom: the smallest unit of an element that retains the properties of that element; comprised of a nucleus (containing positively charged protons plus neutrons possessing a neutral charge) orbited by negatively charged electrons

atomic mass (M): the mass of an isotope of an element measured in atomic mass units; or, the average mass of one mole (6.02×10^{23}) of atoms of an element

atomic mass unit (amu): a unit of mass equal to $\frac{1}{12}$ of the mass of the carbon-12 atom; used to express the mass of one neutron or proton, approximately 1.67×10^{-27} kg

atomic number: the number of protons within the nucleus of one atom of an element; the elements are arranged in order of increasing atomic number in the Periodic Table of the elements

autotroph: an organism that is capable of producing food from simple inorganic materials and energy captured by photosynthesis (or chemosynthesis); e.g., a plant

average speed: the total displacement of an object divided by the time interval over which the displacement occurred; measured in units of m/s

base: aqueous solution that contains hydroxide ions (OH^-) and has a pH of greater than 7

binary fission: the process of cell division used by prokaryotes, e.g., bacteria, to generate multiple identical cells from one parent cell

binary ionic compounds: an ionic compound containing only two elements, one metal and one non-metal

binary molecular compound: a compound containing two non-metallic elements that are joined by a covalent bond

biosphere: an approximately 15 km thick region within and above Earth's crust that supports all life on Earth; composed of the atmosphere, hydrosphere, and lithosphere

boiling point: the temperature at which a substance evaporates (undergoes a phase change from a liquid to a gas)

carbohydrate: a molecule composed of carbon, hydrogen, and oxygen atoms in the form of $C_nH_{2n}O_n$, e.g., glucose.

cathode-ray tube: a vacuum tube in which a stream of electrons are emitted from a piece of metal, and accelerated toward a screen

cell cycle: in eukaryotic cells, the cycle of events between the formation of one cell and its division into two daughter cells; composed of the phases of interphase (including G1, S, and G2) and mitosis (including prophase, metaphase, anaphase, and telophase)

cell membrane: the semipermeable layer of tissue that surrounds the cytoplasm

cellular metabolism: the total of all the cellular processes and chemical reactions involved in the interconversion of matter and energy

cellular respiration: the process by which living organisms release the energy in organic compounds using oxygen (or another reactant) in the mitochondria

cell wall: a membrane that surrounds the outer surface of the cell membrane in plants and some prokaryotes for the purpose of protection and support

charge: a specific amount of electricity that a particle contains, usually as a result of a lack or excess of electrons

chemical bond: a force that joins two or more atoms in a molecule; chemical bonds are classified as ionic (a bond between a non-metal and a metal) or molecular (a bond between two non-metals)

chemical change: a reaction in which new substances having different chemical structures, and different properties, are formed

chemical equation: an expression representing a chemical reaction in which the formulas of the reactants appear on the left and the formulas of the products appear on the right; usually includes the balanced molar quantities of each reactant and product; see also **reaction equation**

chemical formula: a set of chemical symbols that identify a chemical compound; e.g., the chemical formula for glucose is $C_6H_{12}O_6$

chemical potential energy: the energy that is stored in the chemical bonds of an atom; expressed in units of Joules (J)

chemical property: a description of how a substance reacts chemically with another substance;
any characteristic of a compound or an element that is as a result of its chemical structure or composition

chemical reaction: a process in which one or more atoms or molecules change composition to form different molecules, the products having different properties than the starting materials

chemical waste: the unused or unwanted products of a chemical reaction

chemosynthesis: the process used by some organisms (bacteria) to capture energy from inorganic molecules such as hydrogen sulfide, hydrogen, sulfur, and ammonia

chlorophyll: a pigment that absorbs light and is involved in the conversion of light energy into chemical energy; in eukaryotes, chlorophyll is stored in chloroplasts

chloroplast: an organelle in a eukaryotic photosynthetic cell that contains the **chlorophyll pigment**, and functions in the conversion of light energy into chemical energy

chromosome: a strand of DNA in which genetic information of an organism is contained; chromosomes are found in the nucleus of a eukaryotic cell during interphase of the cell cycle, and in the cytoplasm during mitosis

cirrus cloud: **cirrus** means "curl of hair;" the cloud is shaped like a thin wisp or curl

climate: a description of the general trends in weather occurring in a given location over a long time period

closed circulatory system: in an organism, the circulatory fluid is contained and circulated throughout the body within enclosed vessels

closed system: a system that does not exchange matter, but does exchange energy with its surroundings

coefficients (in a reaction equation): the numbers that indicate the relative amounts of each species that take part in a chemical reaction; can be read in terms of molecules or moles

cohesion: a molecular force of attraction between like substances

combustion reaction: also called an **oxidation reaction**, an exothermic chemical reaction in which oxygen is a reactant

compound: a pure substance with constant chemical composition and properties and composed of two
or more joined elements inseparable by ordinary physical methods

concentration gradient: the difference in concentrations between two points

condense: to change the state of a substance from a gas into a liquid; a physical change

conductor: a material through which charged particles, or heat, flow freely; any substance that conducts heat or light

controlled variable: a condition that is kept constant throughout an experiment. Any experimental result, therefore, cannot be attributed to the controlled variable.

convection current: transfer of heat between warm and cool liquids or gases as a result of their difference in density

convection: thermal energy (heat) transfer by circulation in liquids and gases

Coriolis effect: the deflection of Earth's moving air currents caused by Earth's rotation

corrosion: the process in which a substance is worn away gradually through a chemical reaction

covalent bond: a chemical bond formed between two atoms that share electrons

cumulus cloud: cumulus means "pile"; a cloud that is thick and piled horizontally, e.g., the shape of a thundercloud

cytoplasm: region of a cell that is enclosed by the plasma membrane and that includes all cellular organelles except the nucleus

decay: to deteriorate or decompose through a biological or nuclear change

deceleration: a decrease in velocity over time; expressed in units of m/s^2

decomposers: heterotrophs that obtain their energy from non-living plant and animal (organic) remains

decomposition reaction: a chemical change in which a compound is separated into its component parts

density: in **physics**, mass per unit volume expressed in units of g/L; the number of molecules of a substance that occupy a particular volume

deoxyribonucleic acid (DNA): the chemical that composes genetic material

development, biological: the process of cell division, differentiation, and growth of an organism

dialysis: the separation of solutes by a semipermeable membrane; i.e., solutes can be removed from one solution and transmitted into another by diffusion through a semipermeable membrane across which a concentration gradient exists for that particular solute

differentiation: the process by which cells become specialized in structure and function, and the division of labour during development

diffusion: the passive dispersal of molecules; direction of the net movement of molecules of one type is from an area of high concentration to an area of low concentration of the molecule in question. The concentration of molecules of other types in the same areas are disregarded.

digestive system: system in animals by which ingested food is stored and processed by chemical and mechanical means to provide the body with absorbable nutrients, and by which waste materials are excreted

dissolve: when a solid is mixed into a solution, and it subsequently becomes part of the solution

double replacement reaction: a chemical reaction in which two ions exchange places between two reactants

ecosystem: a self-regulating system involving the flow of energy and matter between a community of living organisms and their environment

efficiency: the ratio of useful energy (work accomplished) to the total energy input (energy supplied) during an energy conversion process; often expressed as a percentage

elastic energy: the energy stored in an object that is deformed (stretched, twisted, or compressed) and able to return to its original shape once the forces causing deformation are removed; expressed in units of Joules (J)

electrical energy: the energy of electrical charges; electrical potential energy is derived from the force between charged particles (a force of attraction exists between two particles of unlike charge, and a force of repulsion exists between particles of like charge)

electromagnetic wave: a wave consisting of oscillating (smooth changes in direction back and forth) electric and magnetic fields that travels at the speed of light

electron: a stable, subatomic particle that has a negative charge, and a mass of 9.11×10^{-31} kg

electron cloud: the region in an atom in which there is a probability of an electron being located; this region surrounds the nucleus in the Electron Cloud model of the atom proposed by Louis de Broglie and Erwin Schrodinger in 1930

element: a pure substance that is composed of only one kind of atom, and cannot undergo a decomposition reaction into a simpler substance

endocytosis: method of intake of materials from the environment by a living cell whereby the cell membrane progressively folds inward and around material on the outside surface of the cell until the cell membrane completely wraps around the material taken up; the membrane enclosed material is a food vacuole when it is contained within the cell

endoplasmic reticulum: an organelle in a eukaryotic cell; a network of tubes that functions in the transport of materials and provides a site for some chemical reactions in a cell; rough endoplasmic reticulum possesses associated ribosomes, which smooth endoplasmic reticulum lacks

endothermic reaction: any change that absorbs energy (usually in the form of heat) from its surroundings, resulting in a net chemical potential energy gain in the system

energy: the ability of an object or system to perform work; expressed in units of Joules (J)

environment: the surrounding space in a system, including the atmosphere, land, water and influence of other organisms; or the space surrounding a cell

enzymes: proteins whose function is to catalyze (speed up) a chemical reaction that occurs in an organism

eukaryotes: cells (eukaryotic) that possess a membrane-bound ("true") nucleus, and membrane bound organelles; also, multicellular organisms that are made up of eukaryotic cells

eukaryotic cells: cells that possess a true nucleus and membrane-bound organelles

evaporate: to change the state of a substance from a liquid into a gas; a physical change

excretion: the elimination of metabolic waste from blood and tissue of an organism, e.g., urine in animals

excretory system: the system in animals that is responsible for excretion

exocytosis: method of waste removal from a living cell whereby the membrane of a vacuole containing waste material fuses with the cell membrane such that the contents of the vacuole are exposed to and then diffuse into the external environment

exothermic reaction: any change that releases energy (usually in the form of heat) into its surroundings, resulting in a net chemical potential energy loss in the system

facilitated diffusion: also called facilitated passive transport, the passive movement of molecules across a semipermeable membrane down a concentration gradient, but aided by a protein/channel embedded in the membrane

feedback system: a self-regulated system in which inputs to the system affect the outputs and vice versa, for the purpose of maintaining a steady state

food web: the network of feeding patterns within an ecosystem and in which most or all organisms have more than one food source; distinguished from a food chain in which each organism feeds only on the single organism present in the trophic level below its own

food: any substance (liquid or solid) that is ingested by a living organism to provide nutrients for life

force: an influence that causes an object to accelerate with a magnitude proportional to the object's mass; expressed in units of Newtons (N)

formation reaction: a chemical reaction in which simple elements combine to form larger, more complex compounds; also known as a **synthesis reaction**

freeze: to change the state of a substance from a liquid into a solid; a physical change

freezing point: the temperature at which a substance undergoes a phase change from a liquid to a solid

friction: the force opposing the motion of two surfaces that are in contact

front: the zone of transition between two air masses that differ, e.g., in temperature, humidity

generator: a machine that converts one form of energy to another, especially mechanical energy into electrical energy

glycogen: a carbohydrate that is used for storage of chemical energy in animals

golgi apparatus or **golgi complex:** an organelle in a eukaryotic cell; a network of flattened sacs that function in modification, packaging, and transport of proteins

gradient: a difference in concentration between two areas

gravitational potential energy: the stored energy of an object as a result of its position relative to a gravitational force; expressed in units of Joules (J)

gravity: the force of attraction exerted by a body of mass

group: in the periodic table of the elements, all the elements within a vertical column; elements of a group share similar chemical properties

halogen: a non-metallic element that is a member of group 17 on the periodic table

heat: a form of energy that causes a change in the vibration of a substance's molecules, and can be transferred from one substance to another; also known as **thermal energy**

heat budget: the total amount of energy received and lost by Earth

heat capacity: a measure of the amount of energy that is required to change the temperature of a substance by one degree Celsius (°C)

heat of combustion: the measure of the amount of heat that is released by an exothermic combustion reaction

heat of fusion: the amount of energy that is released by one kilogram of a substance as it undergoes the physical change from a liquid to a solid

heat of vaporization: a measure of the amount of energy that is required to change one kilogram of a substance from a liquid into a vapour

hemoglobin: a molecule in red blood cells that binds and carries oxygen for the purpose of transporting oxygen from the lungs to the tissues of the body

hemolymph: in organisms with open circulatory systems, the fluid that bathes tissues and transports gases and nutrients throughout the body

heterotroph: an organism that obtains its nutrients by consuming autotrophs and/or other heterotrophs (consumers), or by consuming organic remains of dead plants and animals (decomposers)

homeostasis: steady-state of all biological functions maintained in an organism

hormone: a protein that functions to transmit signals within a multicellular body, e.g., growth hormone in humans signals growth, cell division

humidity: the concentration of water vapour in the air

hydrogen bond: a strong non-covalent bond that forms between a hydrogen atom possessing a slight positive charge within a molecule, and an atom possessing a slight negative charge in the same or a different molecule; e.g., water molecules are held together by hydrogen bonds between the hydrogen atoms and the oxygen atoms, which are slightly negatively charged

hydrogen halide: a compound of hydrogen with one of the halogen (group 17) elements

hydrologic cycle: the continuous cycling of water between the atmosphere, land, and ground water, when water evaporates and condenses using solar energy (energy of the sun); also called the **water cycle**

hydrosphere: the portion of Earth's biosphere that is comprised of all of the water on Earth

hypertonic solution: a solution that has a higher concentration of solutes, e.g., salts, when compared to another solution

hypotonic solution: a solution that has a lower concentration of solutes, e.g., salts, when compared to another solution

inefficiency: the fraction of energy lost in an energy conversion process

inertia: the tendency of an object to resist change in motion

inorganic compound: a chemical compound that occurs naturally, but is not usually produced by living organisms; e.g., oxygen, carbon dioxide, water, and minerals are inorganic compounds; an inorganic compound usually does not include covalent bonds between carbon atoms

insoluble: incapable of being dissolved

instantaneous speed: the speed of an object at a defined moment

ion: an atom that has an excess or lack of electrons, and is therefore either positively or negatively charged

ionic bond: the attraction between two or more ions that have opposite charges (a metallic ion and a non-metallic ion)

ionic compound: a compound made up of metallic and non-metallic ions that share ionic bonds

ionic size: the size of a charged atom often referred to by the ionic radius

ionized atom: an atom that has an excess or lack of electrons, and is therefore either positively or negatively charged; an ion

isobar: curved lines on a weather map that connect areas having the same pressure after allowing for differences in height above sea level

isolated system: a system that does not exchange matter or energy with its surroundings

isothermic: having the same temperature

isotonic solution: solutions having the same concentration of a particular solute

isotopes: elements that have the same atomic number but a different mass number; that is, elements that contain the same number of protons but a different amount of neutrons

kinetic energy: energy possessed by an object as a result of its motion; expressed in units of Joules (J)

kinetic molecular theory: the theory that states that all matter is made up of particles that are in constant random motion, and that thermal energy (heat) is produced by the speed of this random motion

latitude: the distance of a point on Earth's surface measured from the equator in either a north or south direction; expressed as an angular distance in degrees

law of conservation of energy: energy cannot be created or destroyed, but it can be converted into another form

law of conservation of mass: matter cannot be created or destroyed during a chemical reaction

laws of thermodynamics: the **first law of thermodynamics** states that energy cannot be created or destroyed, but can be transformed. In any process, the total amount of energy remains the same. The **second law of thermodynamics** states that it is impossible for any process to convert thermal energy from one source entirely into work

lenticel: opening in the stem of a plant through which gas exchange occurs and through which water escapes by transpiration

liquid: a state of matter that identifies the substance as being a fluid and being able to be poured

lithosphere: the portion of Earth's biosphere comprised of all land on Earth, including all land formations

longitude: the distance of a point on Earth's surface measured from the meridian to the Prime Meridian (in Greenwich, England); expressed as an angular distance in degrees

lysosome: a cellular organelle that functions in the degradation and removal of cellular waste in eukaryotes; contains hydrolytic enzymes that digest cell waste; has an acidic internal environment

manipulated variable: the variable in an experiment that is altered between trials; an experiment tests the effect of changing this variable on the experimental outcome

mass: a measure of the quantity of matter that an object contains, mass is one property that all matter possesses

mass number (A): the number of protons plus neutrons in the nucleus of an atom

matter: anything that possesses mass and occupies space

mechanical energy: the sum of the potential and kinetic energies expressed in units of Joules (J)

mechanical mixture: a mixture in which the individual components remain unaltered and visible

meiosis: the process used by eukaryotic cells for sexual reproduction; the process by which one parent cell divides to produce four cells each having half the genetic material of the parent cell

melt: to change the state of a substance from a solid into a liquid; a physical change

melting point: the temperature at which a substance will undergo a physical change from a solid to a liquid; the melting point of a substance is a physical property of that substance

metabolic rate: the rate of energy conversion and use in a living organism

metabolism: all the chemical processes that occur in a living organism and that are responsible for the conversion and use of energy

metal: elements possessing some or all of the following properties: strong, hard, durable, ductile, malleable, reflects light when polished, conducts heat, conducts electricity; usually forms ions that have a positive charge; metals are found on the left side of the periodic table

metalloid: an element that has some properties of a metal and some properties of a non-metal; e.g., silicon and bismuth

mitochondrion: single form of mitochondria, an organelle in a eukaryotic cell that functions in the conversion of chemical energy (e.g., glucose) into useable energy (in the form of ATP); also known as the "powerhouse" of the cell

mitosis: the part of the eukaryotic cell cycle during which one cell divides into two, and during which the genetic material is precisely divided

mixture: a substance made up of one or more pure components that are not chemically bonded to one-another, can be separated by physical means, and whose properties depend on the identity and ratio of the components; one of the two major classifications of matter (the other classification being a **pure substance**)

model: a representation of a system showing how the parts of a system are related; or, a theory or diagram that attempts to simplify a complex idea or system; e.g., Electron Cloud Model of the atom

molar mass: the measure of the mass of one mole (6.02×10^{23}) of molecules of an element of compound, measured in grams per mole (g/mol)

molar ratio: the ratio of moles (coefficients) of individual reactants and products in a balanced chemical equation

mole (mol): the amount of a substance that contains 6.02×10^{23} (Avogadro's number) particles; also, the amount of a substance (expressed in grams (g)) that corresponds to the molecular weight of the substance, usually the mass of one molecule of the substance

molecular compound: a compound that is formed from two or more non-metallic ions that share covalent bonds; molecular compounds usually have a low melting point and are non-conductors; also known as **covalent compounds**

molecular elements: elements that consist of two or more atoms of the same type, e.g., oxygen gas, which is made up of two oxygen atoms (O_2)

molecule: a group of two or more atoms held together by chemical bonds. The smallest particle a compound can be divided into while keeping its chemical and physical properties

momentum: a vector quantity describing the motion of an object as its mass multiplied by its velocity; expressed in units of kg·m/s

motile organism: an organism that is capable of movement independent of other moving bodies

motion: the change in position of an object

multi-thermic: having many different temperatures

mutation: in genetic material, a change in the DNA code that contains information or instructions for the building of proteins, and thereby the normal function of the cell

net charge: the total charge of a particle or an object after all of the positive and negative charges within it have been added together

neutral: **in chemistry**—a substance that is not acidic or basic and has a pH of 7.0; **in physics**—a particle or object that has a net electrical charge of zero

neutralization reaction: a reaction involving an acid and a base in which the products have a pH of 7.0

neutron: a neutrally-charged subatomic particle that is contained within the nucleus and has a mass of approximately 1.68×10^{-27} kg

noble gas: an element with low reactivity that belongs to group 18 on the periodic table

non-ionized atom: an atom that does not have an excess or lack of electrons and is, therefore, neutral in charge

non-metal: an element that lacks the characteristics of a metal, and is found on the right side of the periodic table; they occur naturally in solid, liquid, and gaseous states

non-reactive: a chemical that does not take part in chemical reactions

non-uniform motion: motion that is not at a constant speed

nuclear energy: the potential energy that is stored within the nucleus of an atom, and is released during nuclear reactions such as fission and fusion

nuclear envelope: the semipermeable membrane that encloses the nucleus within a eukaryotic cell; also, **nuclear membrane**

nuclear energy: the potential energy that is contained within the nucleus of an atom, and is released during nuclear reactions, such as fission and fusion

nuclear fission: a highly exothermic nuclear reaction in which the nucleus of an atom splits into two or more smaller fragments

nuclear fusion: a highly exothermic nuclear reaction in which two nuclei are combined to form a larger nucleus

nuclear reaction: a process that causes a change in the nucleus of an atom; see also **nuclear fission** and **nuclear fusion**

nucleus: in biology—organelle in a eukaryotic cell that contains genetic information and controls the operations of the cell; **in chemistry** and **physics**—a dense area in the centre of an atom that contains neutrons and protons

open circulatory system: a circulatory system in which the fluid (hemolymph) is pumped by a heart to different areas of the body in vessels, and then escapes from vessels to the surrounding tissue, bathing cells directly to facilitate the exchange of nutrients and waste

open system: a system that exchanges both matter and energy with its surroundings

organelle: a part of a eukaryotic cell that is enclosed by a semipermeable membrane and possesses a specialized structure and function

organic compound: a substance that is found in, or produced by, a living system and that contains carbon atoms bonded covalently

osmoregulation: the control of the water balance in an organism, which in turn also regulates the ion solute balance

osmosis: the diffusion of water from an area with a higher concentration of water to an area with a lower concentration

oxide: a compound made up of the atoms of oxygen and another element

passive transport: diffusion of substances across a semipermeable membrane; occurs without the use of energy

periods: horizontal rows on the periodic table that consist of elements with increasing atomic numbers

pH: a measure of the concentration of hydrogen ions (H^+) in a solution; a measure of the acidity or alkalinity of a substance

phase change: a physical change in which a substance is transformed from one state to another, e.g., the change of water into ice is a phase change from a solid to a liquid

phloem: in a plant, vascular tissue composed of living cells that functions in the transport of nutrients to other parts of the plant

photosynthesis: the process by which carbon dioxide and water are chemically converted to oxygen and glucose using solar energy; occurs in green plants and other organisms containing pigments (e.g., chlorophyll) that function in capturing light energy

physical change: a change that does not result in either the formation of a new substance or a change in the chemical composition of a substance

physical property: a property of a substance that can be observed without changing it into another substance; e.g., the melting point of a substance

polar molecule: a molecule in which one end possesses a slight charge (either negative or positive) and the opposite end of the molecule possesses a slight opposite charge, e.g., water molecule

potential energy: stored energy as a result of the position or condition of an object; expressed in units of Joules (J)

power: rate of energy consumption; expressed in units of watts (W)

precipitate: a solid that is separated from a solution during a chemical reaction

precipitation: in weather, the conversion of water vapour in the atmosphere into liquid water in the form of rain, snow, or hail

pressure system: a large area of the atmosphere that possesses relatively constant pressure, after allowing for differences in the height above sea level; isobars on weather maps define the area occupied by individual pressure systems

probability: the chance that an event will occur

producer: organisms that convert light (or also thermal) energy into chemical energy that is used by themselves and organisms that consume them in an ecosystem; see **autotroph**

products: substances that are produced as the result of a chemical reaction—products are usually found on the right side of a chemical reaction equation

prokaryote: cells that do not possess a membrane-bound nucleus or other membrane-bound organelles; e.g., bacteria

propagate: a method of producing more cells or organisms from a single cell or organism

protein: a large molecule that is synthesized on the ribosome according to instructions in DNA; made up of amino acids joined in long chains

proton: a positively charged sub-atomic particle that is contained within the nucleus and has a mass of 1.67×10^{-27} kg

pure substance: matter that has a set of definite physical and chemical properties whose components are the same and cannot be separated by physical means

radiation: matter and energy that is released by a nuclear reaction or a radioactive element

radioactivity: the spontaneous release of high energy radiation and particles from the atoms of some elements

reactant: any substance that is changed as a result of a chemical reaction. Reactants are found on the left side of a chemical reaction equation

reactivity: the tendency for a substance to take part in a chemical reaction.

relative reactivity: the reactivity of one substance compared to another. For example, since francium will react more readily than argon, we can say that francium has a higher relative reactivity than argon

replacement reaction: a chemical change in which one or more ions are exchanged to form products that are neither more complex or simpler than the reactants; see **single replacement reaction, double replacement reaction**

respiratory system: a system in an organism that functions on an exchange of oxygen and carbon dioxide gases for the purpose of cellular respiration

responding variable: the variable in an experiment in which a change is detected, and that is caused by a change in the manipulated variable

ribosome: a particle in a cell that is composed of subunits and functions in the synthesis of proteins, both in prokaryotes and eukaryotes

semi-permeable membrane: a membrane such as a biological membrane, through which some, but not all, molecules can pass

sessile organism: an organism that is incapable of movement travel and is attached to a solid substrate

single replacement reaction: a chemical reaction in which one ion is exchanged between one reactant and another

solar energy: energy in the form of heat and radiation that is emitted from the sun; this energy is used in photosynthesis

solid: a state of matter in which its molecules cannot move in relation to one another

solubility: the ability of a compound to dissolve in a specific solvent such as water

solute: a substance that is dissolved in a solvent

solution: a homogeneous mixture of a solute dissolved in a solvent at a particular concentration

solvent: a substance, usually a liquid, in which a solute is dissolved

sound energy: energy due to the uniform vibration (wave vibration) of molecules

specific heat capacity: a measure of the amount of energy that is required to change the temperature of one gram of a substance by one degree Celsius (°C)

speed: a measure of a distance travelled over time; expressed in units such as m/s or km/h

starch: a storage form of a carbohydrate used by plants

state: a physical property of a substance that identifies whether it is a solid, a liquid, or a gas

stoma: singular form of stomata, opening in the surface of a leaf that is capable of opening and closing, through which gas exchange occurs and through which water escapes the plant by transpiration

stratus cloud: **stratus** means "spread out"; a cloud that is spread out across the sky

subatomic particles: particles that are contained within the atoms, specifically protons, neutrons, and electrons

substance: matter that has a specific chemical structure and characteristic properties

surface tension: the tendency of the surface of a liquid to contract to the smallest area because of the force of attraction between like molecules; molecules at the surface of a liquid are pulled toward molecules in the interior of the body of liquid, creating a thin surface film of "compressed" liquid that can support objects, e.g., an insect standing on water or the meniscus (rounded shape of the surface) formed in a narrow tube containing liquid

synthesize: the formation of a new chemical from its component elements

system (in a biological sense): a group of tissues and organs that function cooperatively to accomplish a specialized task

temperature: a measure of the hotness or coldness of a body with respect to some scale

thermal energy: a form of kinetic energy that is due to the random motion of molecules; energy due to the motion of particles making up an object; also referred to as **heat**

total energy: the sum of all energy (of all different types) possessed by an object or system; expressed in units of Joules (J)

transition metal: a metallic element that belongs to groups 3-12 on the periodic table

transpiration: the process by which plants lose water by evaporation and by which water is pulled up from the roots to the higher parts of the plant

turgor pressure: the outward pressure exerted by the water in a cell on the cell wall; the force that maintains the rigidity of a cell, and in plants, is responsible for preventing wilting

uniform motion: motion at a constant speed, i.e., no acceleration is occurring

vacuum: a volume of space that contains no matter

valence electron: an electron that occupies the highest (outermost) energy level of an atom

valence electron shell: the highest (outermost) energy level in an atom that contains electrons

velocity: a vector quantity that describes the change in position over time, expressed in units of m/s.

waste energy: the amount of energy lost in an energy conversion; expressed in units of Joules (J)

weather: a description of the short-term changes in temperature, precipitation, humidity, air pressure, wind direction and velocity, storms, and cloud cover

weight: a measure of the force of gravity on an object

work: the transfer of energy; expressed in units of Joules (J)

Workplace Hazardous Materials Information System (WHMIS): a standardized system that provides specific information on the properties and negative effects of chemicals found in laboratories, industry, and households

***x*-intercept:** the point at which the plot of a graph crosses the x-axis

xylem: dead tubular plant tissue that conducts water and nutrients from the roots to the leaves

***y*-intercept:** the point at which the plot of a graph crosses the y-axis

NOTES

CREDITS

ORDERING INFORMATION

SCHOOL ORDERS

Please contact the Learning Resource Centre (LRC) for school discount and order information.

***THE KEY* Study Guides** are specifically designed to assist students in preparing for unit tests, final exams, and provincial examinations.

***THE KEY* Study Guides** – $29.95 each plus G.S.T.

Senior High		Junior High	Elementary
Biology 30 Chemistry 30 English 30-1 English 30-2 Applied Math 30 Pure Math 30 Physics 30 Social Studies 30-1 Social Studies 30-2	Biology 20 Chemistry 20 English 20-1 Mathematics 20-1 Physics 20 Social Studies 20-1 English 10-1 Math 10 Combined Science 10 Social Studies 10-1	English Language Arts 9 Math 9 Science 9 Social Studies 9 Math 8 Math 7	English Language Arts 6 Math 6 Science 6 Social Studies 6 Math 4 English Language Arts 3 Math 3

Student Notes and Problems (SNAP) Workbooks contain complete explanations of curriculum concepts, examples, and exercise questions.

SNAP Workbooks – $29.95 each plus G.S.T.

Senior High		Junior High	Elementary
Biology 30 Chemistry 30 Applied Math 30 Pure Math 30 Math 31 Physics 30	Biology 20 Chemistry 20 Mathematics 20-1 Physics 20 Math 10 Combined Science 10	Math 9 Science 9 Math 8 Science 8 Math 7 Science 7	Math 6 Math 5 Math 4 Math 3

Visit our website for a tour of resource content and features or order resources online at
www.castlerockresearch.com

#2340, 10180 – 101 Street
Edmonton, AB Canada T5J 3S4
e-mail: learn@castlerockresearch.com

Phone: 780.448.9619
Toll-free: 1.800.840.6224
Fax: 780.426.3917

CASTLE ROCK
RESEARCH CORP

ORDER FORM

THE KEY	QUANTITY
Biology 30	
Chemistry 30	
English 30-1	
English 30-2	
Applied Math 30	
Pure Math 30	
Physics 30	
Social Studies 30-1	
Social Studies 30-2	
Biology 20	
Chemistry 20	
English 20-1	
Mathematics 20-1	
Physics 20	
Social Studies 20-1	
English 10-1	
Math 10 Combined	
Science 10	
Social Studies 10-1	
English Language Arts 9	
Math 9	
Science 9	
Social Studies 9	
Math 8	
Math 7	
English Language Arts 6	
Math 6	
Science 6	
Social Studies 6	
Math 4	
English Language Arts 3	
Math 3	

Student Notes and Problems Workbooks	QUANTITY	
	SNAP Workbooks	Solution Manuals
Math 31		
Biology 30		
Chemistry 30		
Applied Math 30		
Pure Math 30		
Physics 30		
Biology 20		
Chemistry 20		
Mathematics 20-1		
Physics 20		
Math 10 Combined		
Science 10		
Math 9		
Science 9		
Math 8		
Science 8		
Math 7		
Science 7		
Math 6		
Math 5		
Math 4		
Math 3		

TOTALS	
KEYS	
SNAP WORKBOOKS	
SOLUTION MANUALS	
SOLUTION MANUALS	

Learning Resources Centre

Castle Rock Research is pleased to announce an exclusive distribution arrangement with the Learning Resources Centre (LRC). Under this agreement, schools can now place all their orders with LRC for order fulfillment. As well, these resources are eligible for applying the Learning Resource Credit Allocation (LRCA), which gives schools a 25% discount off LRC's selling price. Call LRC for details.

Orders may be placed with LRC by
Telephone: 780.427.2767
Fax: 780.422.9750
Internet: www.lrc.education.gov.ab.ca
Or mail: 12360 – 142 Street NW
Edmonton, AB T5L 4X9

PAYMENT AND SHIPPING INFORMATION

Name: ______
School Telephone: ______
SHIP TO
School: ______
Address: ______
City: ______ Postal Code: ______
PAYMENT
□ by credit card
VISA/MC Number: ______
Expiry Date: ______
Name on card: ______
□ enclosed cheque
□ invoice school P.O. number: ______

#2340, 10180 – 101 Street, Edmonton, AB T5J 3S4 **Phone:** 780.448.9619 Fax: 780.426.3917
Email: learn@castlerockresearch.com **Toll-free:** 1.800.840.6224
www.castlerockresearch.com

CASTLE ROCK RESEARCH CORP